HAMLYN
ALL COLOUR
CASSEROLES

HAMLYN
ALL COLOUR
CASSEROLES

HAMLYN

Front cover shows, left to right:
Elizabethan rabbit (recipe 121), Italian market day (recipe 141),
Veal ragout (recipe 49).

Back cover shows, clockwise from top left:
Chicken Rossini (recipe 81), Portuguese mussel feast (recipe 1),
Jambalaya (recipe 205), Baked ratatouille (recipe 173).

First published in Great Britain 1994 by Hamlyn
an imprint of Reed Consumer Books Limited
Michelin House, 81 Fulham Road, London SW3 6RB
and Auckland, Melbourne, Singapore and Toronto.

Line drawings by Stephen Sweet
Photographs from Reed Consumer Books Picture Library

ISBN 0 600 58273 6

Recipes in this book were first published under other
Reed Consumer Books imprints.

Produced by Mandarin Offset
Printed and bound in China

OTHER TITLES IN THIS SERIES INCLUDE

Hamlyn All Colour Cookbook
Hamlyn New All Colour Cookbook
Hamlyn All Colour Vegetarian Cookbook
Hamlyn New All Colour Vegetarian Cookbook
Hamlyn All Colour Teatime Favourites
Hamlyn All Colour Meals in Minutes
Hamlyn All Colour Barbecues and Summer Food
Hamlyn All Colour Italian Cookbook
Hamlyn All Colour Chinese Cookbook
Hamlyn All Colour Indian Cookbook
Hamlyn All Colour Million Menus Cookbook

CONTENTS

FISH   1 - 48

MEAT   49 - 80

POULTRY   81 - 120

GAME   121 - 140

PASTA, RICE & PULSES   141 - 172

VEGETABLES   173 - 204

SPECIAL OCCASIONS   205 - 240

Useful facts and figures

NOTES ON METRIFICATION

In this book quantities are given in metric and Imperial measures. Exact conversion from Imperial to metric measures does not usually give very convenient working quantities and so the metric measures have been rounded off into units of 25 grams. The table below shows the recommended equivalents.

Ounces	Approx g to nearest whole figure	Recommended conversion to nearest unit of 25	Ounces	Approx g to nearest whole figure	Recommended conversion to nearest unit of 25
1	28	25	9	255	250
2	57	50	10	283	275
3	85	75	11	312	300
4	113	100	12	340	350
5	142	150	13	368	375
6	170	175	14	396	400
7	198	200	15	425	425
8	227	225	16(1lb)	454	450

Note

When converting quantities over 16 oz first add the appropriate figures in the centre column, then adjust to the nearest unit of 25. As a general guide, 1kg (1000g) equals 2.2 lb or about 2 lb 3 oz. This method of conversion gives good results in nearly all cases, although in certain pastry and cake recipes a more accurate conversion is necessary to produce a balanced recipe.

Liquid measures

The millilitre has been used in this book and the following table gives a few examples.

Imperial	Approx ml to nearest whole figure	Recommended ml	Imperial	Approx ml to nearest whole figure	Recommended ml
1/4	142	150ml	1 pint	567	600 ml
1/2	238	300ml	1 1/2 pints	851	900 ml
3/4	425	450ml	1 3/4 pints	992	1000 ml (1 litre)

Spoon measures

All spoon measures given in this book are level unless otherwise stated.

Can sizes

At present, cans are marked with the exact (usually to the nearest whole number) metric equivalent of the Imperial weight of the contents, so we have followed this practice when giving can sizes.

Oven temperatures

The table below gives recommended equivalents.

	°C	°F	Gas Mark		°C	°F	Gas Mark
Very cool	110	225	1/4	Moderately hot	190	375	5
	120	250	1/2		200	400	6
Cool	140	275	1	Hot	220	425	7
	150	300	2		230	450	8
Moderate	160	325	3	Very Hot	240	475	9
	180	350	4				

NOTES FOR AMERICAN AND AUSTRALIAN USERS

In America the 8-fl oz measuring cup is used. In Australia metric measures are now used in conjunction with the standard 250-ml measuring cup. The Imperial pint, used in Britain and Australia, is 20 fl oz, while the American pint is 16 fl oz. It is important to remember that the Australian tablespoon differs from the British and American tablespoons; the table below gives a comparison. The British standard tablespoon, which has been used throughout this book, holds 17.7 ml, the American 14.2 ml, and the Australian 20 ml. A teaspoon holds approximately 5 ml in all three countries.

British	American	Australian
1 teaspoon	1 teaspoon	1 teaspoon
1 tablespoon	1 tablespoon	1 tablespoon
2 tablespoons	3 tablespoons	2 tablespoons
3 1/2 tablespoons	4 tablespoons	3 tablespoons
4 tablespoons	5 tablespoons	3 1/2 tablespoons

AN IMPERIAL/AMERICAN GUIDE TO SOLID AND LIQUID MEASURES

Imperial	American	Imperial	American
Solid measures		**Liquid measures**	
1 lb butter or margarine	2 cups	1/4 pint liquid	2/3 cup liquid
1lb flour	4 cups	1/2 pint	1 1/4 cups
1 lb granulated or caster sugar	2 cups	1/4 pint	2 cups
1 lb icing sugar	3 cups	1 pint	2 1/2 cups
8 oz rice	1 cup	1 1/2 pints	3 3/4 cups
		2 pints	5 cups (2 1/2 pints)

NOTE: WHEN MAKING ANY OF THE RECIPES IN THIS BOOK, ONLY FOLLOW ONE SET OF MEASURES AS THEY ARE NOT INTERCHANGEABLE.

INTRODUCTION

The great appeal of casseroles is that they can be prepared and cooked in advance, which makes them ideal for the busy cook. This new addition to the Hamlyn All-Colour Series is a highly varied collection of casseroles to suit all tastes, from the dedicated meat-eater to the dedicated vegetarian. Every recipe is illustrated, to help in making a selection, and the Cook's Tip gives advice on difficult techniques, unusual ingredients and alternatives. Preparation and cooking times help in advance planning and calorie counts are included as additional aids to healthy eating.

Casserole cooking is international. It is, after all, one of the oldest forms of cooking - long, slow enclosed simmering over a fire or in an oven - and many casseroles, including a good few in this book, are foreign in origin, coming from many of the countries of Europe, from Asia, Africa and even the Pacific.

The traditional concept of a casserole is a meat-based dish, and there is in this book a chapter which includes many of the traditional hearty casseroles. But in fact, casserole cooking, which produces a richly flavoured, perfectly tender dish, is also ideal for cooking game, poultry, vegetables, pasta and fish.

Fish casseroles need a much shorter cooking time than meats and both fish and shellfish respond well to the moist, enclosed casserole system of cooking. You will find a surprising varied array of fish casseroles for summer and winter eating in this book.

There is a whole chapter on game, now widely available all year round, in supermarkets, fresh or frozen. Game is an ideal subject for the casserole treatment: pheasant, venison and wild duck for instance tend to be dry meats, so the long, slow simmering in liquid helps to keep them tender, moist and full of flavour. Chicken, turkey and duck, all widely available all year round, are also ideal for casserole cooking. Duck can be a fatty bird, but removing the skin, or draining off the fat after browning, will solve the problem.

There is a complete chapter on vegetable casseroles, containing a great diversity of dishes, most of them suitable for vegetarian diets. Vegetarians must also take note of their protein intake, so there is a chapter on nutritious dishes containing rice and pulses, proving that vegetarian casseroles can also be delicious. Pasta is also increasing in popularity, and so we have included a selection of attractive, filling baked pastas, easy to assemble and cook.

Our final chapter is a selection of dishes for special occasions. Casseroles can be homely and old-fashioned, but they can also be elegant and impressive. These are dishes you can be proud to put in front of your guests - and you can also feel a little smug, knowing how little trouble they took to cook, thanks to the casserole.

FISH

Possibly a surprising chapter in a casseroles book, and surprising, too, in the number and variety of the recipes. There are everyday, nourishing dishes such as the many variations on fish pie, exciting Mediterranean fish stews, classic dishes of salmon and trout and, of course, shell fish.

1 PORTUGUESE MUSSEL FEAST

Preparation time:
45 minutes, plus marinating

Cooking time:
30 minutes

Oven temperature:
190C/375F/gas 5

Serves 4

Calories:
366 per portion

YOU WILL NEED:
450 g/1 lb hake or cod, cut into
   5 cm/2 inch pieces
1 kg/2 lb mussels, cleaned
1 x 200 g/7 oz can pimentos,
   drained and sliced
4 large tomatoes, skinned and
   quartered
2 tablespoons tomato purée
8 tablespoons dry white wine
3 tablespoons fresh white
   breadcrumbs
FOR THE MARINADE
6 tablespoons olive oil
2 teaspoons red wine vinegar
2 tablespoons chopped parsley
½ teaspoon dried thyme
large pinch of cayenne
1 garlic clove, crushed (optional)
1 small onion, chopped
1 bay leaf

Mix the marinade ingredients in a deep flameproof casserole, add the hake, cover and set aside for at least 2 hours. Cover and bake the fish in the marinade in a preheated oven for 15 minutes.

Add the mussels, pimentos, tomatoes, tomato purée, wine and breadcrumbs. Stir carefully without breaking up the fish and cook, uncovered for 10 minutes. Taste the sauce and adjust the seasoning, if necessary. Serve with plenty of French bread.

■ COOK'S TIP

Wash mussels thoroughly under running cold water, then scrub vigorously with a stiff brush. Discard any that are even slightly opened. Scrape off the black 'beard' with a small sharp knife.

2 HONEY AND ALMOND FISH STEAKS

Preparation time:
15 minutes

Cooking time:
20 minutes

Serves 4

Calories:
455 per portion

YOU WILL NEED:
4 cod or halibut steaks, about
   175-200 g/6-7 oz each, frozen
2 tablespoons plain flour
salt and pepper
½ teaspoon ground coriander
3 tablespoons oil
150 ml/¼ pint sweet cider
4 tablespoons lemon juice
3 tablespoons clear honey
1 garlic clove, crushed (optional)
1 teaspoon dried rosemary, finely
   crumbled
50 g/2 oz seedless raisins
50 g/2 oz blanched almonds,
   toasted
sprigs of coriander, to garnish

Wash and dry the fish. Season the flour with salt, pepper and coriander, then coat the fish thoroughly. Heat the oil in a shallow flameproof casserole and fry the fish over moderate heat for 3-4 minutes on each side, until evenly golden. Remove from the heat.

Put the cider, lemon juice, honey, garlic, if using, rosemary and raisins into a small pan. Boil for 2 minutes, then pour over the fish, cover and simmer for 5 minutes. Scatter the almonds over the fish and garnish with coriander.

■ COOK'S TIP

Serve this dish with saffron rice: add ½ teaspoon of saffron powder to rice cooked by the boiling water method, or a large pinch if steaming rice.

3 CRAB-STUFFED ROLLS

Preparation time:
20 minutes, plus
marinating

Cooking time:
40 minutes

Oven temperature:
180C/350F/gas 4

Serves 6

Calories:
593 per portion

YOU WILL NEED:
6 x 100 g/4 oz skinned fillets of sole
250 ml/8 fl oz dry white wine
40 g/1½ oz butter
1 medium onion, finely chopped
100 g/4 oz mushrooms, chopped
225 g/8 oz cooked white crabmeat
40 g/1½ oz chopped parsley
2 tablespoons dried breadcrumbs
salt and white pepper
1 tablespoon sieved hard-boiled
egg yolk
½ teaspoon paprika
cheese sauce, see Cook's Tip

Place the sole fillets in a dish, cover with the white wine. Marinate for 1 hour, then remove, reserving the wine. Melt the butter in a large frying pan. Add the onion and mushrooms and cook for 10 minutes, stirring occasionally. Transfer to a large bowl and stir in the crabmeat, 25 g/1 oz parsley, breadcrumbs, salt and pepper.

Place an equal amount of stuffing on each fillet and roll up. Transfer the fillets, seam-side down, to a casserole and cover with the reserved wine. Cover the casserole with greaseproof paper, transfer to a preheated oven and cook for 10 minutes.

While the fish is cooking, make the cheese sauce. Remove the fillets from the oven, and stir the liquid into the sauce. Pour the sauce over the fillets and sprinkle with paprika. Return to the oven and continue cooking for another 15 minutes. Serve sprinkled with the remaining parsley and egg yolk.

■ COOK'S TIP

For cheese sauce, melt 50 g/ 2 oz butter over medium heat Blend in 4 tablespoons flour and cook for 2-3 minutes, stirring. Gradually whisk in 250 ml/8 fl oz single cream. Blend in 225g/8 oz grated Gruyère until melted, then add 2 tablespoons lemon juice.

4 MALAYSIAN FISH CURRY

Preparation time:
30 minutes, plus
soaking

Cooking time:
25 minutes

Serves 4

Calories:
489 per portion

YOU WILL NEED:
450 g/1 lb desiccated coconut
450 ml/¾ pint hot water
1 medium onion, finely chopped
1 garlic clove, crushed (optional)
2.5 cm/1 inch fresh root ginger,
    peeled and finely chopped
2 dried red chillies, cored, seeded
    and finely chopped
4 tablespoons tomato purée
6 tablespoons oil
750 g/1½ lb fillet cod, cut into
    4 cm/1½ inch slices
175 g/6 oz okra, trimmed
3 tablespoons lemon juice
salt

Soak the coconut in the hot water for 2 hours. Liquidize in a blender or food processor then pass through a sieve. Add more water if necessary to make 300 ml/½ pint.

Process the onion, garlic, ginger, chillies, 2 tablespoons tomato purée and 1 tablespoon oil in a food processor. Heat the remaining oil in a shallow flameproof casserole and fry the spice paste over moderate heat for 3-4 minutes. Add the fish and turn in the paste to coat thoroughly.

Add the remaining tomato purée, the okra, coconut 'milk' and lemon juice and season with salt. Bring to the boil, cover and simmer over low heat for 10 minutes, turning the fish in the sauce once or twice. Serve with lemon quarters, rice and sliced bananas tossed in lemon juice.

■ COOK'S TIP

Okra are best cooked whole, as they tend to have a slimy texture if cut up. Choose small ones if possible.

5 COD AND CHEDDAR CASEROLE

Preparation time:	YOU WILL NEED:
45 minutes	50 g/2 oz butter
	1 medium onion, finely chopped
Cooking time:	100 g/4 oz mushrooms, sliced
1 hour	50 g/2 oz plain flour
	350 ml/12 fl oz milk
Oven temperature:	50 ml/2 fl oz dry white wine
200C/400F/gas 6	175 g/6 oz Cheddar cheese, grated
	salt and white pepper
Serves 4	750 g/1½ lb thick cod or
	haddock fillets, skinned
Calories:	1 red pepper, cored, seeded and
670 per portion	diced
	8 topping balls (see Cook's Tip)

Melt the butter, add the onion and mushrooms then cook for 10 minutes, stirring occasionally. Blend in the flour and cook for 2-3 minutes, stirring frequently. Using a whisk, gradually stir in the milk and white wine. Bring the sauce to the boil and simmer for 2-3 minutes until smooth and thick. Add the cheese, salt and pepper and cook until the cheese has just melted. Remove from the heat and set aside.

Place the cod fillets in a large casserole. Sprinkle with the red pepper. Pour the sauce over the cod.

Place the topping balls on the casserole. Cover and cook for 20 minutes or until the topping is cooked and the fish flakes easily.

6 SALMON IN RED WINE

Preparation time:	YOU WILL NEED:
15 minutes	4 salmon steaks, about 2.5 cm/
	1 inch thick
Cooking time:	salt and pepper
about 35 minutes	1 bay leaf
	2-3 spring onions, trimmed and
Oven temperature:	finely chopped
180C/350F/gas 4	1 small carrot, sliced
	150 ml/¼ pint light red wine
Serves 4	2 tablespoons water
	25 g/1 oz butter
Calories:	2-3 tablespoons whipping cream
336 per portion	2 teaspoons finely chopped parsley
	wedges of lemon and cucumber
	twists, to garnish

Place the salmon in a shallow, buttered ovenproof dish just large enough to take the steaks in a single layer. Sprinkle with salt and pepper and add the bay leaf.

Scatter the spring onions and carrot slices over the salmon, pour in the red wine and water and dot with butter. Cover closely with a lid or foil and cook in the centre of a preheated oven for 30 minutes or until the salmon is cooked through. Carefully transfer the salmon to a serving dish and keep hot.

Strain the cooking liquid into a clean pan and boil rapidly until it is reduced to about 2 tablespoons. Remove from the heat and stir in the cream and parsley. Check the seasoning, then pour over the cooked salmon. Garnish with wedges of lemon and cucumber twists.

■ COOK'S TIP

To make the topping, mix 50 g/2 oz self-raising flour, 50 g/2 oz breadcrumbs, 2 tablespoons parsley, 2 teaspoons lemon rind, salt and pepper in a large bowl.

Make a well in the centre and add 1 beaten egg. Quickly combine into the dough and shape into 8 balls.

■ COOK'S TIP

You could also cook a whole fish - perhaps a salmon trout - using this recipe.

7   WILD RICE FISH CASSEROLE

Preparation time:	YOU WILL NEED:
30 minutes	275 g/10 oz wild rice
	750 ml/1¼ pints beef stock
Cooking time:	50 g/2 oz butter
40 minutes, plus 1	225 g/8 oz cooked, shelled prawns
hour for the rice	225 g/8 oz cooked white crabmeat
	FOR THE MUSHROOM SAUCE
Oven temperature:	35 g/1¼ oz butter
160C/325F/gas 3	100 g/4 oz mushrooms, sliced
	4 tablespoons chopped shallots
Serves 6	1½ teaspoons curry powder
	1½ tablespoons plain flour
Calories:	300 ml/8 fl oz milk
572 per portion	175 ml/6 fl oz double cream
	2 tablespoons Chinese oyster sauce

Place the rice, stock and butter, in the top of a double boiler. Cover and steam for 45 minutes to 1 hour over a medium-low heat. Remove from the heat and gently stir in the butter.

For the mushroom sauce, melt the butter over a medium heat. Add the mushrooms and shallots, and cook for 10 minutes, stirring. Stir in the curry powder, blend in the flour and cook for 2-3 minutes, stirring constantly. Gradually whisk in the milk. Cook until thick and smooth. Blend in the double cream and oyster sauce. Cook, stirring, for 5 minutes.

Spoon half of the wild rice mixture on to the bottom of an oval casserole. Cover evenly with the prawns and crab. Add the remaining rice mixture, smoothing the top down. Spoon the mushroom sauce over the rice. Transfer the casserole to a preheated oven and cook for 30 minutes, until heated through.

▪ COOK'S TIP

Wild rice is not rice, but the long, narrow, dark brown grain of a native American grass. It is expensive. If it is unavailable, brown rice may be used instead.

8   HADDOCK WITH GRAPEFRUIT AND MUSHROOMS

Preparation time:	YOU WILL NEED:
10 minutes	4 haddock fillets, skinned
	50 g/2 oz butter
Cooking time:	3 spring onions, chopped
30 minutes	salt and pepper
	2 grapefruit
Oven temperature:	100 g/4 oz mushrooms, sliced
180C/350F/gas 4	
Serves 4	
Calories:	
229 per portion	

Arrange the haddock fillets in a greased casserole. Mash the butter with the spring onions and salt and pepper to taste. Grate the rind from the grapefruit and beat into the butter. Spread this over the haddock fillets. Cover with the mushrooms.

Squeeze the juice from one grapefruit and peel and segment the other. Pour the grapefruit juice over the mushrooms and place the grapefruit segments on top.

Cover and cook in a preheated moderate oven for about 30 minutes or until the fish is cooked.

▪ COOK'S TIP

Pilau rice and a green salad would be a good choice to serve with this exotic dish.

9 COTRIADE

Preparation time:
25 minutes

Cooking time:
1½ hours

Serves 4

Calories:
395 per portion

YOU WILL NEED:
1.5 kg/3 lb mixed fish fillets
2 tablespoons orange juice
1 tablespoon cider vinegar
2 large onions, sliced
2 garlic cloves, finely chopped
225 g/8 oz potatoes, sliced
1 bouquet garni
salt and pepper
2 tablespoons oil
FOR THE FISH STOCK
1 carrot, trimmed and quartered
2 celery stocks, sliced
1 medium onion, quartered
2 bay leaves
2 sprigs fresh parsley
900 ml/1½ pints water
salt and pepper

For the stock, put the fish trimmings into a large saucepan with all the other ingredients. Bring to the boil and skim off any foam. Cover and simmer for 45 minutes. Strain the stock through a colander lined with cheesecloth.

Put the fish stock, orange juice, vinegar, onions, garlic, potatoes and the bouquet garni into a pan. Season with salt and pepper and bring to the boil. Cover the pan and simmer for 20 minutes. Cut the fish fillets into bite-sized pieces, add them to the pan, pour on the oil and bring to the boil again. Cover and simmer for 10 minutes, until the fish feels firm. Serve very hot in deep plates, garnished with croûtons.

■ COOK'S TIP

You can use a selection of white fish such as cod, haddock and whiting together with a small herring or mackerel. Too high a proportion of oily fish will give the dish a strong, almost bitter flavour.

10 RAINBOW TROUT WITH BROWN BUTTER

Preparation time:
15 minutes

Cooking time:
about 45 minutes

Oven temperature:
160C/325F/gas 3

Serves 4

Calories:
498 per portion

YOU WILL NEED:
4 rainbow trout, cleaned
salt and pepper
50 g/2 oz butter
50 g/2 oz blanched almonds, roughly chopped
2 tablespoons lemon juice
FOR THE STUFFING BALLS
75 g/3 oz fresh breadcrumbs
2 tablespoons grated onion
grated rind of ½ lemon
25 g/1 oz blanched almonds, finely chopped
1 tablespoon chopped fresh parsley
1 egg yolk
lemon wedges, to garnish

Lightly grease an ovenproof dish. Sprinkle the fish inside with salt and pepper and lay in the dish in a single layer. Melt the butter in a pan and fry the almonds until lightly browned. Remove from the heat, stir in the lemon juice and pour quickly over the fish.

For the stuffing balls, place the breadcrumbs in a bowl with the onion, lemon rind, chopped nuts and parsley. Add salt and pepper and bind with the egg yolk. Divide into 8, shape into balls and arrange round the fish. Cover and cook in a preheated oven for about 45 minutes or until the fish are tender. Serve garnished with lemon wedges.

■ COOK'S TIP

Trout are always served with their heads on, unless smoked. If you find this unappealing, cover the eye with a slice of stuffed olive or tiny sprig of parsley.

11 SMOKED HADDOCK AND BACON POT PIE

Preparation time:
20 minutes

Cooking time:
40 minutes

Oven temperature:
180C/350F/gas 4

Serves 2-3

Calories:
458-306 per portion

YOU WILL NEED:
450 g/1 lb smoked haddock fillets
½ teaspoon freshly ground black
   pepper
4 rashers back bacon, rinded and
   diced
40 g/1½ oz butter
350 g/12 oz tomatoes, skinned,
   quartered and seeded
75 g/3 oz fine fresh white
   breadcrumbs

Place the haddock fillets in a large frying pan, pour in boiling water just to cover and poach gently for 10 minutes. Remove from the heat and cool slightly, then flake, removing skin and any bones. Season with the pepper. Fry the bacon without added fat, until softened.

Grease a baking dish with one-third of the butter. Place the fish in the dish, then the tomatoes and the bacon. Sprinkle with the breadcrumbs and dot with the remaining butter. Bake in a preheated oven for 30 minutes, until the topping is crisp and golden brown.

12 FISH BOULANGERE

Preparation time:
10 minutes

Cooking time:
50 minutes

Oven temperature:
180C/350F/gas 4

Serves 4

Calories:
339 per portion

YOU WILL NEED:
450 g/1 lb potatoes
salt and pepper
50 g/2 oz butter
1 garlic clove, very finely chopped
750 g/1½ lb white fish fillets,
   skinned and cut into chunks
1 large onion, thinly sliced

Parcook the potatoes in boiling salted water for 10 minutes. Drain and slice thinly.

Cream half the butter with the garlic and spread over the bottom of a casserole. Arrange the fish chunks on top and sprinkle with salt and pepper. Cover with the onion and then the potato slices. Dot with the remaining butter.

Cook in a preheated moderate oven for about 40 minutes or until the fish and potatoes are tender.

■ COOK'S TIP

Baked potatoes would go well with this traditional Welsh fisherman's dish.

■ COOK'S TIP

Smoked fish, say Arbroath smokies, would give an added tang to this dish.

13 PRAWN GUMBO WITH RICE

Preparation time:	YOU WILL NEED:
30 minutes	2 tablespoons oil
	2 sticks celery, finely sliced
Cooking time:	1 onion, diced
1¼ hours	1 green pepper, seeded and diced
	1 garlic clove, crushed
Oven temperature:	1 tablespoon Worcestershire sauce
160C/325F/gas 3	1 x 425 g/15 oz can tomatoes
	300 ml/½ pint tomato juice
Serves 8	salt and pepper
	100 g/4 oz long-grain rice
Calories:	100 g/4 oz okra, stem removed,
181 per portion	sliced
	225 g/8 oz peeled prawns, fresh or
	frozen
	225 g/8 oz dressed crabmeat, fresh
	or frozen
	4 tablespoons dry sherry
	croûtons and chopped fresh
	parsley, to garnish

Heat the oil in a flameproof casserole, cook the celery, onion and pepper gently for 5 minutes. Add the garlic, Worcestershire sauce, tomatoes, tomato juice, and season with salt and pepper.

Stir in the rice and okra, and bring gently to simmering point. Cover, and cook in a preheated oven for 1 hour.

Gently stir in the prawns, crabmeat and sherry (if the rice looks a little dry, add more tomato juice). Re-cover and return to the oven for 15 minutes. Pour into a heated serving dish, group the croûtons at either end and sprinkle with parsley.

■ COOK'S TIP

This dish comes originally from the American Deep South. Use Tabasco instead of Worcestershire sauce for a more authentic flavour.

14 PLAICE PAUPIETTES WITH SMOKED SALMON

Preparation time:	YOU WILL NEED:
20 minutes	4 plaice (about 350 g/12 oz each)
	filleted
Cooking time:	salt and pepper
50 minutes	100 g/4 oz smoked salmon
	40 g/1½ oz butter or margarine
Oven temperature:	40 g/1½ oz flour
180C/350F/gas 4	150 ml/¼ pint dry white wine
	300 ml/½ pint milk
Serves 4	3 tablespoons single cream
	1 tablespoon lemon juice
Calories:	8 whole prawns and sprigs of
573 per portion	parsley, fennel or dill (optional),
	to garnish

Wipe the 8 plaice fillets and sprinkle lightly with salt and pepper. Divide the smoked salmon into 8 pieces and lay 1 piece on the skin side of each fillet. Roll up loosely towards the tail and place in a lightly greased, shallow ovenproof dish.

Melt the butter or margarine in a pan, stir in the flour and cook for 1 minute. Gradually add the wine, followed by the milk and bring to the boil for 2 minutes. Add plenty of salt and pepper, stir in the cream and lemon juice and pour this sauce over the fish.

Cover the dish with foil or a lid and cook in a preheated oven for about 50 minutes or until cooked through.

Remove the foil and garnish the plaice rolls with whole prawns and parsley, fennel or dill (if using).

■ COOK'S TIP

If you prefer to remove the plaice skin, it is quite simple. Place on a wooden board and, using a sharp knife, begin at the tail and carefully run the knife *along towards the head, keeping the blade slanting downwards and working away from you. The fillet will then lift away from the skin.*

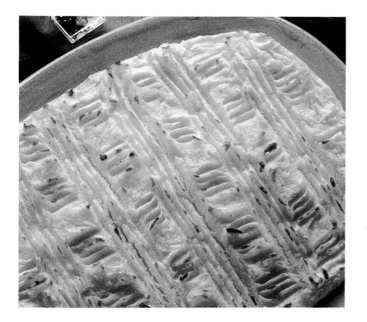

15   FISH PIE

Preparation time:	YOU WILL NEED:
15 minutes plus cooling	1 kg/2 lb potatoes, peeled and cut into chunks
	750 g/1½ lb cod, hake or haddock
Cooking time:	fillets, skinned and cut into 4
50 minutes	equal pieces
	salt and pepper
Oven temperature:	900 ml/1½ pints milk
180C/350F/gas 4	75 g/3 oz butter
	40 g/1½ oz plain flour
Serves 4	

Calories:
660 per portion

Boil the potatoes in salted water until tender. Meanwhile, grease a shallow ovenproof dish and add the fish in two layers. Season and pour over 750 ml/1¼ pints of the milk. Cover with foil and bake in a preheated oven for 25 minutes.

Drain the potatoes, add 40 g/1½ oz butter and 150 ml/¼ pint milk and beat until soft and creamy.

Melt 25 g/1 oz of the butter in a medium saucepan, sprinkle in the flour and cook, stirring, for 1-2 minutes. Remove from the heat. Strain the cooking liquid and gradually stir into the butter and flour mixture. Return to the heat and cook, stirring, for 2-3 minutes. Pour the sauce over the fish.

Spoon the potato over the fish and lightly smooth the surface, then mark the top in a pattern with the fork. Dot with the remaining butter. Bake near the top of the preheated oven for about 25 minutes, until the topping is browned.

▮ COOK'S TIP

For a richer dish, add 85 ml/3 fl oz white wine to the roux before adding the milk and 2 tablespoons of double cream to the sauce before pouring it over the fish.

16   CREAMED SCALLOPS FANTASIA

Preparation time:	YOU WILL NEED:
10 minutes	8 large or 16 small scallops
	150 ml/¼ pint dry white wine
Cooking time:	1 x 225 g/8 oz can pineapple slices
20 minutes	1 tablespoon cornflour
	300 ml/½ pint single cream
Oven temperature:	1 tablespoon finely chopped
160C/325F/gas 3	parsley
	2-3 teaspoons lemon juice
Serves 4	salt and pepper
	2 tomatoes, skinned, seeded and
Calories:	chopped
259 per portion	100 g/4 oz peeled prawns

Cut large scallops into 4 slices or small scallops in half. Place in a pan with the white wine and 2 tablespoons of the pineapple syrup. Cover and simmer gently for 5 minutes.

Transfer the scallops to a buttered, shallow casserole and keep the cooking liquid on one side. Blend the cornflour with a little of the cream, then add to the reserved liquid together with the parsley and the remainder of the cream. Bring slowly to simmering point and simmer for 1 minute. Season to taste and add lemon juice.

Reserve 1 pineapple ring and 8 prawns for garnish. Chop the rest of the pineapple rings and add to the casserole with the tomatoes and the rest of the prawns. Stir together. Pour the sauce over the prepared ingredients until completely coated. Garnish with the reserved pineapple and prawns. Cover and cook in a preheated oven for 15 minutes.

▮ COOK'S TIP

If you dislike the sweet taste of fruit syrup use pineapple canned in pure fruit juice instead. This dish is good served with boiled rice.

17 BAKED MACKEREL WITH RHUBARB SAUCE

Preparation time:	YOU WILL NEED:
15 minutes	4 mackerel, cleaned and filleted
	4 bay leaves
Cooking time:	12 black peppercorns
30-40 minutes	300 ml/½ pint dry cider
	225 g/8 oz prepared rhubarb
Oven temperature:	4 tablespoons cider
180C/350F/gas 4	1 teaspoon lemon juice
	pinch of ground mace
Serves 4	pinch of ground cinnamon
	2 tablespoons butter
Calories:	
403 per portion	

Put the mackerel fillets into an ovenproof dish with a bay leaf on each, then scatter the peppercorns around. Barely cover the fish with cider and bake in the preheated oven for about 30-40 minutes. When cooked, keep hot.

Put the rhubarb and all the other ingredients except the butter into a small saucepan. Cook until puréed. Before serving, add the butter in pieces so that it melts through the hot purée.

18 GREEK PRAWN CASSEROLE

Preparation time:	YOU WILL NEED:
10 minutes	300 ml/½ pint water
	juice of ½ lemon
Cooking time:	1 kg/2 lb unshelled raw prawns
30 minutes	3 tablespoons olive oil
	1 onion, finely chopped
Oven temperature:	1 garlic clove, crushed
180C/350F/gas 4	2 x 397 g/14 oz can tomatoes,
	drained and chopped
Serves 4	¼ teaspoon dried oregano
	salt and pepper
Calories:	75 g/3 oz Feta cheese, crumbled
268 per portion	

Bring the water and lemon juice to the boil in a saucepan. Add the prawns and simmer for 5 minutes or until pink. Drain, reserving the liquid, cool slightly, then remove the shells. Boil the liquid until reduced to 150 ml/¼ pint.

Heat the oil in a flameproof casserole. Add the onion and garlic and fry until softened. Stir in the tomatoes, oregano, reserved prawn cooking liquid and salt and pepper to taste. Simmer until the sauce is reduced and thickened.

Fold the prawns into the sauce. Sprinkle the cheese on top and cook in a preheated moderate oven for 15 minutes.

■ COOK'S TIP

Rhubarb is very acidic so it is healthier to cook it in a stainless steel pan, rather than aluminium.

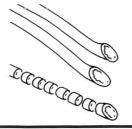

■ COOK'S TIP

If raw prawns are unobtainable, substitute 450 g/1 lb frozen, shelled prawns. Do not precook; simply thaw and add them to the cooked sauce. For the *cooking liquor use 150 ml/¼ pint water and 2 teaspoons lemon juice.*

19 CREAMY FINNAN HADDIE CASSEROLE

Preparation time:	YOU WILL NEED:
15 minutes	450 g/1 lb boneless finnan haddie
	750 ml/1¼ pints boiling water
Cooking time:	50 g/2 oz butter
35 minutes	50 g/2 oz plain flour
	350 ml/12 fl oz single cream
Oven temperature:	¼ teaspoon paprika
190C/375F/gas 5	salt (optional)
	white pepper
Serves 4	50 g/2 oz Cheddar cheese, grated
	15 g/½ oz butter, for greasing
Calories:	25 g/1 oz soft white breadcrumbs
535 per portion	25 g/1 oz Cheddar cheese, grated

Place the fish in a medium saucepan. Cover with the boiling water. Simmer over a low heat for 10 minutes, until the fish flakes easily. Drain, then flake the fish into a medium bowl.

Melt the butter in a small saucepan over a moderate heat. Blend in the flour and cook for 2-3 minutes, stirring constantly. Using a whisk, gradually stir in the cream. Bring the sauce to a simmer and cook, stirring constantly, until thick and smooth. Remove from the heat, then add paprika, salt, and pepper.

Blend the sauce with the fish. Add the cheese and stir well. Grease a medium casserole with the butter. Pour the fish mixture into the casserole. Top with the breadcrumbs and cheese. Place in a preheated oven and cook for 20-25 minutes, until the top is brown. Serve with lemon wedges, toast and a cucumber salad.

■ COOK'S TIP

Finnan haddock is a speciality of Arbroath in Scotland. If unavailable, use ordinary smoked haddock, though the flavour's not so fine.

20 SALMON CORN CASSEROLE

Preparation time:	YOU WILL NEED:
10 minutes	25 g/1 oz butter
	3 x 285 g/10½ oz cans cream-style corn
Cooking time:	
1 hour	1 x 425 g/15 oz can salmon
	3 eggs, beaten
Oven temperature:	25 g/1 oz cheese cracker crumbs
180C/350F/gas 4	salt and pepper
	6 lemon wedges and sprig parsley,
Serves 6	to garnish

Calories:
323 per portion

Grease a medium-size casserole with 1 tablespoon of the butter. Set aside.

Combine the corn, salmon, eggs, cracker crumbs, salt and pepper in a large bowl, reserving 1 tablespoon of cracker crumbs for the topping. Transfer the mixture to the casserole. Top the casserole with the reserved cracker crumbs and dot with the remaining butter. Transfer the uncovered casserole to a preheated oven and cook for 1 hour.

Garnish the casserole with the lemon wedges and parsley. Serve with a green salad for a quick light meal.

■ COOK'S TIP

This is a super-fast casserole to put together. If preferred you could use fresh-cooked, flaked salmon instead of canned.

21 HERRINGS POTTED IN GUINNESS

Preparation time:
30 minutes

Cooking time:
40 minutes

Oven temperature:
180C/350F/gas 4

Serves 4

Calories:
280 per portion

YOU WILL NEED:
4 fresh herrings, filleted
2 bay leaves
1 onion, sliced
4 whole cloves
6 black peppercorns
6 white peppercorns
150 ml/¼ pint Guinness or stout
150 ml/¼ pint malt vinegar
1 teaspoon sea salt

Roll up the herring fillets with a piece of bay leaf inside each and arrange in an ovenproof dish. Arrange the onion rings on top and scatter the cloves and peppercorns around.

Carefully pour over the Guinness or stout and vinegar. Scatter over the sea salt, cover with foil and bake in the centre of the preheated oven for 40 minutes.

Cool in the liquid and serve cold.

■ COOK'S TIP

These herrings are delicious served with buttered brown soda bread. They will keep in the refrigerator for 1 week.

22 SCOT'S HADDIE

Preparation time:
20 minutes

Cooking time:
about 45 minutes

Oven temperature:
180C/350F/gas 4;
then
220C/425F/gas 7

Serves 4-6

Calories:
608-405 per portion

YOU WILL NEED:
750 g/1½ lb smoked haddock
*   fillets*
300 ml/½ pint water
oatmeal topping (see Cook's Tip)
50 g/2 oz butter
50 g/2 oz plain flour
300 ml/½ pint milk
2 hard-boiled eggs, chopped
2 tablespoons finely chopped
*   parsley*
freshly ground black pepper
1 hard-boiled egg, sliced
sprigs of parsley, to garnish

Place the fish in a lightly greased casserole and pour in the water. Cover and cook in a preheated oven for 20 minutes. Meanwhile, make the topping.

Drain the fish, setting aside the liquid. Flake the haddock, discarding skin and bones, and return to the casserole.

Melt the butter, stir in the flour and cook for 1 minute. Blend in the milk and the reserved cooking liquid, bring to the boil and simmer for 1 minute, stirring. Add the hard-boiled eggs and parsley and season with pepper. Pour over the flaked fish in the casserole. Scatter the oatmeal topping over the fish and sauce so the surface is completely covered. Sprinkle with the remaining cheese. Increase the oven temperature. Cook, uncovered for 15-20 minutes or until the top is crisp and brown. Garnish with the egg slices and parsley.

■ COOK'S TIP

Grate hard cheeses like Cheddar and pack into freezer bags. Store for up to 6 months and use straight from the freezer for sauces and toppings.

23 MARIO'S CASSEROLE

Preparation time:
20 minutes

Cooking time:
40-50 minutes

Oven temperature:
180C/350F/gas 4

Serves 4-6

Calories:
410-274 per portion

YOU WILL NEED:
175 g/6 oz coley fillets
175 g/6 oz cod fillets
175 g/6 oz swordfish fillets
175 g/6 oz lemon sole fillets
450 g/1 lb potatoes, peeled
2 tablespoons oil
1 onion, chopped
1 garlic clove, crushed
1 stick celery, chopped
*50 g/2 oz streaky bacon, rinded
    and diced*
150 ml/¼ pint dry white wine
450 g/1 lb tomatoes, chopped
1 canned red pimiento, sliced
2 tablespoons chopped parsley
½ teaspoon dill
salt and pepper
100 g/4 oz peeled prawns
1 x 150 g/5 oz jar mussels, drained

Cut the fish into 2.5 cm/1 inch cubes. Cook the potatoes in boiling salted water for 10 minutes until parboiled. Drain well then dice. Heat the oil in a flameproof casserole, add the onion, garlic, celery and streaky bacon and cook gently for 5 minutes. Add the wine, tomatoes, red pimiento, parsley and dill and season. Simmer for 2-3 minutes. Stir in the fish and potatoes.

Cover and cook in a preheated oven for 15-25 minutes or until cooked through. Add the prawns and mussels, cook for a further 5 minutes. Serve garnished with shredded lemon rind.

■ COOK'S TIP

For a simpler dish for six people, increase the quantity of fish to 1 kg/2 lb, but omit the red pimiento and the prawns and mussels. Serve the casserole *garnished with lemon slices and celery leaves.*

24 CHINESE CRAB AND RICE CASSEROLE

Preparation time:
15 minutes

Cooking time:
35 minutes

Oven temperature:
180C/350F/gas 4

Serves 4

Calories:
383 per portion

YOU WILL NEED:
1 tablespoon oil
1 onion, chopped
2 celery sticks, sliced
350 g/12 oz cooked long-grain rice
50 g/2 oz frozen peas
*1 x 225 g/8 oz can water-
    chestnuts, drained*
225 g/8 oz crabmeat
25 g/1 oz butter
50 g/2 oz blanched almonds
150 ml/¼ pint tomato juice
1 tablespoon light soy sauce
salt and pepper

Heat the oil in a pan, add the onion and celery and cook until soft, then add to the rice in a mixing bowl with the peas, water chestnuts and crabmeat.

Melt the butter in a pan, fry the almonds until lightly browned, then add to the rice mixture with the tomato juice, soy sauce, salt and pepper and mix well.

Put the mixture into a casserole. Cover, put into a preheated oven and cook for 25 minutes.

■ COOK'S TIP

For a complete Chinese meal serve with stir-fried mushrooms and beansprouts.

25 BACCALA

Preparation time:	YOU WILL NEED:
15 minutes, plus	450 g/1 lb salt cod
soaking	2 tablespoons olive oil
	1 onion, chopped
Cooking time:	1 green pepper, cored, seeded and
1½ hours	chopped
	1 garlic clove, crushed
Oven temperature:	1 x 400 g/14 oz can chopped
180C/350F/gas 4	tomatoes, juice reserved
	2 tablespoons chopped fresh
Serves 4	parsley
	salt and pepper
Calories:	450 g/1 lb cooked potatoes, sliced
301 per portion	2 hard-boiled eggs, shelled and cut
	into wedges, to garnish

Soak the cod in cold water for 24 hours, changing the water 3 or 4 times.

Drain the fish and put into fresh cold water, bring to the boil then simmer for 15-20 minutes, until the fish flakes easily. Drain, then leave until cool enough to handle. Skin, bone and flake the fish.

Heat the oil in a pan, add the onion, pepper and garlic and cook for 2 minutes. Add the tomatoes and their juice, parsley, a little salt and the pepper, bring to the boil, then add the fish.

Layer the potatoes and fish mixture in a casserole, starting with potatoes and ending with fish. Cover the casserole, put into a preheated oven and cook for 1 hour.

Serve garnished with the wedges of hard-boiled egg.

■ COOK'S TIP

If salt cod is unavailable, use 450 g/1 lb fresh cod and omit the initial soaking.

26 MACKEREL WITH SESAME AND ORANGE

Preparation time:	YOU WILL NEED:
10 minutes	grated rind and juice of 1 orange
	150 ml/¼ pint water
Cooking time:	1 tablespoon soy sauce
30 minutes	15 g/½ oz butter
	1 tablespoon sesame oil
Oven temperature:	4 large mackerel fillets, approx
190C/375F/gas 5	175 g/6 oz each
	2 teaspoons cornflour
Serves 4	½ teaspoon ground ginger
	salt and pepper
Calories:	1 tablespoon sesame seeds,
525 per portion	to garnish

Put the orange rind, juice, water and soy sauce into a pan, bring to the boil and simmer for 3 minutes.

Heat the butter and sesame oil in a large frying pan and lightly fry the mackerel for 1 minute on each side. Transfer the fish to a shallow casserole, skin side down.

Strain the orange juice mixture into the frying pan and reserve the rind. Mix the cornflour with a little water, then add it to the pan with the ginger, salt and pepper. Bring to the boil, then pour over the fish.

Cover the casserole, put into a preheated oven and cook for 20 minutes. Serve sprinkled with the reserved orange rind and sesame seeds.

■ COOK'S TIP

This would make a very elegant starter for a summer party. Follow with a dish with a blander flavour, such as a quiche.

27 PRAWN AND OKRA IN COCONUT SAUCE

Preparation time: 15 minutes	YOU WILL NEED: 2 tablespoons oil 1 small onion, finely chopped
Cooking time: 45 minutes	1 small green pepper, wiped clean and finely chopped 450 g/1 lb small, even-sized okra,
Oven temperature: 180C/350F/gas 4	stalk end removed 50 g/2 oz creamed coconut 300 ml/½ pint boiling water
Serves 4	1 tablespoon chilli sauce 1 tablespoon tomato purée
Calories: 265 per portion	salt and pepper 225 g/8 oz peeled prawns

Heat the oil in a flameproof casserole, add the onion and green pepper and cook until soft. Add the okra to the casserole and cook for a further minute.

Dissolve the creamed coconut in the boiling water, then add the chilli sauce, tomato purée, salt and pepper.

Pour the coconut mixture into the casserole, bring to the boil, cover and put into a preheated oven. Cook for 30 minutes.

Add the prawns to the casserole, mixing them well in. Cook the casserole, covered, for a further 10 minutes.

28 HERRINGS MARINATED AND BAKED IN TEA

Preparation time: 30 minutes	YOU WILL NEED: 8 herrings, cleaned 8 bay leaves
Cooking time: approximately 1 hour	1 tablespoon brown sugar 15 whole black peppercorns 150 ml/¼ pint white vinegar
Oven temperature: 180C/350F/gas 4	150 ml/¼ pint cold, milkless tea
Serves 4	
Calories: 350 per portion	

Lay the fish in an ovenproof dish and put a bay leaf, crumbled, into each one. Sprinkle evenly with the brown sugar and peppercorns.

Combine the vinegar and tea, then pour the mixture over the fish so that they are barely covered. Cover loosely with foil and bake in the preheated oven for about 1 hour.

Leave to get cold in the liquor, which will jell slightly. Serve a little of the jelly with each portion.

■ COOK'S TIP

This exotic dish is best served with stir-fried rice, tossed with soy sauce before serving.

■ COOK'S TIP

This is an excellent West Country method of pickling fish. Mackerel, sprats or pilchards can also be cooked in this way.

29 MEDITERRANEAN STOVE POT

Preparation time:
20 minutes

Cooking time:
30 minutes

Serves 4

Calories:
296 per portion

YOU WILL NEED:
750 g/1½ lb cod or haddock fillet
2 tablespoons plain flour
salt and pepper
1 teaspoon dried oregano
40 g/1½ oz butter
1 tablespoon oil
1 red and 1 green pepper, cored,
   seeded and sliced
2 medium onions, sliced
1 garlic clove, crushed
1 x 425 g/15 oz can tomatoes
1 teaspoon tomato purée
1 bay leaf
1 teaspoon sugar
2 tablespoons chopped fresh parsley
50 g/2 oz stuffed green olives

Skin the fish and cut into 5 cm/2 inch slices. Season the flour, add the oregano and coat the fish thoroughly.

Heat the butter and oil in a flameproof casserole and fry the peppers, onion and garlic gently for 3-4 minutes, stirring. Remove with a slotted spoon. Add the fish and fry for about 2-3 minutes on each side until golden. Remove and keep warm.

Tip the tomatoes into the casserole and stir in the tomato purée. Add the bay leaf, sugar and parsley. Bring to the boil and cook, uncovered, for 5 minutes to reduce the liquid slightly. Return the vegetables and fish to the casserole, bring back to the boil, cover and simmer for 15 minutes, until the fish is firm. Scatter the olives (cut in half) on top and serve.

■ COOK'S TIP

*Serve this hearty fish stew
with rice or boiled potatoes
and a green salad.*

30 GREEK COD WITH COURGETTES

Preparation time:
30 minutes, plus
soaking

Cooking time:
1 hour

Oven temperature:
180C/350F/gas 4

Serves 4

Calories:
351 per portion

YOU WILL NEED:
750 g/1½ lb dried salt cod
6 tablespoons olive oil
2 green peppers, cored, seeded and
   thickly sliced
2 medium onions, sliced
4 garlic cloves, chopped
450 g/1 lb tomatoes, skinned and
   chopped
1 tablespoon lemon juice
freshly ground black pepper
225 g/8 oz courgettes, trimmed
   and thinly sliced
2 tablespoons chopped parsley

Soak the fish (see below) then skin the fish and remove the bones. Cut into 5 cm/2 inch slices and dry on kitchen paper.

Heat 5 tablespoons of the oil in a flameproof casserole and fry the fish over moderate heat for 2-3 minutes on each side. Lift out the fish and set it aside.

Add the remaining oil and sauté the green peppers and onions for 3-4 minutes, stirring once or twice. Stir in the garlic and tomatoes and bring to the boil. Add the fish and lemon juice, season with pepper and cover the dish. Cook in a preheated oven for 30 minutes.

Add the courgettes, cover and continue cooking for 15 minutes. Adjust the seasoning and stir in the parsley.

■ COOK'S TIP

*Dried salt cod looks like old
leather and must be well
soaked before use. Soak for
2 days in a large bowl of
cold water, changing the
water several times.*

31 SMOKED FISH CURRY

Preparation time:	YOU WILL NEED:
10 minutes	*750 g/1½ lb smoked haddock,*
	skinned and cut into chunks
Cooking time:	*2 tablespoons oil*
30 minutes	*1 onion, finely chopped*
	1 garlic clove, crushed
Oven temperature:	*1 teaspoon turmeric*
180C/350F/gas 4	*1 tablespoon mild curry powder*
	25 g/1 oz creamed coconut
Serves 4	*150 ml/¼ pint boiling water*
	1 tablespoon mango chutney
Calories:	*salt and pepper*
300 per portion	*25 g/1 oz toasted desiccated*
	coconut

Put the fish into a casserole. Heat the oil in a pan, add the onion and garlic and cook until soft. Add the turmeric and curry powder to the pan and cook for 1 minute.

Dissolve the creamed coconut in the water. Add the coconut water and mango chutney to the pan, bring to the boil, add salt and pepper to taste, then pour over the fish. Mix well.

Cover the casserole and cook for 25 minutes. Serve sprinkled with the toasted coconut.

32 SEAFOOD CASSEROLE

Preparation time:	YOU WILL NEED:
10 minutes	*450 g/1 lb haddock or cod fillet,*
	skinned
Cooking time:	*225 g/8 oz smoked haddock fillet,*
40-45 minutes	*skinned*
	100 g/4 oz peeled prawns
Oven temperature:	*3-4 scallops, quartered or 1 x 150*
180C/350F/gas 4	*g/5 oz jar mussels, drained*
	1 x 325 g/11 oz can sweetcorn
Serves 6	*kernels, drained*
	1-2 canned red pimentos, sliced
Calories:	*(optional)*
293 per portion	*40 g/1½ oz butter or margarine*
	40 g/1½ oz flour
	300 ml/½ pint milk
	1 teaspoon made English mustard
	1 tablespoon lemon juice
	4 tablespoons soured cream
	salt and pepper
	whole prawns, to garnish

Cut the white and smoked fish into 2.5 cm/1 inch cubes. Place in a large, fairly shallow casserole with the prawns, scallops or mussels, sweetcorn and pimentos (if using).

Melt the butter or margarine in a pan, stir in the flour and cook for 1 minute. Gradually add the milk and bring to the boil. Stir the mustard, lemon juice, soured cream and plenty of salt and pepper into the sauce and pour into the casserole.

Cook in a preheated oven for about 40 minutes or until the fish is cooked. Garnish the casserole with whole prawns.

■ COOK'S TIP

Plain boiled rice with pistaccio nuts would make a good accompanying dish for this tangy curry.

■ COOK'S TIP

Use all white fish in place of the smoked haddock and add 1-2 teaspoons anchovy essence to the sauce instead of the mustard. Use anchovy fillets as garnish.

33 BAKED RED MULLET IN PORT WINE

Preparation time:	YOU WILL NEED:
15 minutes	75 g/3 oz butter
	1 tablespoon chopped parsley
Cooking time:	1 tablespoon finely chopped shallot
30 minutes	4 red mullet
	1 teaspoon anchovy sauce
Oven temperature:	2 teaspoons Worcestershire sauce
180C/350F/gas 4	350 ml/12 fl oz port
	40 g/1½ oz flour
Serves 4	225 g/8 oz tomatoes, stewed in
	300 ml/½ pint water and sieved
Calories:	1 tablespoon double cream
536 per portion	1 tablespoon milk

Butter a shallow baking dish, and sprinkle with half the parsley and shallot. Lay on the mullet and sprinkle the remainder of the parsley and shallot over them. Pour in the anchovy and Worcestershire sauces and the port.

Cover with foil and bake in a preheated oven for 15 minutes, then uncover and bake for a further 10-15 minutes.

Meanwhile, make a roux with the remaining 50 g/2 oz of butter and the flour. Stir in the tomatoes, cream and enough milk to give the consistency of very thick cream. Season well and keep warm.

Lift the fish on to a warmed serving dish and pour the liquid from the baking dish into the sauce, stirring well. Pour the sauce over the mullet and serve.

34 MUSSELS IN CIDER

Preparation time:	YOU WILL NEED:
20 minutes	4.5 litres (4 quarts) fresh mussels
	50 g/2 oz butter
Cooking time:	2 onions, finely chopped
about 20 minutes	2 carrots, finely chopped
	1-2 garlic cloves, crushed
Oven temperature:	450 ml/¾ pint medium cider
200C/400F/gas 6	1 tablespoon lemon juice
	salt and pepper
Serves 4	2 bay leaves
	4 teaspoons cornflour
Calories:	3 tablespoons double cream
321 per portion	chopped fresh parsley, to garnish

Wash and scrub the mussels in several bowls of cold water, making sure they are thoroughly clean. The water should be clear when they are ready. Pull away the beard; drain.

Melt the butter in a large flameproof casserole and fry the onions, carrots and garlic gently until soft but not coloured. Add the cider and lemon juice and bring to the boil. Add salt, pepper and bay leaves.

Add the mussels and mix well. Cover the casserole tightly and cook in a preheated oven for about 20 minutes, or until the mussels have opened. (Discard any which do not open.)

Blend the cornflour with the cream and stir into the sauce. Bring slowly to the boil until slightly thickened.

Ladle the mussels and the sauce into large bowls and serve generously sprinkled with parsley and with fresh crusty bread.

■ COOK'S TIP

This very delicate fish was much prized in England in the eighteenth and nineteenth centuries. Traditionally, it was served on Feast nights in several Cambridge colleges and this is one of the recipes used.

■ COOK'S TIP

When preparing mussels, discard any that feel very heavy (they are probably full of sand) or any that will not close when tapped sharply with a knife.

35 MATELOTE NORMANDE

Preparation time:	YOU WILL NEED:
20 minutes	*1 kg/2 lb freshwater fish fillets*
	75 g/3 oz butter
Cooking time:	*3 tablespoons Calvados, or brandy*
30 minutes	*300 ml/½ pint dry cider*
	300 ml/½ pint fish stock
Serves 6	*1 tablespoon cider vinegar*
	salt and pepper
Calories:	*2 tablespoons chopped fresh parsley*
464 per portion	*1 tablespoon plain flour*
	6 tablespoons double cream
	1 x 200 g/7 oz can mussels in brine
	100 g/4 oz mushrooms, sliced

Cut the fish into 5 cm/2 inch slices. Melt 25 g/1 oz of the butter in a flameproof casserole and sauté the fish over moderate heat for 3 minutes each side. Warm the Calvados or brandy in a ladle, pour it over the fish and set light to it. Shake the casserole to distribute the flames evenly. Pour on the cider, stock and vinegar and seasoning. Stir in half the parsley. Cover and simmer gently for 10 minutes, until the fish feels firm.

Beat 15 g/½ oz of the remaining butter with the flour to form a thick paste. Stir into the casserole a little at a time over low heat, taking care not to break the fish. Stir in the cream and heat gently without boiling. Adjust the seasoning.

Heat the mussels in the liquor from the can. Melt the remaining butter in a small pan over moderate heat and fry the mushroom slices for 2-3 minutes, stirring them once or twice.

Transfer the stew to a serving dish, arrange the mussels and mushrooms on top and sprinkle with the remaining parsley.

▪ COOK'S TIP

Use the heads, skin and bones from the fish to make fish stock. Place in a pan with 600 ml /1 pint water, a bay leaf and an onion quartered. Bring to the boil, *simmer gently for 30 minutes, then strain.*

36 TUNA CAROUSEL

Preparation time:	YOU WILL NEED:
15 minutes	*15 g/½ oz butter, for greasing*
	1 x 200 g/7 oz can tuna, drained
Cooking time:	*and flaked*
40 minutes	*225 g/8 oz frozen peas, thawed*
	100 g/4 oz button mushrooms,
Oven temperature:	*cleaned and sliced*
180C/350F/gas 4	*1 garlic clove, finely chopped*
	¼ teaspoon dillweed
Serves 4	*¼ teaspoon celery seed*
	350 g/12 oz cooked noodles
Calories:	*25 g/1 oz fresh white breadcrumbs*
458 per portion	FOR THE SAUCE
	50 g/2 oz butter
	50 g/2 oz plain flour
	475 ml/16 fl oz milk
	2 tablespoons dry sherry

Grease a medium casserole and stir in the tuna, peas, mushrooms, garlic, dillweed, celery seed, salt and pepper.

For the sauce, melt the butter over a moderate heat. Add the flour and cook for 2-3 minutes, stirring constantly. Gradually whisk in the milk. Cook until smooth and thickened. Blend in the sherry. Remove from the heat.

Stir half of the sauce into the tuna mixture. Spread the noodles over the tuna. Pour the remaining sauce into the noodles. Sprinkle the breadcrumbs over the noodles. Transfer the uncovered casserole to a preheated oven and cook for 30 minutes until hot and bubbly.

▪ COOK'S TIP

This easy casserole is ideal for a quick supper dish. You could use macaroni, or pasta quills (penne) instead of the noodles, if liked.

37 HADDOCK COBBLER

Preparation time:	YOU WILL NEED:
15 minutes	550 g/1¼ lb haddock fillet, cut in
	5 x 2.5 cm/ 2 x 1 inch pieces
Cooking time:	100 g/4 oz peeled prawns
about 45 minutes	25 g/1 oz butter or margarine
	25 g/1 oz flour
Oven temperature:	300 ml/½ pint milk
180C/350F/gas 4;	salt and pepper
200C/400F/gas 6	2 teaspoons dry mustard
	1 tablespoon wine vinegar
Serves 4	2 hard-boiled eggs, quartered
	scone topping (see Cook's Tip)
Calories:	whole prawns and parsley sprigs,
500 per portion	to garnish

Place the fish and prawns in a greased, shallow casserole.

Melt the fat in a pan, stir in the flour and cook for 1 minute. Gradually add the milk and bring to the boil for 1 minute. Add plenty of salt and pepper, mustard and vinegar, then pour over the fish. Cover the casserole and cook in a preheated oven for 25 minutes. Remove the lid, add the eggs and give the fish a stir to mix evenly.

Meanwhile, make the scone dough (see Cook's Tip). Turn on to a floured surface. Roll or pat the dough out to about 1 cm/½ inch thick and cut into 4-5 cm/1½-2 inch triangles or squares. Arrange around the edge of the casserole over the fish and brush with milk.

Increase the oven temperature and return the casserole, uncovered, to the oven for about 20 minutes or until the scones are well risen. Serve garnished with whole prawns and parsley.

▪ COOK'S TIP

For the scone topping, sift together 175 g/6 oz granary flour, 1 tablespoon baking powder and ½ teaspoon dried thyme. Rub in 40g/1½ oz butter. Add 1 egg and about 2 tablespoons milk to make a softish dough.

38 HADDOCK WITH CIDER AND VEGETABLES

Preparation time:	YOU WILL NEED:
30 minutes	250 ml/8 fl oz dry cider
	2 medium onions, thinly sliced
Cooking time:	750 g/1 ½ lb haddock fillets, cut
30 minutes	into 10 cm/4 inch pieces
	1 green pepper, cored, seeded and
Oven temperature:	diced
160C/325F/gas 3	3 medium tomatoes, peeled,
	seeded and chopped
Serves 4	1 tablespoon chopped parsley
	1 tablespoon chopped marjoram
Calories:	salt and pepper
204 per portion	4 tablespoons fresh white
	breadcrumbs
	25 g/1 oz grated Parmesan cheese
	2 lemon wedges, to garnish

Place the cider in a saucepan over a high heat. Bring to the boil, then reduce the heat to medium. Add the onions. Simmer for 5 minutes, or until the cider has reduced by a quarter.

Place the fish in a flameproof casserole. Stir in the cider mixture, green pepper, tomatoes, parsley, marjoram, salt and pepper. Cover the casserole and bring to the boil. Place in a preheated oven and cook for 15 minutes, or until the fish flakes easily. Mix the breadcrumbs and cheese in a small bowl. Remove the casserole from the oven and sprinkle with the breadcrumb mixture. Place under a preheated grill and cook for 2-3 minutes, until browned. Garnish with lemon wedges.

▪ COOK'S TIP

If short of time, use canned, chopped tomatoes - the flavour will be equally good.

39 PRAWN, GARLIC AND HERB CASSEROLE

Preparation time:	YOU WILL NEED:
30 minutes, plus	*120 ml/4 fl oz olive oil*
cooling and	*120 ml/4 fl oz dry white vermouth*
marinating	*or dry white wine*
	85 ml/3 fl oz lemon juice
Cooking time:	*4 garlic cloves, finely chopped*
30 minutes	*15 g/½ oz finely chopped fresh*
	parsley
Oven temperature:	*2½ tablespoons finely chopped*
190C/375F/gas 5	*fresh oregano*
	salt and pepper
Serves 4	*750 g/1½ lb large prawns, peeled,*
	deveined and tails left intact
Calories:	*4 lemon twists and 4 sprigs*
351 per portion	*parsley, to garnish*

Combine the oil, vermouth or wine, lemon juice, garlic, parsley, and oregano in a saucepan. Bring to the boil over a medium-high heat, stirring frequently. Remove from the heat and season to taste. Set aside and let cool for 30 minutes.

Put the prawns in a flameproof casserole. Pour over the vermouth mixture. Cover and marinate at room temperature for 1 hour.

Cook the prawns, in the marinade, in a preheated oven for 10-15 minutes, until pink and firm. Arrange the prawns on a serving platter and keep them warm. Reduce the liquid in the casserole until thickened. Pour the sauce over the prawns, then garnish with the lemon twists and parsley sprigs.

■ COOK'S TIP

Large peeled prawns are now available frozen. Defrost thoroughly before use and dry on absorbent kitchen paper.

40 FISH WITH HORSERADISH CREAM

Preparation time:	YOU WILL NEED:
10 minutes	*1 kg/2 lb white fish cutlets*
	300 ml/½ pint fish or chicken
Cooking time:	*stock*
45 minutes	*1 tablespoon lemon juice*
	40 g/1½ oz butter
Oven temperature:	*40 g/1½ oz plain flour*
200C/400F/gas 6	*150 ml/¼ pint single cream*
	1 tablespoon horseradish sauce
Serves 4	*salt and pepper*
	chopped chives, to garnish
Calories:	
365 per portion	

Arrange the fish in one layer in a baking dish. Pour over the stock and lemon juice and cook in a preheated for 15-20 minutes or until almost cooked.

Drain off the cooking liquid into a saucepan; keep the fish warm. Boil the liquid until it is reduced to 150 ml/¼ pint.

Melt the butter in a clean saucepan. Add the flour and cook, stirring for 2 minutes. Gradually stir in the reduced cooking liquid and bring to the boil, stirring. Stir in the cream, horseradish sauce and salt and pepper to taste. Pour this sauce over the fish and return to the oven. Cook for a further 15 minutes. Serve garnished with chives.

■ COOK'S TIP

You can make your own horseradish, if you are able to find fresh horseradish root. Grate firmly and mix with mayonnaise or single cream to a stiff consistency.

41   POACHED SALMON

Preparation time:	YOU WILL NEED:
5 minutes	1 salmon, about 5.5 kg/12 lb
	1.75 litres/3 pints court bouillon:
Cooking time:	1 medium onion
1 hour	1 carrot, scraped
	3 sprigs each parsley, thyme
Serves 10	and tarragon
	1 bay leaf
Calories:	150 ml/1/4 pint dry white wine
780 per portion	1 teaspoon salt
	5 peppercorns
	1 tablespoon olive oil
	½ cucumber, peeled and thinly
	sliced

Remove the fins from the salmon and reserve.

Put 1.75 litres/3 pints of cold water into a fish kettle and add the court bouillon ingredients. Put in the fins and bring to the boil. Boil for 30 minutes.

Remove from the heat and add the olive oil (which helps to keep the skin of the fish from breaking). Carefully lower the salmon into the liquid, which should just cover it.

Bring back to the boil and simmer gently for 30 minutes. Test with a skewer to see if the flesh leaves the bone easily. Lift out on to a serving dish, garnish with the cucumber slices and serve with Hollandaise sauce, if liked, if it is to be eaten hot.

If the salmon is to be eaten cold, it should be allowed to cool in the bouillon and then lifted out and allowed to become quite cold in the refrigerator. Serve chilled with Mayonnaise.

■ COOK'S TIP

A recipe for a large party. If using a whole fish it will require a fish kettle, which can be obtained from most good kitchen shops. This recipe works equally well *with a middle cut of salmon, in which case use a normal casserole.*

42   HALIBUT A LA GRECQUE

Preparation time:	YOU WILL NEED:
15 minutes	4 halibut steaks
	salt and pepper
Cooking time:	2 tablespoons oil
35-40 minutes	1 medium onion, chopped
	2 carrots, peeled and diced
Oven temperature:	1 garlic clove, crushed
180C/350F/gas 4	1 bay leaf
	6 tablespoons white wine
Serves 4	175 g/6 oz button mushrooms,
	trimmed
Calories:	tomatoes and chopped fresh
241 per portion	mixed herbs to garnish

Lay the halibut steaks in a lightly greased shallow ovenproof dish or casserole and season.

Heat the oil in a pan and fry the onion, carrots and garlic gently until soft but not coloured. Add the bay leaf, wine and salt and pepper to taste. Bring to the boil for 1 minute. Cut any large mushrooms in half, then add them all to the pan. Pour over the fish.

Cover the casserole and cook in a preheated oven for 35-40 minutes or until the fish is tender. Discard the bay leaf and garnish with quarters or slices of tomato and sprinkle liberally with chopped herbs.

■ COOK'S TIP

For a cheaper dish use another firm-fleshed fish, such as cod.

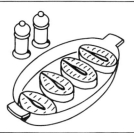

43 MULLET MORNAY

Preparation time:	YOU WILL NEED:
20 minutes	450 g/1 lb spinach
	salt and pepper
Cooking time:	50 g/2 oz butter
45 minutes	100 g/4 oz mushrooms, sliced
	750 g-1 kg/1½-2 lb mullet or
Oven temperature:	other fish fillets, skinned
180C/350F/gas 4	40 g/1½ oz plain flour
	450 ml/¾ pint milk
Serves 4	grated nutmeg
	50 g/2 oz Gruyère cheese, grated
Calories:	50 g/2 oz Cheddar cheese, grated
628 per portion	parsley sprigs, to garnish

Cook the spinach, with only the water clinging to the leaves after washing, until tender. Drain well, pressing out all excess water, then chop. Season with salt and pepper to taste and stir in 15 g/½ oz of the butter. Spread the spinach over the bottom of a greased casserole. Cover with the mushrooms and arrange the fish fillets on top.

Melt the remaining butter in a saucepan. Add the flour and cook, stirring, for 1 minute. Gradually stir in the milk and bring to the boil. Simmer, stirring, until thickened. Season to taste with salt, pepper and nutmeg, then stir in all but 2 tablespoons of the cheeses.

Pour the cheese sauce over the fish and sprinkle the reserved cheese on top. Cook in a preheated moderate oven for about 30 minutes or until the fish is tender. Garnish with parsley and serve.

44 MEDITERRANEAN FISH STEAKS

Preparation time:	YOU WILL NEED:
10 minutes	4 tablespoons olive oil
	2 onions, thinly sliced
Cooking time:	1 garlic clove, finely chopped
55 minutes	1 green pepper, cored, seeded and
	sliced in rings
Oven temperature:	4 large tomatoes, skinned and sliced
180C/350F/gas 4	2 teaspoons dried basil
	salt and pepper
Serves 4	4 white fish steaks
	2 teaspoons lemon juice
Calories:	6 tablespoons dry white wine
271 per portion	

Heat the oil in a frying pan and fry the onions and garlic until softened. Add the green pepper rings and continue frying for 3 minutes. Remove from the heat and place half the mixture in a casserole.

Arrange half the tomato slices on top and sprinkle with half the basil and salt and pepper to taste. Place the fish steaks on top and sprinkle with the lemon juice. Add the rest of the tomato slices, basil and onion and green pepper mixture. Pour in the wine.

Cover and cook in a preheated moderate oven for about 45 minutes or until the fish is tender.

■ COOK'S TIP

Mullet is a very bony fish, so it would be advisable to ask your fishmonger to fillet it for you.

■ COOK'S TIP

To add to the Mediterranean flavour, serve with a fresh tomato and basil salad, if fresh basil is available, with a vinaigrette dressing.

45 BAKED SEA TROUT

Preparation time:	YOU WILL NEED:
5 minutes	1 sea trout, about 750 g/1¼ lb, cleaned
Cooking time:	15 g/½ oz butter
35 minutes	2 teaspoons plain flour
	salt and pepper
Oven temperature:	1 teaspoon lemon juice
200C/400F/gas 6	1 sprig each parsley, fennel, marjoram and tarragon or 1
Serves 4-6	bouquet garni
	½ cucumber, finely sliced
Calories:	sprigs of fennel and tarragon, to
206-138 per portion	garnish

Spread out a piece of foil large enough to wrap up the fish well. Butter it well and sprinkle with flour, salt and pepper. Lay the fish in the centre.

Rub the inside of the fish with salt and pepper, sprinkle in the lemon juice and add the fresh herbs, if available. Wrap up the fish, making a close parcel that will keep the juices in. Lay on a baking sheet and put in a preheated oven for 30 minutes.

Remove from the oven and undo the parcel, allowing the juice to run into the baking sheet. Lift the fish very carefully, supporting it at both ends so that it does not break, on to a hot, ovenproof dish.

Strain the juice and pour it over. Put the fish back into the oven for 4 minutes, so that the top of the skin is lightly crisped.

Serve with slices of cucumber and sprigs of fresh herbs arranged round it.

■ COOK'S TIP

This fish is often referred to as salmon trout because the flesh is pink, but it is thought by many people to be more delicately flavoured than salmon. The finest of all are caught in the sea lochs of Scotland.

46 SMOKED HADDOCK SPECIAL

Preparation time:	YOU WILL NEED:
30 minutes	750 g/2 lb smoked haddock fillets, skinned and halved
Cooking time:	2 teaspoons lemon juice
40 minutes	salt and pepper
	25 g/1 oz butter
Oven temperature:	1 medium onion, finely chopped
160C/325F/gas 3	150 ml/¼ pint milk
	1 bay leaf
Serves 4	1 tablespoon cornflour
	150 ml/¼ pint single cream
Calories:	1 x 225 g/8 oz packet frozen
447 per portion	mixed vegetables (including sweetcorn), thawed
	2 tablespoons chopped fresh parsley
	50 g/2 oz Cheddar cheese, grated
	skinned tomato slices, to garnish

Place the fish in a flameproof casserole, pour over the lemon juice and season with salt and pepper.

Melt the butter in a frying pan, add the onion and fry until softened. Pour the onion over the fish and add the milk and bay leaf. Cover and cook in a preheated oven for 20 minutes. Remove the bay leaf. Dissolve the cornflour in the cream and pour into the casserole. Bring to the boil on top of the stove, stirring gently. Remove from the heat. Add the vegetables and parsley. Adjust the seasoning. Sprinkle the cheese over the top.

Return to the oven and bake for a further 20 minutes or until the vegetables are cooked and the cheese topping golden. Garnish with tomato slices.

■ COOK'S TIP

This colourful fish is ideal for a family supper. Serve with new potatoes, tossed in butter and lemon juice and sprinkled with parsley.

47 MIXED FISH CASSEROLE WITH MUSTARD CREAM

Preparation time:
20 minutes

Cooking time:
35 minutes

Oven temperature:
160C/325F/gas 3

Serves 4

Calories:
366 per portion

YOU WILL NEED:
50 g/2 oz butter
3 medium onions, finely chopped
1 bouquet garni
2 cloves
150 ml/¼ pint dry white wine
150 ml/¼ pint fish stock
juice of ½ lemon
salt and pepper
750 g/1¼ lb mixed white fish
    fillets, skinned and cut into 5
    cm/2 inch pieces
100 g/4 oz button mushrooms,
    sliced
100 g/4 oz fresh or frozen peas
1 teaspoon Dijon mustard
4 tablespoons double cream
puff pastry crescents, to garnish

Melt the butter in a frying pan, add the onions and fry gently until softened. Stir in the bouquet garni, cloves, white wine and stock. Bring to the boil and simmer 5 minutes. Cool slightly, then pour into a casserole. Stir in the lemon juice and salt and pepper to taste. Add the fish pieces. Cover and cook in a preheated oven for 25 minutes. Add the mushrooms and peas and cook for 10 minutes. Discard the bouquet garni.

Stir the mustard into the cream and stir into the casserole carefully. Garnish with pastry crescents and watercress.

■ COOK'S TIP

If available, use the heads, bones and skin of the fish to make the fish stock. Simmer gently for 30 minutes, then strain.

48 SEAFOOD PIE

Preparation time:
50 minutes

Cooking time:
50 minutes

Oven temperature:
180C/350F/gas 4;
then
200C/400F/gas 6

Serves 4

Calories:
464 per portion

YOU WILL NEED:
225 g/8 oz cod fillet, skinned and
    cut into 5 cm/2 inch pieces
225 g/8 oz huss, cut into 5 cm/2
    inch lengths
4 scallops, opened and cleaned
100 g/4 oz crabmeat
300 ml/½ pint hot parsley sauce
    (see Cook's Tip)
2 teaspoons chopped fresh dill or
½ teaspoon dried dill
salt and pepper
2 tablespoons tomato purée
750 g/1½ lb creamed potato
50 g/2 oz Cheddar cheese, grated
few unpeeled prawns and chopped
    parsley, to garnish

Arrange the cod, huss and scallops in a casserole.

Stir the crabmeat into the parsley sauce, add the dill and taste and adjust the seasoning. Mix well together, pour over the fish, cover and cook in a preheated oven for 30 minutes.

Meanwhile, beat the tomato purée into the creamed potato. Taste and adjust the seasoning.

Remove the lid from the casserole, raise the oven temperature, pipe or spoon the potato over the fish, leaving a space in the centre, into which sprinkle the cheese. Return the dish to the oven for about 20 minutes, uncovered, until golden and bubbling. Do not leave it to cook any longer as this will toughen the scallops. Garnish with prawns and parsley.

■ COOK'S TIP

To make parsley sauce melt 25 g/1 oz butter in a pan, stir in 25 g/1 oz flour and gradually add 300 ml/½ pint milk. Simmer for 10 minutes then stir in 3 tablespoons chopped fresh parsley.

MEAT

All the old favourites of meat cookery - beef and veal, lamb and pork - are here, plus a few new ones to try. These are mainly hearty, filling dishes that require little else to go with them. Most could happily be served with plain rice, baked potatoes or French bread and salad.

49 VEAL RAGOUT

Preparation time:
25 minutes

Cooking time:
2 hours

Serves 6

Calories:
373 per portion

YOU WILL NEED:
2 tablespoons vegetable oil
1 kg/2 lb stewing veal, cubed
3 tablespoons plain flour
1 garlic clove, finely chopped
900 ml/1½ pints chicken stock
2 tablespoons tomato purée
1 tablespoon chopped parsley
1 tablespoon fresh thyme leaves
1 bay leaf, crushed
salt and pepper
40 g/1½ oz butter
3 medium onions, quartered
4 medium carrots, chopped
1 tablespoon sugar
6 medium new potatoes, halved
2 tablespoons chopped chives

Heat the oil in a flameproof casserolet. Add the veal and brown for 10 minutes. Sprinkle the flour over the meat. Continue cooking for 5 minutes, until the flour is brown.

Add the garlic to the casserole. Pour in the stock and stir well. Add the tomato purée, parsley, thyme, bay leaf, salt and pepper. Cover and simmer gently for 30 minutes.

Melt the butter in a frying pan. Add the onions and carrots and cook for 5 minutes. Sprinkle with the sugar and cook for 5 minutes, stirring constantly. Transfer the vegetables to the veal mixture. Cover and cook for 30 minutes. Add the potatoes, cover and continue cooking for 30 minutes. Sprinkle with the chives and serve immediately.

■ COOK'S TIP

The casserole may be prepared up to a day in advance, covered and kept chilled. Reheat for 20 minutes over a medium heat until hot.

50 GOULASH

Preparation time:
15 minutes

Cooking time:
1¼-2 hours

Oven temperature:
160C/325F/gas 3

Serves 4

Calories:
335 per portion

YOU WILL NEED:
2 tablespoons oil
450 g/1 lb braising steak,cubed
2 teaspoons paprika
2 teaspoons flour
300 ml/1½ pint stock
25 g/1 oz butter
225 g/8 oz onions, diced
225 g/8 oz carrots, diced
1 bay leaf
good pinch of thyme
1 x 396 g/14 oz can tomatoes
1 tablespoon tomato purée
1 teaspoon lemon juice
salt and pepper
1 potato, peeled and diced
8 small onions, peeled
1 tablespoon soured cream
1 tablespoon chopped parsley

Heat the oil in a frying pan and brown the meat. Reduce the heat, sprinkle in the paprika and flour, turning the meat to absorb the flour. After about 2-3 minutes add the stock and stir gently. Pour into a casserole with the meat and meat particles.

Rinse the pan, melt the butter and sweat the onions and carrots gently. Add the herbs, tomatoes, purée, lemon juice and seasoning. Add the potato and pour the tomato mixture over the meat, cover the casserole and cook in the oven for 1 hour. Add the onions and continue cooking for 45 minutes. Remove the bay leaf, stir in the cream and sprinkle with parsley.

■ COOK'S TIP

Soured cream is traditional, but if preferred you could use plain, unsweetened yogurt.

51 NOISETTES WITH HAZELNUT SAUCE

Preparation time:
15 minutes

Cooking time:
about 1 hour

Oven temperature:
180C/350F/gas 4

Serves 4

Calories:
506 per portion

YOU WILL NEED:
8 noisettes of lamb, about
750 g/1 ½ lb
salt and pepper
½ teaspoon ground coriander
50 g/2 oz butter
1 tablespoon finely chopped onion
150 ml/¼ pint chicken stock
3 tablespoons white vermouth
3 tablespoons orange juice
1 teaspoon dried marjoram
2 teaspoons cornflour
150 ml/¼ pint single cream
50 g/2 oz hazelnuts, toasted and
finely chopped
hazelnuts, to garnish

Sprinkle the lamb with salt, pepper and coriander. Heat the butter in a flameproof casserole and brown the meat quickly. Drain and set aside. Fry the onion in the pan, add the stock, vermouth, juice and marjoram and bring to the boil. Replace the lamb in the casserole, cover and cook in a preheated oven for about 40-45 minutes or until the lamb is tender.

Arrange the meat on an ovenproof serving dish and keep hot. Blend the cornflour with the cream and stir into the juices remaining in the casserole. Add the chopped hazelnuts, bring to the boil and simmer for 1 minute, stirring. Coat the meat with the prepared sauce and garnish with hazelnuts.

■ COOK'S TIP

*To continue the nutty
theme, serve with a salad
dressed with hazelnut or
walnut oil.*

52 BOEUF A L'ORANGE

Preparation time:
30 minutes

Cooking time:
about 2½ hours

Oven temperature:
160C/325F/gas 3

Serves 4

Calories:
317 per portion

YOU WILL NEED:
3 tablespoons oil
675 g/1½ lb braising steak, cubed
225 g/8 oz button onions, peeled
1 garlic clove, crushed
2 tablespoons flour
300 ml/½ pint beef stock
2 oranges
1 tablespoon tomato purée
3 tablespoons brandy
1 tablespoon black treacle
salt and pepper
100 g/4 oz mushrooms, sliced
sprigs of parsley and orange
wedges or slices, to garnish

Heat the oil in a pan and fry the meat until well sealed. Transfer to a casserole. Fry the onions and garlic in the same fat until golden brown, then transfer to the casserole. Stir the flour into the fat in the pan and cook for 1 minute. Gradually add the stock and bring to the boil.

Pare the rind thinly from the oranges and cut into julienne strips. Add to the sauce with the juice from both oranges. Add the tomato purée, brandy and black treacle to the sauce and add plenty of salt and pepper. Pour over the beef and cover the casserole tightly. Cook in a preheated oven for about 2 hours.

Add the mushrooms, adjust the seasoning and add a little extra stock if necessary. Return to the oven for about 30 minutes or until tender. Garnish with parsley and orange.

■ COOK'S TIP

*If possible, add a small
glass of orange-flavoured
liqueur (such as Curaçao)
to enhance the orange
flavour.*

53 TAGINE

Preparation time:	YOU WILL NEED:
15 minutes, plus soaking	2 tablespoons oil
	500 g/1¼ lb lean lamb, diced
	1 large onion, chopped
Cooking time:	1 garlic clove, crushed
1 hour 40 minutes	1 teaspoon ground ginger
	1 teaspoon ground cinnamon
Oven temperature:	25 g/1 oz plain flour
180C/350F/gas 4	300 ml/½ pint lamb stock
	salt and pepper
Serves 4	225 g/8 oz pitted prunes, soaked
	overnight and drained
Calories:	1 tablespoon toasted sesame
362 per portion	seeds, to garnish

Heat the oil in a frying pan, add the meat and cook until it is brown on all sides. Remove the meat from the pan with a slotted spoon and put into a casserole. Fry the onions and garlic in the pan until soft, then add the spices and cook for 1 minute. Sprinkle the flour into the pan and cook for 1 minute, then add the stock, salt and pepper. Bring to the boil, then pour over the lamb. Cover the casserole, place in a preheated oven and cook for 1 hour.

Add the prunes to the casserole and cook for a further 30 minutes. Transfer the lamb and prunes to a warmed serving dish and sprinkle with the sesame seeds before serving.

54 LANCASHIRE HOT POT

Preparation time:	YOU WILL NEED:
25 minutes	1 kg/2 lb middle neck of lamb
	cutlets
Cooking time:	3 tablespoons plain flour
2½ hours	salt and pepper
	4 onions, peeled and finely sliced
Oven temperature:	2 lamb's kidneys, cored and sliced
180C/350F/gas 4	225 g/8 oz carrots, diced
	750 g/1½ lb potatoes, scrubbed
Serves 4	and sliced
	450 ml/¾ pint light stock
Calories:	1 bay leaf
914 per portion	½ teaspoon dried marjoram
	½ teaspoon dried thyme

Trim any excess fat off the lamb and coat with the flour, seasoned with salt and pepper. Place layers of meat, onions, kidneys, carrots and potatoes in a large casserole, seasoning each layer lightly with salt and pepper. Finish with a layer of potatoes.

Heat the stock and add the herbs. Pour into the casserole and cook, covered, in a preheated oven for 2 hours, until the meat is tender. Remove the lid and cook for a further 30 minutes to brown the potatoes.

■ COOK'S TIP

This traditional Moroccan stew is cooked in a tagine, a round and shallow earthenware pot with a conical lid. Kitchenware shops sometimes sell them.

■ COOK'S TIP

This traditional dish is very filling. Serve with a fresh green salad to counteract the heaviness of the meat.

55 SWEET AND SOUR PORK HONG KONG STYLE

Preparation time:
15 minutes

Cooking time:
1¼ hours

Oven temperature:
180C/350F/gas 4

Serves 4

Calories:
363 per portion

YOU WILL NEED:
2-3 tablespoons oil
1 large onion, chopped
1 large green pepper, cored,
    seeded and chopped
1 garlic clove, crushed
500 g/1¼ lb lean pork, diced
3 tablespoons cornflour
1 x 425 g/15 oz can lychees in syrup
2 tablespoons wine vinegar
1 tablespoon soft brown sugar
1 tablespoon tomato ketchup
2 tablespoons soy sauce
salt and pepper

Heat the oil in a frying pan, add the onion, pepper and garlic and cook until soft. Transfer to a casserole with a slotted spoon. Coat the pork in 2 tablespoons of the cornflour and fry in the oil until brown. Add the pork to the casserole.

Drain the syrup from the lychees: there should be about 250 ml/8 fl oz. Mix the syrup with the vinegar, brown sugar, tomato ketchup, soy sauce, salt and pepper and the remaining cornflour. Mix well, then pour into the pan, bring to the boil and strain into the casserole. Cover the casserole, put into a preheated oven and cook for 1 hour. Add the lychees to the casserole and cook for a further 10 minutes.

▪ COOK'S TIP

To freeze, cook as above, but do not add lychees. Freeze for up to 6 months; defrost and reheat, adding the lychees when almost warmed through.

56 PAUPIETTES DE VEAU

Preparation time:
30 minutes

Cooking time:
1½ hours

Oven temperature:
180C/350F/gas 4

Serves 8

Calories:
242 per portion

YOU WILL NEED:
8 x 50 g/2 oz veal escalopes
100 g/4 oz Parma ham, cut to fit
    the escalopes
8 fresh sage leaves
salt and pepper
bacon sauce (see Cook's Tip)
1 tablespoon butter
1 tablespoon oil
1 bunch watercress, to garnish

Place the veal escalopes on a working surface. Place 1 slice of Parma ham on each escalope. Top each with 1 sage leaf. Roll up the escalopes and secure with metal skewers or wooden toothpicks. Season each escalope with salt and pepper and set aside.

Make the bacon sauce (see Cook's Tip).

Heat the butter and oil in a flameproof casserole. Add the escalopes and brown on all sides for 5 minutes, turning occasionally. Drain off the excess fat and discard. Coat the escalopes with the sauce, cover and place in a preheated oven. Cook for 45 minutes. To serve, place the escalopes on a heated platter. Taste the sauce and adjust the seasoning if necessary, then pour over the escalopes. Serve immediately, garnished with watercress.

▪ COOK'S TIP

Bacon sauce: fry 225 g/8 oz diced bacon until crisp, then drain. Melt 15 g/½ oz butter and cook 3 diced tomatoes, 2 diced carrots and 1 sliced onion until soft. Blend in 4 tablespoons flour, 750 ml/1¼ pints stock and 120 ml/4 fl oz Madeira. Add pinch of dried thyme and a bay leaf. Stir in the bacon.

57   POT ROAST LEG OF LAMB

Preparation time:	YOU WILL NEED:
15 minutes	1 leg of lamb, about 1.75 kg/4 lb
	4 garlic cloves, peeled and cut
Cooking time:	into spikes
about 2 hours	few sprigs of fresh rosemary or 1
	tablespoon dried rosemary
Oven temperature:	350 g/12 oz pickling onions, peeled
190C/375F/gas 5	300 ml/½ pint beef stock
	salt and pepper
Serves 6	1 kg/2 lb potatoes, peeled and diced
	fresh sprigs of rosemary, to garnish
Calories:	
1112 per portion	

Wipe the lamb all over, then make deep cuts over the surface of the skin into the flesh. Stick the garlic spikes and small pieces of rosemary into the cuts in the meat. If dried rosemary is used, sprinkle it over the skin after spiking with garlic. Place the joint in a roasting tin and arrange the onions around it. Bring the stock to the boil, add plenty of salt and pepper and pour over the lamb. Cover with foil and cook in a preheated oven for 1 hour.

Remove the foil, baste the joint and sprinkle the skin with salt and pepper. Arrange the diced potatoes around the lamb with the onions. Return to the oven, covered with foil and cook for 45 minutes. Baste the joint again and return to the oven uncovered for 15-20 minutes or until the meat is tender and the potatoes are cooked. Serve the lamb garnished with fresh rosemary.

■ COOK'S TIP

If liked, pour off some liquid once the meat is cooked, skim off fat, and beat in beurre manié to thicken. Simmer 5 minutes then return to the casserole.

58   CRISPED LOIN OF LAMB

Preparation time:	YOU WILL NEED:
15 minutes	1 loin of lamb, about
	1.25-1.5 kg/2 ½-3 lb, chined
Cooking time:	salt and pepper
1¼-2 hours	1 tablespoon oil or dripping
	1 onion, peeled and diced
Oven temperature:	2 carrots, peeled and diced
180C/350F/gas 4;	1-2 leeks, trimmed and sliced
200C/400F/gas 6	150 ml/¼ pint beef stock
	1-2 tablespoons wine vinegar
Serves 4	FOR THE TOPPING
	50 g/2 oz fresh breadcrumbs
Calories:	1 tablespoon chopped fresh mint
323 per portion	sprigs of fresh mint or parsley,
	to garnish

Trim the lamb and sprinkle lightly with salt and pepper. Heat the oil in a frying pan, then add the lamb and fry evenly to seal the fat. Remove from the pan. Fry the onion and carrots gently in the same pan until beginning to soften, then transfer to a casserole with the leeks. Place the lamb joint on the vegetables and add the stock and vinegar, salt and pepper. Cover the casserole and cook in a preheated oven for 1¼ hours.

Remove the cover and baste the joint. Combine the breadcrumbs, mint, salt and pepper and spoon over the fat. Increase the oven temperature and return to the oven for about 30 minutes or until the topping is crisp and the lamb tender.

Serve the lamb cut into slices, or as a whole joint, surrounded by the vegetables and garnished with fresh mint or parsley. Serve the juices in a small jug.

■ COOK'S TIP

A loin of lamb must be chined to make carving into chops possible. Chining means to remove or loosen the chine bone (back bone) attached to the chops. If *loosened it can be removed easily once the joint is cooked. Do not take off before cooking as the meat will shrink from the bones and look shrivelled.*

59 KIDNEYS VICTORIA

Preparation time:
15 minutes

Cooking time:
30 minutes

Serves 4

Calories:
529 per portion

YOU WILL NEED:
50 g/2 oz butter
2 tablespoons blanched almonds,
  halved
2 medium onions, peeled and sliced
100 g/4 oz small button
  mushrooms, trimmed
12 lambs' kidneys, halved,
  skinned, cored, washed and dried
2 tablespoons plain flour
300 ml/½ pint beef stock, hot
4 tablespoons dry sherry
salt and pepper
225 g/8 oz long-grain rice, cooked
sprigs of watercress, to garnish

Melt the butter in a flameproof casserole and sauté the almonds over moderate heat, stirring often, until they are deep golden brown. Remove the almonds with a draining spoon and set aside. Fry the onion in the casserole for 3 minutes, stirring once or twice. Add the mushrooms and fry for 2-3 minutes. Remove the vegetables with a draining spoon and set aside.

Sauté the kidneys in the fat for 2-3 minutes, stirring once or twice. Return the vegetables to the casserole, sprinkle on the flour and stir to blend. Gradually stir in the hot stock and the sherry. Bring just to the boil, season, cover the casserole and simmer over low heat for 5 minutes.

Make a ring of rice on a serving dish and spoon the kidney mixture into the centre. Scatter the almonds on top and garnish with watercress sprigs.

■ COOK'S TIP

With its low cooking time this dish is a good choice when time is short. To make the sauce richer still, you can use port in place of the sherry.

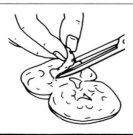

60 PAPRIKA VEAL

Preparation time:
25 minutes

Cooking time:
1¼-1½ hours

Oven temperature:
180C/350F/gas 4

Serves 4

Calories:
482 per portion

YOU WILL NEED:
25 g/1 oz butter or margarine
2 tablespoons oil
675 g/1½ lb pie veal, cubed
2 large onions, peeled and sliced
1 tablespoon paprika
25 g/1 oz flour
300 ml/½ pint chicken stock
1 tablespoon tomato purée
1 tablespoon lemon juice
salt and pepper
1 x 425 g/15 oz can tomatoes
50 g/2 oz raisins
5 cm/2 inch piece cucumber
4-6 tablespoons soured cream

Melt the fat with 1 tablespoon of the oil in a pan and fry the veal until browned. Transfer to a casserole. Add the rest of the oil to the pan and fry the onions until golden brown. Stir in the paprika and flour and cook for 1 minute, then gradually add the stock and bring to the boil. Add the tomato purée, lemon juice, salt and pepper, tomatoes together with their liquid and the raisins, then simmer for 1 minute. Pour over the veal. Cover the casserole tightly and cook in a preheated oven for 1¼-1½ hours or until tender. Taste and adjust the seasoning.

Coarsely grate the cucumber, without peeling; or finely dice if preferred. Mix with the soured cream and spoon over the casserole. For an alternative presentation, spoon the soured cream over the casserole and sprinkle with the cucumber.

■ COOK'S TIP

When using paprika or other ground spices, test that it has not lost its flavour, before using. Ground spices quickly lose fragrance - renew regularly.

61 OXTAIL WITH BLACK OLIVES

Preparation time:	YOU WILL NEED:
about 20 minutes,	2 oxtails, cut up and trimmed
plus chilling	3 tablespoons olive oil
	4 tablespoons brandy
Cooking time:	1 onion, sliced
4½ hours	1 garlic clove, crushed
	200 ml/7 fl oz dry white wine
Oven temperature:	2 bay leaves
160C/325F/gas 3	salt and pepper
	grated rind of ½ orange
Serves 6-8	juice of ½ orange
	600 ml/1 pint beef stock
Calories:	225 g/8 oz stoned black olives
561-421 per portion	50 g/2 oz butter or margarine
	50 g/2 oz flour

Heat the oil in a pan and brown the meat. Transfer to a casserole. Warm the brandy, pour over the oxtail and ignite. Fry the onion and garlic in the pan until golden brown. Add the wine and bring to the boil. Pour over the oxtail and add the bay leaves, salt and pepper, orange rind and juice. Bring the stock to the boil and add enough to cover the oxtail. Cover the casserole and cook in a preheated oven for 3 hours.

Pour the liquid into a bowl and chill. Discard the bay leaves, cool and chill the oxtail overnight. Remove the fat from the liquid, bring back to the boil and pour over the oxtail; add the olives. Cover and cook for 1-1½ hours or until tender.

Blend the butter and flour together. Strain off the juices and reserve 600 ml/1 pint. Whisk the beurre manié into the sauce, to thicken; bring back to the boil and pour over the oxtail.

■ COOK'S TIP

Oxtail can be rather fatty. It needs long slow cooking, so it is ideal for casseroles and stews. Choose an oxtail with bright red flesh and creamy white fat.

62 PIQUANT LIVER

Preparation time:	YOU WILL NEED:
15 minutes	2 tablespoons plain flour
	1 teaspoon dried thyme
Cooking time:	salt and pepper
25 minutes	450 g/1 lb lamb's liver, sliced
	25 g/1 oz butter
Serves 4	1 tablespoon oil
	1 small onion, sliced
Calories:	1 green pepper, seeded and sliced
371 per portion	100 g/4 oz mushrooms, sliced
	1 x 200 g/7 oz can tomatoes
	2 teaspoons lemon juice
	2 teaspoons dark brown sugar
	2-3 drops red pepper sauce
	150 ml/¼ pint red wine
	50 g/2 oz stuffed green olives

Put the flour, thyme, salt and pepper into a heavy polythene bag, shake well and toss in the liver slices, one at a time, to coat them thoroughly.

Heat the butter and oil in a flameproof casserole and fry the onion, green pepper and mushrooms over moderate heat for 2-3 minutes. Add the liver slices and brown them lightly on both sides. Remove from the casserole. Stir in the tomatoes, lemon juice, sugar and pepper sauce and the wine and bring to the boil. Return the liver to the casserole and bring the sauce to simmering point again. Cover the casserole and cook over low heat for 15 minutes. Add the olives and heat them thoroughly. Taste the sauce and adjust the seasoning, if necessary. Serve the dish with a green vegetable such as spinach or cabbage.

■ COOK'S TIP

It is important not to over-cook liver, as it becomes dry and tasteless. Brown the liver slices quickly and keep the casserole over a very low heat when cooking.

63 ORANGE AND LIVER CASEROLE

Preparation time:
20 minutes

Cooking time:
40 minutes

Oven temperature:
140C/275F/gas 1

Serves 8

Calories:
338 per portion

YOU WILL NEED:
25 g/1 oz plain flour
salt and pepper
1 kg/2 lb lamb's liver, thinly sliced
40 g/1½ oz butter
2 tablespoons vegetable oil
1 medium onion, thinly sliced
1 garlic clove, chopped
2 oranges, thinly sliced, seeded
250 ml/8 fl oz dry red wine
250 ml/8 fl oz orange juice
2 tablespoons orange marmalade
1 teaspoon dried thyme
2 tablespoons double cream
1 tablespoon chopped parsley,
  to garnish

Combine the flour, salt and pepper. Coat the liver with the flour. Heat the butter and oil in a frying pan. Add the onion and garlic and cook for 5 minutes. Transfer to a casserole.

Add the liver slices to the pan. Cook for 2-3 minutes on each side. Transfer the liver to the casserole. Cook the orange slices in the pan for 1-2 minutes, turning. Put the orange slices over the liver in the casserole. Add the wine, orange juice, marmalade, thyme, salt and pepper to the frying pan. Bring to the boil, stirring occasionally, then pour over the ingredients in the casserole. Cover and cook in a preheated oven for 30 minutes. Stir in the cream. Garnish with the parsley.

■ COOK'S TIP

The liver for this recipe should be very thinly sliced. Fresh liver is sometimes not sliced thinly enough, so you may prefer to buy frozen liver. When it has partially thawed, carefully slice it with a sharp knife.

64 SPARE RIBS

Preparation time:
10 minutes

Cooking time:
1¼ hours

Oven temperature:
200C/400F/gas 6

Serves 4

Calories:
648 per portion

YOU WILL NEED:
1½ kg/3 lb Chinese-style spare ribs
4 tablespoons soy sauce
2 tablespoons orange marmalade
1 garlic clove, crushed
1 large onion, sliced
salt and pepper
300 ml/½ pint stock or water
1 tablespoon vinegar

Brown the spare ribs under a high grill. Mix the soya sauce, marmalade, and crushed garlic together and spread over the ribs. Place sliced onion on the bottom of a casserole, place ribs on top, season well. Pour over stock and vinegar. Cover and cook for 1½ hours. Remove lid to allow to crisp before serving. Taste and adjust the seasoning.

■ COOK'S TIP

For a spicier finish, add a few drops of Tabasco sauce to the mixture before coating the spare ribs.

65   ORANGE LAMB WITH RICE

Preparation time:	YOU WILL NEED:
15 minutes	2 oranges
	675 g/1½ lb lean boneless lamb,
Cooking time:	cubed
1 hour	salt and pepper
	1 tablespoon oil
Oven temperature:	1 large onion, sliced
180C/350F/gas 4	450 ml/¾ pint beef stock
	50 g/2 oz raisins
Serves 4	pinch of garlic powder
	¼ teaspoon ground coriander
Calories:	175 g/6 oz long-grain rice
528 per portion	40 g/1½ oz toasted almond slivers
	orange twists and watercress,
	to garnish

Pare the rind from 1 orange and cut into julienne strips. Cut away the white pith and ease away segments from between the membranes. Squeeze the juice from the second orange.

Sprinkle the lamb lightly with salt and pepper. Heat the oil in a pan and fry the lamb until well sealed and lightly browned; remove from the pan. Fry the onion in the same pan until lightly browned, then add the orange rind, segments and juice, the stock and raisins and bring to the boil. Add plenty of salt and pepper, the garlic powder and coriander.

Place the rice in a lightly greased ovenproof dish, add the onion mixture and mix well. Lay the meat on top, cover and cook in a preheated oven for 1 hour. Lightly mix the rice and meat together and sprinkle over the nuts. Garnish with orange twists and watercress.

■ COOK'S TIP

Lamb can often be very fatty. Choose shoulder meat, leg meat or lamb fillet for this recipe as they are the leanest cuts.

66   OLD ENGLISH CASSEROLE

Preparation time:	YOU WILL NEED:
45 minutes	750 g/1½ lb stewing steak,
	trimmed and cubed
Cooking time:	225 g/8 oz ox kidney, skinned,
about 2½ hours	cored and cut into small pieces
	25 g/1 oz plain flour
Oven temperature:	2 teaspoons dry mustard
160C/325F/gas 3	salt and pepper
	50 g/2 oz dripping
Serves 4	100 g/4 oz button onions, peeled
	2 celery sticks, chopped
Calories:2075	175 g/6 oz carrots, sliced
519 per portion	600 ml/1 pint beef stock
	2 teaspoons dried marjoram
	8 pickled walnuts, drained and
	sliced
	dumplings (see Cook's Tip)

Coat the steak and kidney with flour seasoned with mustard, salt and pepper. Heat the dripping in a pan, and fry the onions, celery and carrots for 4-5 minutes. Add the meat and continue frying until sealed all over. Remove the pan from the heat and blend in the beef stock and the marjoram. Return to the heat, bring to the boil and simmer for 1 minute, stirring. Transfer to a casserole and cover closely. Cook in a preheated oven for 2 hours or until the meat is tender.

Meanwhile, make up the dumpling mixture and shape into 8 balls. Stir the pickled walnuts into the casserole, then add the dumplings. Cover and cook for 25-30 minutes or until the dumplings are cooked.

■ COOK'S TIP

Dumplings: mix 50 g/2 oz self-raising flour, 50 g/2 oz breadcrumbs, 2 tablespoons suet, 1 tablespoon parsley, 2 teaspoons lemon rind. Bind with 1 beaten egg.

67 ALABAMA CHILLI

Preparation time:	YOU WILL NEED
20 minutes	1 tablespoon oil
	450 g/1 lb minced beef
Cooking time:	2 onions, peeled and diced
1 hour	1 carrot, peeled and diced
	1 pepper, seeded and diced
Serves 4	1 chilli, seeded and diced
	1 x 396 g/14 oz can tomatoes
Calories:	2-3 tablespoons tomato purée
475 per portion	150 ml/¼ pint stock
	1 bay leaf
	½ teaspoon chilli powder
	½ teaspoon mixed herbs
	salt and pepper
	225 g/8 oz frozen sweetcorn
	1 x 396 g/14 oz can red kidney
	beans, drained

Heat the oil in a frying pan and brown the meat. Transfer to a casserole. Sauté the onion, carrot, pepper and chilli and add to meat. Add remaining ingredients, except the sweetcorn and kidney beans; season well. Cover and bring to the boil and simmer over a low heat for 45 minutes. Add the sweetcorn and kidney beans and simmer for a further 15 minutes. Remove the bay leaf, taste and adjust the seasoning. Chilli powder may be adjusted to taste; a mild mixture will only require ¼ teaspoon. Serve with boiled rice or pasta.

68 HERRIES PORK

Preparation time:	YOU WILL NEED:
15 minutes	50 g/2 oz butter or margarine
	675 g/1 ½ lb lean pork, cubed
Cooking time:	1 onion, finely chopped
about 1 hour	4 sticks celery, thinly sliced
	1 large red pepper, seeded and
Oven temperature:	thinly sliced
180C/350F/gas 4	1-2 garlic cloves, crushed
	4 tablespoons medium sherry
Serves 4	2 tablespoons soy sauce
	1 tablespoon lemon juice
Calories:	about 175 ml/6 fl oz beef stock
526 per portion	salt and pepper
	1 x 225 g/8 oz can water
	chestnuts, drained and sliced
	nut topping (see Cook's Tip)
	chopped fresh parsley, to garnish

Melt half the butter in a pan and brown the pork cubes. Transfer to a casserole. Melt the remaining butter in the pan and add the onion, celery, pepper and garlic. Cook over a high heat for 2 minutes, stirring, then transfer to the casserole. Combine the sherry, soy sauce and lemon juice and make up to 300 ml/½ pint with stock. Add salt and pepper, then the water chestnuts. Sir into onion mixture. Pour the sauce over the pork, mix well, cover and cook in a preheated oven for 50-60 minutes or until tender. Taste and adjust the seasoning.

Meanwhile, make the topping (see Cook's Tip). Serve the casserole with the topping spooned over and garnished with chopped fresh parsley.

▇ COOK'S TIP

Chillies vary a great deal in hotness - the hottest part is the seeds, so be sure to remove them all, and wash your hands afterwards.

▇ COOK'S TIP

Topping: melt 40 g/1½ oz butter in a frying pan and fry 40 g/1½ oz breadcrumbs until brown. Add 40 g/1½ oz chopped almonds and fry till brown.

69 CASSEROLED BACON JOINT

Preparation time:	YOU WILL NEED:
10-15 minutes	1.5 kg/3¼-3½ lb bacon joint
	25 g/1 oz butter
Cooking time:	1 large onion, chopped
about 2¼ hours	1 garlic clove, crushed (optional)
	1 x 425 g/15 oz can tomatoes
Oven temperature:	150 ml/¼ pint dry cider
180C/350F/gas 4;	2 large sour-sweet gherkins,
then 200C/400F/gas 6	chopped
	2 teaspoons capers, chopped
Serves 4	freshly ground black pepper
	2-3 tablespoons demerara sugar
Calories:	½ teaspoon powdered cinnamon
1176 per portion	1 teaspoon dry mustard
	1 tablespoon clear honey
	whole cloves

Put the bacon in a large pan and cover with cold water. Bring to the boil, then discard the cooking liquid. Melt the butter in a flameproof casserole, add the onion and garlic and fry for 2-3 minutes until tender. Add the tomatoes, cider, gherkins, capers and pepper. Arrange the bacon joint on top. Cover and cook in a preheated oven for 1½ hours. Increase the oven temperature.

Remove the bacon from the casserole, strip off the skin and score the fat into a trellis pattern. Mix together the demerara sugar, cinnamon, mustard and honey and spread over the fat. Stud with cloves. Carefully return the joint to the casserole and cook, uncovered for a further 30 minutes until the top is browned and the bacon cooked. Serve the bacon on a serving dish. Skim any fat from the sauce and pour round the bacon.

■ COOK'S TIP

If there is a very thick layer of fat, trim some off before spreading with the sugar mixture, to give a less fatty dish.

70 PORK 'N' PEARS

Preparation time:	YOU WILL NEED:
10 minutes, plus	50 g/2 oz seedless raisins
soaking overnight	2 tablespoons dark rum
	750 g/1½ lb pork fillet, sliced
Cooking time:	diagonally
55 minutes-1 hour	salt and pepper
	1 tablespoon butter
Oven temperature:	1 tablespoon oil
180C/350F/gas 4	3 firm dessert pears, peeled, cored
	and sliced
Serves 4	150 ml/¼ pint chicken stock
	1 tablespoon lemon juice
Calories:	150 ml/¼ pint whipping cream
490 per portion	2 teaspoons cornflour
	asparagus tips, to garnish

Soak the raisins in the rum overnight. Place the pork slices between sheets of greaseproof paper and beat flat with a rolling pin. Season. Heat the butter and oil in a and quickly fry the pork slices on both sides until sealed. Transfer to a casserole.

Fry the pear slices for 2-3 minutes in the fat in the pan. Place in the casserole with the pork. Add the raisins, rum, chicken stock and lemon juice to the pan. Bring to the boil, simmer for 1 minute and pour over the pork and pears. Cover and cook in a preheated oven for 30 minutes or until tender.

Transfer the pork and pears to a serving dish and keep hot. Blend the cream with the cornflour and stir into the juices remaining in the casserole. Return to the oven for 10-15 minutes until the sauce has thickened. Pour over the pork and pears and garnish with cooked asparagus tips.

■ COOK'S TIP

For a less expensive dish use boneless pork chops. Trim off all fat and slice thinly in strips before cooking.

71 BEEF CARBONADE

Preparation time:	YOU WILL NEED:
15 minutes	675 g/1½ lb chuck or braising steak, cubed
	3 tablespoons seasoned flour
Cooking time:	salt and pepper
about 1 3/4 hours	4 tablespoons vegetable oil
	2 large onions, thinly sliced
Oven temperature:	1-2 garlic cloves, crushed
160C/325F/gas 3	300 ml/½ pint brown ale
	300 ml/½ pint beef stock
Serves 4	1 tablespoon tomato purée
	pinch of ground mace or nutmeg
Calories:	1 bay leaf
444 per portion	2 teaspoons brown sugar
	2 teaspoons vinegar
	1½ teaspoons French mustard
	3-4 carrots, cut into sticks
	100 g/4 oz button mushrooms
	chopped fresh parsley, to garnish

Coat the meat with the flour. Heat 3 tablespoons of the oil in a pan and brown the meat. Transfer to a casserole. Fry the onions and garlic in the pan with the remaining oil added, until lightly coloured, then stir in the remaining seasoned flour and cook for 1 minute. Gradually add the ale and stock and bring to the boil. Add the purée, mace, salt and pepper, bay leaf, sugar, vinegar and mustard and pour over the beef. Add the carrots, mix well, cover tightly and cook in a preheated oven for 1¼ hours. Add the mushrooms and return to the oven for 25-30 minutes until quite tender. Serve sprinkled with parsley .

■ COOK'S TIP

To add to the fruity flavour use Guinness instead of brown ale.

72 LAMB'S KIDNEYS IN RED WINE

Preparation time:	YOU WILL NEED:
10 minutes, plus	8 lambs' kidneys
soaking time	900 ml/1½ pints water
	salt
Cooking time:	25 g/1 oz butter
40 minutes	2 tablespoons plain flour
	300 ml/½ pint dry red wine
Oven temperature:	300 ml/½ pint beef or lamb stock
180C/350F/gas 4	3 tablespoons finely chopped fresh parsley
Serves 4	1 garlic clove, finely chopped
	freshly ground black pepper
Calories:	
215 per portion	

Place the kidneys in a medium bowl. Cover with the water, then add the salt. Soak for 3 minutes. Drain the kidneys. Remove the skin and cut the kidneys in half. Remove the white core then set the kidneys aside.

Melt the butter over a medium-high heat in a flameproof casserole. Add the kidneys and cook for 2-3 minutes, stirring frequently. Sprinkle the flour on the kidneys and stir well to combine. Gradually stir in the wine and stock. Bring the sauce to the boil, stirring continuously, then add the parsley, garlic, salt and pepper. Cover the casserole and place in a preheated oven. Cook for 30 minutes. Serve with hot, buttered toast.

■ COOK'S TIP

If your budget can stretch to veal kidneys, try substituting them for the lambs' kidneys. Pre-soaking is not necessary.

73   BACON STEWPOT

Preparation time:
20 minutes, plus
soaking overnight

Cooking time:
1¼ hours

Oven temperature:
180C/350F/gas 4

Serves 4

Calories:
770 per portion

YOU WILL NEED:
750 g/1½ lb unsmoked bacon,
    collar or 'slipper'
25 g/1 oz butter
225 g/8 oz small onions, peeled
4 medium leeks, trimmed and
    thinly sliced
2 tablespoons plain flour
450 ml/¾ pint chicken stock, hot
2 medium carrots, sliced
225 g/8 oz dried haricot beans,
    soaked overnight and drained
    (see Cook's tip)
225 g/8 oz potatoes, peeled and
    sliced
freshly ground black pepper
pinch of dried sage

Remove the rind and visible fat from the bacon and cut the meat into 2.5 cm/1 inch cubes. Melt the butter in a flameproof casserole and gently fry the onions and leeks over moderate heat until the onions are translucent. Stir in the flour, then gradually pour on the hot stock, stirring constantly. Simmer for 2-3 minutes.

Add the bacon, carrots, beans and potatoes. Season well with pepper, add the sage and bring to the boil and boil for 3 minutes. Cover the casserole and cook in a preheated oven for 1½ hours. Taste the sauce and adjust the seasoning if necessary. Serve with a green vegetable.

■ COOK'S TIP

Soak the beans in a large bowl of cold water (they absorb about 2½ times their dried weight) for several hours or overnight. Or, to speed up the process, put them in a large pan of water, bring to the boil and boil for 2 minutes. Leave to cool in the water, then drain them.

74   BEEF AND BUTTER BEAN MARMITE

Preparation time:
20 minutes, plus
soaking overnight

Cooking time:
3½ hours

Oven temperature:
180C/350F/gas 4

Serves 4-6

Calories:
483-322 per portion

YOU WILL NEED:
3 tablespoons plain flour
salt and pepper
1 teaspoon dried oregano
1.25 kg/2½ lb stewing beef, cut
    into 4 cm/1½ inch cubes
225 g/8 oz shallots or small
    onions, peeled
3 celery sticks, thinly sliced
2 medium carrots, thinly sliced
100 g/4 oz dried butter beans,
    soaked overnight and drained
600 ml/1 pint brown ale
1 tablespoon soft dark brown sugar
1 tablespoon chopped fresh
    parsley, to garnish

Put the flour in a bag and season with salt and pepper and the dried herbs. Toss the meat in the seasoned flour to coat it thoroughly.

Put the meat into a casserole, add the fresh vegetables and dried beans and pour on the beer. Stir in the sugar and cover the dish. Cook in a preheated oven for 3½ hours. Taste the sauce and adjust the seasoning if necessary. Skim off the fat from the surface.

Garnish with the chopped parsley. Serve with small potatoes boiled in their skins.

■ COOK'S TIP

This is an ideal recipe for a slow cooker, and a good choice if you are trying to limit the amount of fat in your diet.

75 OXTAIL WITH RED KIDNEY BEANS

Preparation time:
15 minutes, plus soaking

Cooking time:
about 4 hours, plus reheating

Oven temperature:
150C/300F/gas 2

Serves 4

Calories:
512 per portion

YOU WILL NEED:
225 g/8 oz red kidney beans, soaked overnight
1 large oxtail, jointed
40 g/1½ oz flour
salt and pepper
1 teaspoon dry mustard
2 tablespoons oil
1 large onion, chopped
2 carrots, sliced
2 celery sticks, chopped
600 ml/1 pint beef stock
2 tablespoons tomato purée
1 tablespoon creamed horseradish
2 tablespoon medium sherry
bouquet garni

Strain the red kidney beans, cover with fresh water. Bring to the boil and boil rapidly for 15-20 minutes. Drain.

Coat the oxtail in flour seasoned with salt, pepper and mustard. Heat the oil in a flameproof casserole and fry the onion, carrots, and celery for 3-4 minutes. Add the oxtail and fry for 4-5 minutes, to brown the joints. Gradually blend in the stock, purée, horseradish and sherry. Bring to the boil and simmer 1 minute. Stir in the beans and the bouquet garni. Cover and cook in the oven for 3½-4 hours, until the oxtail is tender. When cold, remove the fat, discard the bouquet garni. Cover and cook in a preheated oven for 1 hour before serving.

■ COOK'S TIP

It is most important to boil red kidney beans for 15-20 minutes before using in any recipe. The boiling kills a toxic enzyme which is present in the beans.

76 PAPRIKA PORK CHOPS

Preparation time:
25 minutes

Cooking time:
1 hour

Oven temperature:
190C/375F/gas 5

Serves 4

Calories:
674 per portion

YOU WILL NEED:
25 g/1 oz plain flour
2 tablespoons Hungarian paprika
¼ teaspoon cayenne pepper
salt and pepper
4 x 175 g/6 oz loin pork chops
1 tablespoon vegetable oil
4 medium potatoes, peeled and thinly sliced
1 large onion, thinly sliced
300 ml/½ pint beef stock
300 ml/½ pint soured cream
2 tablespoons plain flour
watercress and caraway seeds

Combine the flour, paprika, cayenne pepper, salt and pepper and coat the pork chops in the mixture. Set aside. Heat the oil in a flameproof casserole. Add the pork chops and brown for 10 minutes. Remove the chops and set aside. Lay the potato and onion slices on the bottom of the casserole. Place the pork chops on top. Pour the stock into the casserole. Cover and cook in a preheated oven for 45 minutes.

Combine the soured cream and flour until smooth. Set aside. Remove the pork chops and vegetables from the casserole. Arrange on a serving platter and keep warm. Place the casserole over a medium-low heat. Using a whisk, stir in the soured cream mixture. Cook until just heated through. Remove the sauce from the heat and pour over the chops. Garnish with the watercress and caraway seeds.

■ COOK'S TIP

This dish could also be made with lamb chump chops. Trim all fat off pork or lamb before cooking.

77 BOEUF A LA BOURGUINONNE

Preparation time:
about 25 minutes,
plus marinating

Cooking time:
about 3 hours

Oven temperature:
160C/325F/gas 3

Serves 4

Calories:
601 per portion

YOU WILL NEED:
1 kg/2 lb chuck steak, cubed
2-3 tablespoons oil
175 g/6 oz bacon, cut in strips
2 onions, sliced
2 carrots, sliced
1 garlic clove, crushed
25 g/1 oz seasoned flour
2 tablespoons brandy
150 ml/¼ pint stock
1 bouquet garni
25 g/1 oz butter
225 g/8 oz small button mushrooms
225 g/8 oz button onions, peeled
1 teaspoon sugar
4 tablespoons red Burgundy

Marinate the steak (see Cook's Tip). Heat 1 tablespoon of the oil in a pan and brown the bacon. Transfer to a casserole. Fry the onions, carrots and garlic in the pan for 10-15 minutes. Add to the casserole. Strain the marinade and reserve. Dry the meat and toss in the flour. Add the remaining oil to the pan and brown the meat. Add to the casserole. Stir the marinade, brandy and stock into the pan, scraping up the sediment. Bring to the boil and simmer 1 minute. Add to the casserole. Add the bouquet garni. Cover and cook in a preheated oven 2½ hours.

Melt the butter and fry the mushrooms and onions for 4-5 minutes. Stir in the sugar and cook for 1 minute, add the wine and bring to the boil. Add the mixture to the casserole. Cover and cook for 30 minutes. Remove the bouquet garni.

■ COOK'S TIP

*To marinate the beef, place
in a bowl and cover with
300 ml/½ pint red wine, 2
tablespoons oil and ½
teaspoon dry thyme. Cover
and leave for 2-3 hours.*

78 MOROCCAN LAMB

Preparation time:
15 minutes, plus
soaking

Cooking time:
about 2½ hours

Oven temperature:
160C/325F/gas 3

Serves 4

Calories:
660 per portion

YOU WILL NEED:
*225 g/8 oz chick peas, soaked
    overnight*
*75 g/3 oz dried apricots, soaked
    overnight*
3 tablespoons oil
750 g/1½ lb boneless lamb, cubed
1 large onion, chopped
1 garlic clove, crushed
300 ml/½ pint chicken stock
salt and pepper
2 tablespoons honey
1 teaspoon ground cinnamon
½ teaspoon ground allspice
½ teaspoon cumin seeds
finely peeled rind of ½ orange
50 g/2 oz halved almonds, fried

Drain the chick peas. Drain the apricots and cut into pieces.

Heat 2 tablespoons of the oil in a flameproof casserole and fry the lamb until lightly browned. Remove from the pan and set aside. Add the remaining oil, the onion and the garlic to the pan and fry very gently for about 5 minutes until soft. Add the chicken stock and stir well.

Return the meat to the casserole and stir in the chick peas. Cover and cook in the centre of a preheated oven for 1 hour. Stir in the honey, cinnamon, allspice, cumin seeds, orange rind and apricots. Cover and return to the oven for a further 1-1 ½ hours or until the lamb is tender. Discard the orange rind. Transfer to a serving dish. Scatter the almonds over the top.

■ COOK'S TIP

*If liked, use canned chick
peas to save time. Drain
and add with the honey
and spices. Toasted sesame
seeds make a tasty extra
garnish for this dish.*

79   SWEET AND SOUR BEEF

Preparation time:
20 minutes, plus
marinating

Cooking time:
about 1-1¼ hours

Oven temperature:
180C/350F/gas 4

Serves 4-6

Calories:
395-263 per portion

YOU WILL NEED:
500-750 g/1¼-1½ lb topside of
beef, cubed and marinated
(see Cook's Tip)
2 tablespoons corn oil
2 medium onions, diced
1 green and 1 red pepper, cored,
seeded and diced
2 teaspoons cornflour
150 ml/¼ pint syrup from
canned pineapple
150 ml/¼ pint beef stock
1 tablespoon light soy sauce
salt and pepper
6-8 canned pineapple rings, cut
into segments

Lift the beef out of the marinade; strain and retain the marinade. Heat the oil in a pan, cook the beef and diced onions gently for 10 minutes, take out of the pan and place in a casserole. Add half the peppers to the casserole.

Blend the cornflour with the pineapple syrup and stock, heat steadily in the pan; stir until thickened then add the soy sauce and marinade and seasoning, if necessary. Add a little more honey or vinegar if necessary. Pour the sauce over the beef and vegetables. Cover the casserole and cook in the centre of a preheated moderate oven for 40 minutes.

Remove the lid, stir in the remaining peppers and the pineapple. Replace the lid and cook for a further 10 minutes.

■ COOK'S TIP

Marinade: blend together 1 crushed garlic clove, 1 chopped onion, 1 tablespoon honey, 2 tablespoons vinegar, 2 tablespoons pineapple syrup, 1 teaspoon ginger, 1 teaspoon cinnamon and pinch of cayenne. Stir in the beef and leave for 1½-2 hours. Turn the beef twice while marinating.

80   LAMB AND DILL HOT POT

Preparation time:
15 minutes

Cooking time:
about 2 hours

Oven temperature:
180C/350F/gas 4;
200C/400F/gas 6

Serves 6

Calories:
795 per portion

YOU WILL NEED:
2 tablespoons oil or dripping
1.25 kg/2½ lb scrag end neck of
lamb, chopped
2 onions, sliced
2 carrots, sliced
1 tablespoon flour
150 ml/¼ pint white wine
300 ml/½ pint beef stock
1 tablespoon tomato purée
1 tablespoon demerara sugar
salt and pepper
1-1½ teaspoons dried dillweed
675 g/1½ lb potatoes, peeled
and thinly sliced
15 g/½ oz melted butter or
margarine

Heat the oil in a pan and fry the pieces of lamb until well browned, then place in a large casserole. Fry the onions and carrots in the same fat for 2 minutes, then stir in the flour and cook for 1 minute. Gradually add the wine and stock and bring to the boil, stirring frequently. Add the tomato purée, sugar, plenty of salt and pepper and the dillweed and pour into the casserole. Mix well with the lamb and level the top.

Arrange the sliced potatoes evenly over the contents of the casserole and brush the top layer with melted fat. Cover with a lid or foil. Cook in a preheated oven for 1½ hours. Increase the oven temperature, uncover the casserole and return to the oven for about 30 minutes or until the potatoes are golden brown.

■ COOK'S TIP

Dill has a strong distinctive flavour; if you prefer a more definite taste of dill use the larger amount than what is suggested here.

POULTRY

The sheer variety of poultry dishes is enormous, from the classics to the exotic. There is something here for everyone, whether you want a simple family meal or something a little more exciting. None of the dishes is difficult to prepare, and poultry takes less time to cook than red meat. Most recipes have serving suggestions, though often rice and a salad will be enough.

81 CHICKEN ROSSINI

Preparation time:	YOU WILL NEED:
15 minutes	4 boneless chicken breasts
	salt and pepper
Cooking time:	about 100 g/4 oz firm pâté
about 40 minutes	40 g/1½ oz butter
	175 g/6 oz mushrooms, sliced
Oven temperature:	3 tablespoons brandy
180C/350F/gas 4	6 tablespoons chicken stock
	3 tablespoons double cream
Serves 4	4 slices bread
	25 g/1 oz butter
Calories:	2 tablespoons oil
586 per portion	watercress

Skin the chicken and flatten a little. Sprinkle lightly with salt and pepper. Cut the pâté into 4 even slices and wrap up in pieces of chicken. Secure with fine string or wooden cocktail sticks. Melt the butter in a pan and brown the chicken lightly. Transfer to a casserole. Fry the mushrooms gently in the same fat for about 1 minute, then add the brandy and stock and bring to the boil. Add salt and pepper and pour over the chicken. Cover the casserole and cook in a preheated oven for about 40 minutes or until cooked through.

Cut the bread into ovals about the size of the chicken pieces and fry in a mixture of butter and oil until golden. Place the croûtons on a serving dish and top each with a portion of chicken (string or cocktail sticks removed). Add the cream to the sauce and reheat. Spoon over the chicken. Garnish the dish with watercress.

■ COOK'S TIP

To flatten the chicken breasts, place between sheets of greaseproof paper and roll lightly with a rolling pin. Be careful not to break the flesh.

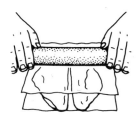

82 CHICKEN AND BROCCOLI ROLL-UPS

Preparation time:	YOU WILL NEED:
35 minutes	65 g/ ½ oz butter
	6 x 150 g/5 oz chicken thighs,
Cooking time:	boned and skinned
1¼ hours	6 small fresh broccoli spears
	120 ml/4 fl oz chicken stock
Oven temperature:	salt and pepper
180C/350F/gas 4	2 small onions, thinly sliced
	2 tablespoons plain flour
Serves 6	½ tablespoon chopped basil
	¼ teaspoon celery salt
Calories:	120 ml/ 4 fl oz milk
354 per portion	6 x 25 g/1 oz Swiss cheese

Melt 2 tablespoons of the butter and brown the chicken thighs. Set aside. Dip the broccoli spears into the chicken stock, sprinkle with salt and set aside. Reserve the chicken stock.

Melt 2 tablespoons of the butter in a small pan and cook the onion for 5-10 minutes, until tender. Sprinkle the onions with the flour, basil, celery salt, salt and pepper. Cook 2-3 minutes, stirring. Gradually whisk in the reserved chicken stock and milk. Cook for 5 minutes, stirring, until thick and smooth.

To assemble each roll-up, wrap a slice of cheese round a broccoli spear. Wrap a chicken thigh around each one, securing with a cocktail stick. Put the roll-ups in a greased casserole and pour over the sauce. Cover and cook in a preheated oven for 20 minutes. Cook uncovered for another 20 minutes. Serve hot.

■ COOK'S TIP

For a special occasion, used boned, skinned chicken breasts in stead of the thighs in this recipe.

83 DUCK FESANJAN

Preparation time:	YOU WILL NEED:
15 minutes	3 pomegranates
	chicken stock
Cooking time:	1 tablespoon oil
50 minutes-1 hour	4 boneless duck breasts, about
	175 g/6 oz each, skinned
Oven temperature:	1 small onion, chopped
180C/350F/gas 4	2 teaspoons lemon juice
	½ teaspoon ground cinnamon
Serves 4	pinch chilli powder
	1 tablespoon clear honey
Calories:	salt and pepper
357 per portion	seeds of 1 pomegranate
	25 g/1 oz chopped walnuts

Cut the pomegranates in half, put the seeds into a sieve and push through to extract the juice. Discard the pips and make the pomegranate juice up to 300 ml/½ pint with the chicken stock. Heat the oil in a frying pan. Fry the duck breasts for 1 minute on each side, then transfer them to a shallow casserole.

Add the onion to the pan and cook for 1 minute. Add the pomegranate juice, lemon juice, cinnamon, chilli powder, honey, salt and pepper to the pan, bring to the boil and pour over the duck. Cover the casserole and put into a preheated oven. Cook for 40-50 minutes until the duck is tender.

Take the duck breasts out of the casserole with a slotted spoon, place on a warmed serving dish and keep warm. Pour the juices from the casserole into a small saucepan and boil until reduced by half. Pour over the duck and sprinkle with the pomegranate seeds and chopped walnuts.

■ COOK'S TIP

This Middle Eastern dish should be served with couscous, or plain boiled rice.

84 STEWED CHICKEN

Preparation time:	6 tablespoons vegetable oil
40 minutes	8 pieces chicken
	1 medium carrot,chopped
Cooking time:	1 large onion, chopped
2¾ hours	1 celery stick, finely chopped
	900 ml/1/1½ pints chicken stock
Serves 8	250 ml/8 fl oz dry white wine
	fresh vegetables (see Cook's Tip)
Calories:	6 tablespoons chopped fresh herbs
529 per portion	225 g/8 oz broccoli florets
	100 g/4 oz thawed frozen pea
	salt and pepper
	3 egg yolks
	120 ml/4 fl oz double cream

Heat half the oil in a pan and brown the chicken. Transfer to a flameproof casserole. Add the carrot, onion and celery to the pan and cook for 10 minutes. Add 250 ml/8 fl oz stock and bring to the boil, scraping the bottom to incorporate the bits. Pour into the casserole. Add the remaining stock and wine to the casserole. Bring to the boil, then reduce the heat to a simmer. Cook the chicken, partially covered, for 1½ hours.

Brown the chosen vegetables and put in the casserole with the herbs. Cook 15-25 minutes, until the chicken is tender. Add the broccoli and peas. Cook 4-5 minutes. Remove the chicken and vegetables to a deep platter. Skim the fat off the casserole. Whisk the egg yolks and cream together. Whisk in 120 ml/4 fl oz of the cooking liquid. Slowly stir the egg mixture into the casserole. Cook over a very low heat for 3 minutes, stirring. Do not boil. Pour over the chicken.

■ COOK'S TIP

Suggested fresh vegetables: about 6 each small onions, carrots, turnips and new potatoes, all trimmed and cut into bite-sized pieces.

85   KENTISH DUCKLING

Preparation time:	YOU WILL NEED:
35 minutes	*1 x 2.5 kg/5 ½ lb duckling with*
	giblets
Cooking time:	*3 large oranges*
2½ hours	*450 ml/¾ pint duckling giblet*
	stock (see Cook's Tip)
Oven temperature:	*40 g/1½ oz plain flour*
190C/375F/gas 5;	*salt and pepper*
160C/325F/gas 3	*3 tablespoons red wine*
	3 Cox's Orange Pippins, cored
Serves 4	*and cut in segments*
Calories:	
653 per portion	

Roast the duckling in a preheated oven 45-50 minutes. Prick the skin lightly after 30 minutes so the surplus fat drains out.

Cut the duckling into 4 joints and put them into a casserole with the skin side uppermost. Halve one orange, squeeze the juice and add to the stock. Spoon 2 tablespoons of the duckling fat from the roasting tin into a saucepan. Stir in the flour and cook for 2-3 minutes then blend in the orange-flavoured stock. Bring to the boil and cook until thick. Add the wine and seasoning. Pour this sauce around the duckling portions. Cover the casserole and cook for 1 hour in the centre of the oven, reducing the heat to moderate.

Remove the lid, add the apple segments, replace the lid and cook for 15 minutes. Cut the rind from 2 oranges, cut out the orange segments, and arrange over the duckling.

■ COOK'S TIP

To make giblet stock, wash giblets and place in a pan with 600 ml/1 pint water, salt, pepper, 3 sage leaves and 1 small onion. Simmer for 45 minutes, then strain.

86   TURKEY OLIVES

Preparation time:	YOU WILL NEED:
25 minutes, plus	*4 turkey escalopes*
soaking overnight	*stuffing (see Cook's Tip)*
	25 g/1 oz flour
Cooking time:	*salt and pepper*
1 hour 20 minutes	*50 g/2 oz butter or margarine*
	whole walnuts, to garnish
Oven temperature:	*FOR THE SAUCE*
160C/325F/gas 3	*2 teaspoons Dijon mustard*
	300 ml/½ pint turkey or chicken
Serves 4	*stock*
	4 tablespoons prune liquid
Calories:	*4 tablespoons dry sherry*
628 per portion	*3 tablespoons redcurrant jelly*
	8-10 prunes, soaked overnight and
	drained

Spread the turkey escalopes with the stuffing, then form the escalopes into neat rolls (olives). Secure with cotton or fine string. Season the flour with salt and pepper and coat the olives. Heat the butter or margarine in a frying pan and gently fry the olives for 10 minutes or until golden in colour. Lift into a deep casserole.

Put all the ingredients for the sauce, except the prunes, into the pan in which the olives were fried, stir well to absorb any fat and flour. Bring the sauce to boiling point, then lower the heat and simmer gently until the redcurrant jelly has dissolved, the add the prunes. Pour over the turkey olives and cover the casserole. Cook in the centre of a preheated oven for 1 hour. Remove the cotton or string. Garnish with whole walnuts.

■ COOK'S TIP

For the stuffing, blend together in a liquidizer 2 diced bacon rashers, 8 soaked and drained prunes, 25 g/1 oz walnut pieces, 225 g/8 oz pork sausagemeat, *50 g/2 oz breadcrumbs and 1 tablespoon chopped chives or spring onions.*

87 TUSCANY DUCKLING

Preparation time:
15 minutes

Cooking time:
about 1¼ hours

Oven temperature:
180C/350F/gas 4;
then 200C/400F/gas 6

Serves 4

Calories:
615 per portion

YOU WILL NEED:
4 duckling portions
salt and pepper
25 g/1 oz plain flour
2 tablespoons oil
2 large onions, thinly sliced
¼ teaspoon ground cloves
600 ml/1 pint duckling stock
2 tablespoons chopped fresh mint
50 g/2 oz sultanas
50 g/2 oz sugar
4 tablespoons water
2 tablespoons wine vinegar
sprigs of fresh mint, to garnish

Cut the duckling into 4 portions, season and coat with the flour. Heat the oil in a flameproof casserole and gently fry the onions until soft. Add the duckling portions and brown on both sides. Sprinkle with the ground cloves. Pour in the stock and gradually bring to the boil. Cover and cook in a preheated oven for 1¼ hours. Remove the casserole from the oven and increase the heat. Drain the duck portions, transfer to an ovenproof dish and return to the oven to finish cooking.

Meanwhile prepare the sauce. Skim any fat from the liquid in the casserole then stir in the mint and sultanas. Heat the sugar with the water in a small, heavy pan until it turns a deep golden caramel. Stir this carefully into the casserole. Stir in the vinegar and simmer uncovered for 5-10 minutes until the sauce is well reduced. Pour the sauce around the duck on the serving dish and garnish with sprigs of fresh mint.

■ COOK'S TIP

*When boiling the sugar and
water for the caramel,
watch it carefully as it may
give a bitter flavour to the
sauce if allowed to turn
really dark brown.*

88 POULET CHEZ-MOI

Preparation time:
15 minutes

Cooking time:
50-55 minutes

Oven temperature:
180C/350F/gas 4

Serves 4

Calories:
357 per portion

YOU WILL NEED:
4 boneless chicken breasts
25 g/1 oz butter
1 tablespoon oil
1 large onion, thinly sliced
25 g/1 oz plain flour
3 teaspoons ground ginger
450 ml/¾ pint chicken stock
1 tablespoon Dijon mustard
1 tablespoon wholegrain mustard
1 tablespoon sherry
100 g/4 oz button mushrooms,
    wiped, trimmed and sliced
salt and pepper
1 bunch watercress
2 tablespoons cream

Skin the chicken, if preferred. Heat the butter and oil in a pan and brown the chicken. Drain and transfer to a casserole.

Add the onion to the pan and cook gently for 2-3 minutes until soft. Sprinkle in the flour and ginger and cook, stirring, for 1 minute. Remove from the heat and gradually blend in the stock, mustards and sherry. Return to the heat, bring to the boil and simmer for 1 minute, stirring. Add the mushrooms and seasoning. Pour into the casserole. Cover and cook in a preheated oven for 40-45 minutes or until the chicken is tender.

Reserve half the watercress for garnish and chop the rest finely. Transfer the chicken breasts to a serving dish, stir the chopped watercress and cream into the sauce and pour over the chicken. Garnish with sprigs of watercress.

■ COOK'S TIP

*For an inexpensive family
meal, replace the chicken
breasts with chicken thighs,
allowing two per person.
Chicken thighs skin very
easily.*

89 POULET EN COCOTTE

Preparation time:	YOU WILL NEED:
15 minutes	50 g/2 oz butter
	1.75 kg/4 lb oven-ready chicken,
Cooking time:	dressed and trussed
about 2¼-2½ hours	100 g/4 oz thick rashers streaky
	bacon, cut into strips
Oven temperature:	225 g/8 oz button onions, peeled
150C/300F/gas 2	350 g/12 oz small new carrot
	3 celery sticks, sliced
Serves 4	salt and pepper
	3 sprigs fresh tarragon
Calories:	2-3 tablespoons port (optional)
635 per portion	finely chopped parsley, to garnish

Heat 25 g/1 oz of the butter in a frying pan and brown the chicken slowly, turning it carefully to avoid breaking the skin. Transfer to a casserole just a little larger than the chicken. Add the bacon, cover and cook in a preheated oven for 15 minutes.

Meanwhile, add the onions, carrots and celery to the fat remaining in the pan and cook gently for 5 minutes, stirring occasionally to avoid sticking. Arrange the vegetables in the casserole and spread the remaining butter over the chicken breast. Sprinkle with salt and pepper and add the tarragon. Cover the casserole return to the oven for 2 hours or until the chicken and vegetables are quite tender.

Transfer the chicken to a hot serving dish. Remove the vegetables from the casserole with a slotted spoon and arrange around the chicken. Skim the fat from the juices in the casserole, add the port, and boil the juices rapidly until reduced. Spoon over the chicken and sprinkle with parsley.

■ COOK'S TIP

If you dislike the taste of port, use red wine or sherry instead to boost the flavour of the sauce.

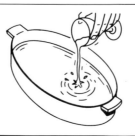

90 STOVED CHICKEN

Preparation time:	YOU WILL NEED:
30 minutes	50 g/2 oz flour
	salt and pepper
Cooking time:	1 x 1½ kg/3½ lb chicken, cut
2¼ hours	into 8 pieces
	50 g/2 oz butter
Oven temperature:	1¼ kg/2½ lb potatoes, thinly sliced
150C/300F/gas 2	25 g/1 oz melted butter
	1 large onion, thinly sliced
Serves 4	600 ml/1 pint chicken stock
	2 tablespoons chopped fresh
Calories:	parsley, to garnish
641 per portion	

Combine the flour, salt and pepper and coat the chicken pieces in the mixture. Melt the butter in a flameproof casserole and brown the chicken pieces for 10 minutes. Transfer the chicken pieces to a plate. Remove the casserole from the heat.

Arrange one-third of the potato slices in the casserole. Brush with one-third of the melted butter. Season with the salt and pepper. Arrange half the onion slices on the potatoes. Place 4 of the chicken pieces on the onions. Arrange one-third of the potato slices over the chicken pieces. Brush with one third of the melted butter, then season. Repeat the onion, chicken and potato layers. Brush with the remaining butter, then season. Pour the stock over to just cover the potatoes. Cover with greased greaseproof paper and the casserole lid. Cook in a preheated oven for 2 hours.

Uncover the casserole and continue to cook for 30 minutes. Garnish with the parsley.

■ COOK'S TIP

This dish can be prepared earlier in the day, giving the 2 hours' cooking time in the oven. Return to the oven, uncovered, for the final 30 minutes.

91 COCONUT CHICKEN

Preparation time:
20 minutes

Cooking time:
1 hour

Oven temperature:
180C/350F/gas 4

Serves 4

Calories:
436 per portion

YOU WILL NEED:
4 tablespoons desiccated coconut
150 ml/¼ pint boiling water
4 chicken portions
salt and pepper
25 g/1 oz butter or margarine
1 tablespoon oil
1 onion, sliced
1 garlic clove, crushed
2 sticks celery, sliced
2 tablespoons flour
300 ml/½ pint chicken stock
few strands of saffron or
  ¼ teaspoon turmeric
½ teaspoon ground coriander
toasted shredded coconut and
  parsley sprigs, to garnish

Put the coconut into a small bowl, pour on the water, mix well and leave to stand for 10 minutes.

Trim the chicken portions and sprinkle with salt and pepper. Heat the butter and oil in a pan and fry chicken until well browned. Transfer to a casserole. Fry the onion, garlic and celery gently in the same fat until soft. Stir in the flour and cook for 1 minute. Add the stock followed by the coconut mixture and bring to the boil. Stir in the saffron or turmeric, coriander and plenty of salt and pepper and pour over the chicken. Cover the casserole and cook in a preheated oven for 1 hour until tender. Spoon off any excess fat and garnish with toasted shredded coconut and parsley.

▧ COOK'S TIP

If liked, replace the
desiccated coconut and
water with 150 ml/¼ pint
coconut milk and add
about 50 g/2 oz freshly
grated coconut to the sauce.

92 ITALIAN HUNTERS' CHICKEN

Preparation time:
20 minutes, plus
soaking

Cooking time:
55 minutes

Serves 8

Calories:
395 per portion

YOU WILL NEED:
25 g/1 dried porcini mushrooms
50 ml/2 fl oz olive oil
8 chicken pieces
2 leeks, white part only, sliced
1 large onion, chopped
75 g/3 oz unsmoked ham, cubed
2 garlic cloves, finely chopped
2½ tablespoons mixed herbs
  (see Cook's Tip)
400 ml/14 fl oz chicken stock
120 ml/4 fl oz dry red wine
1 tablespoon tomato purée
salt and pepper
2 tablespoons cornflour
50 ml/2 fl oz red wine

Reconstitute the mushrooms (see recipe 122). Strain and retain the soaking liquid. Heat the oil in a flameproof casserole and brown the chicken. Remove from the casserole and set aside. Add the leeks and onion to the casserole. Cook 5 minutes. Add the ham, garlic and herbs. Cook 1 minute. Stir in the mushrooms and soaking liquid, stock, wine, and tomato purée

Season the chicken and return to the casserole. Cover and cook over medium-low heat for 25 minutes. Remove the chicken pieces from the casserole and keep warm on a serving platter. Skim the fat off the sauce thoroughly, then bring it to the boil. Mix the cornflour and wine in a cup until smooth, then whisk into the sauce. Simmer for 2 - 3 minutes, until thick and smooth. Pour the sauce over the chicken before serving.

▧ COOK'S TIP

Choose fresh herbs, for
instance, marjoram,
rosemary, thyme and
savory, all finely chopped.

93   DRUMSTICKS IN BARBECUE SAUCE

Preparation time:
15 minutes, plus marinating

Cooking time:
about 50 minutes

Oven temperature:
150C/350F/gas 4;
then 200C/400F/gas 6

Serves 4

Calories:
386 per portion

YOU WILL NEED:
8 chicken drumsticks
marinade (see Cook's Tip)
25 g/1 oz butter
1 large onion, finely chopped
1 large carrot, grated
2 celery sticks, finely chopped
225 g/8 oz tomatoes, peeled and
   chopped
150 ml/¼ pint chicken stock
spring onion curls, to garnish

Make deep cuts diagonally across each drumstick and arrange in a shallow casserole. Pour the marinade over the prepared chicken and leave to stand for 1 hour.

Heat the butter in a pan and fry the onion for 2-3 minutes until tender. Add the carrot and celery and continue cooking for a further 2-3 minutes. Add the tomatoes and chicken stock. Bring to the boil, then pour over the chicken. Spoon the sauce over the drumsticks until all the ingredients are well mixed.

Cover and cook in a preheated oven 30 minutes. Increase the oven temperature, uncover the casserole and cook for another 15 minutes, until the chicken is tender and the sauce reduced. Skim off any fat and garnish with spring onion curls.

■ COOK'S TIP

Marinade: mix together 2 tablespoons each oil, wine vinegar, demerara sugar, soy sauce and dry sherry,4 tablespoons tomato ketchup, 1 crushed garlic clove, 1 teaspoon five-spice powder and 1 tablespoon English mustard.

94   TURKEY MOLE

Preparation time:
25 minutes

Cooking time:
1¼ hours

Oven temperature:
180C/350F/gas 4

Serves 4

Calories:
439 per portion

YOU WILL NEED:
2 tablespoons cooking oil
750 g/1½ lb diced turkey breast
1 onion, chopped
300 ml/½ pint chicken stock
1 small green chilli, seeded and
   chopped
1 green pepper, seeded and
   chopped
2 tomatoes, skinned, seeded and
   chopped
50 g/2 oz blanched almonds
50 g/2 oz raisins
1 teaspoon ground coriander
½ teaspoon ground anise
pinch ground cloves
½ teaspoon ground cinnamon
¼ teaspoon dried red pepper
   flakes
15 g/1 oz plain chocolate
salt and pepper

Heat the oil in a pan, brown the turkey and transfer it to a casserole. Add the onion to the pan and cook until soft. Put the stock, chilli, green pepper, tomatoes, almonds, raisins, spices and pepper flakes in a blender and blend until smooth. Pour into the frying pan, add the chocolate and salt and pepper, and stir until the chocolate has melted. Bring to the boil and cook for 5 minutes. Pour over the turkey and mix well. Cover the casserole, put into a preheated oven and cook for 1 hour.

■ COOK'S TIP

Freeze this for up to 3 months. Defrost overnight in the refrigerator or for 4-6 hours at room temperature. Reheat at 180C/350F/gas 4 for 30 minutes.

95 TURKEY CINZANO

Preparation time:
15 minutes

Cooking time:
45-50 minutes

Oven temperature:
180C/350F/gas 4

Serves 4

Calories:
251 per portion

YOU WILL NEED:
4 thick turkey escalopes or breast
   fillets
salt and pepper
garlic powder
25 g/1 oz butter or margarine
1 x 425 g/15 oz can tomatoes
1 tablespoon tomato purée
125 ml/4 fl oz Cinzano Bianco
2 teaspoons lemon juice
2 bay leaves
FOR THE GARNISH
fresh bay leaves or sprigs of parsley
lemon slices

Sprinkle the turkey escalopes with salt, pepper and garlic powder. Melt the butter in a pan and fry the escalopes until lightly browned. Transfer to a shallow ovenproof casserole.

Liquidize or purée the canned tomatoes and add to the residue in the pan with the tomato purée. Cook until reduced by almost half and thickened. Add the Cinzano and lemon juice to the pan, bring to the boil and add plenty of salt, pepper and garlic powder. Pour over the turkey, add the bay leaves and cover with foil or a lid. Cook in a preheated oven for 45-50 minutes or until tender.

Adjust the seasoning, discard the bay leaves and serve garnished with bay leaves or parsley, and slices of lemon.

96 PLUM DUCK

Preparation time:
10 minutes

Cooking time:
about 1½ hours

Oven temperature:
200C/400F/gas 6

Serves 4

Calories:
667 per portion

YOU WILL NEED:
1 x 2.25-2.75 kg/5-6 lb duck
salt and pepper
garlic powder
1 x 550 g/1¼ lb can red plums in
   syrup
2 teaspoons Worcestershire sauce
1 tablespoon wine vinegar
watercress, to garnish

Remove any excess fat from the duck and place in a large casserole or roasting tin. Prick the skin all over with a fork, then sprinkle with salt, pepper and powdered garlic. Cook in a preheated oven for 30 minutes. Spoon off all the fat from the pan, leaving just the pan juices around the duck.

Drain the juice from the plums, add the Worcestershire sauce, vinegar and salt and pepper and make up to 300 ml/½ pint with water. Pour over the duck, cover with foil and return to the oven for 45 minutes. Baste the duck with the juices again and arrange the plums around the bird. Cover and return to the oven for 15 minutes or until tender. The cover may be left off for the last 10 minutes to crisp up the skin.

Transfer the duck to a serving dish with the plums around and garnish with watercress. Spoon the fat off the pan juices, adjust the seasoning and serve in a sauce boat.

■ COOK'S TIP

Serve with plain boiled rice
and a green salad.

■ COOK'S TIP

To help drain off the fat
from the duck, place on a
wire rack in the roasting tin
so that it is not sitting in its
own fat.

97 GINGERED CITRUS CHICKEN

Preparation time:	YOU WILL NEED:
15-20 minutes	4 x 150 g/5 oz boneless chicken
	breasts, skinned
Cooking time:	½ teaspoon Hungarian paprika
45-50 minutes	salt and pepper
	25 g/1 oz butter
Oven temperature:	175 ml/6 fl oz orange juice
180C/350F/gas 4	50 ml/2 fl oz lemon juice
	grated rind of 1 lemon
Serves 4	1 teaspoon chopped fresh ginger
	2 teaspoons cornflour
Calories:	2 tablespoons chicken stock
282 per portion	2 tablespoons toasted slivered
	almonds
	4 lemon twists and 4 sprigs
	parsley, to garnish

Sprinkle the chicken breasts with the paprika, salt and pepper.
Melt the butter in a flameproof casserole and brown the
chicken for 5-10 minutes. Drain off the excess fat. Blend in the
juices, lemon rind and ginger. Cover and cook in a preheated
ovenfor 25-30 minutes, until the chicken is cooked through.

Remove the chicken from the casserole and keep warm on
a serving platter. Pour the juice mixture into a small saucepan
over a medium-high heat. Combine the cornflour and stock in a
small cup until smooth. Whisk into the juice mixture. Cook,
stirring, until the mixture comes to the boil. Cook for 1
minute, stirring. To serve, coat the chicken with the sauce.
Sprinkle with the almonds, and garnish with lemon twists and
fresh parsley.

■ COOK'S TIP

*You might find it easier to
grate the fresh ginger. Use a
fine grater and remove all
the ginger with a stiff
brush.*

98 CHINESE FIVE SPICED CHICKEN LEGS

Preparation time:	YOU WILL NEED:
10 minutes	1 tablespoon sesame oil
	8 chicken drumsticks, skinned
Cooking time:	1 small bunch spring onions, sliced
1 hour 10 minutes	1 x 225 g/8 oz can bamboo shoots,
	drained
Oven temperature:	2 teaspoons cornflour
180C/350F/gas 4	2 tablespoons soy sauce
	3 tablespoons dry sherry
Serves 4	85 ml/3 fl oz water
	2 teaspoons five-spice powder
Calories:	salt and pepper
253 per portion	

Heat the oil in a pan and lightly fry the chicken drumsticks in
it. Transfer them to a casserole, then add the spring onions,
reserving 1 tablespoonful for garnish, and the bamboo shoots.

Mix the cornflour with the soy sauce, sherry, water and
five-spice powder, add to the oil remaining in the pan, bring to
the boil, taste and adjust the seasoning, then pour over the
chicken drumsticks. Cover the casserole, then put into a
preheated oven and cook for 1 hour. Serve garnished with the
reserved spring onions.

■ COOK'S TIP

*Serve with egg noodles or
egg-fried rice for an
authentic Chinese meal.*

99 TURKEY RICE CASSEROLE

Preparation time:	YOU WILL NEED:
25 minutes	*50 g/2 oz butter*
	2 medium onions, chopped
Cooking time:	*225 g/8 oz button mushrooms,*
1 hour	*cleaned and sliced*
	225 g/8 oz cooked turkey, cubed
Oven temperature:	*150 g/5 oz stuffing, cubed or*
190C/375F/gas 5	*crumbled*
	100 g/4 oz ham, diced
Serves 4	*2 tablespoons chopped parsley*
	½ tablespoon fresh thyme leave
Calories:	*salt and pepper*
526 per portion	*200 g/7 oz long-grain rice*
	1 tablespoon mild curry powder
	475 ml/16 fl oz hot turkey or
	chicken stock

Melt 40 g/1½ oz of the butter in a saucepan. Add the onions and cook for 5 minutes, stirring frequently. Add the mushrooms and continue to cook for 5 minutes, stirring frequently. Place the vegetable mixture in a medium casserole. Add the turkey, stuffing, ham, parsley, thyme, salt and pepper, then stir well to combine. Set aside.

In the saucepan used to cook the onions, melt the remaining butter. Add the rice and curry powder. Brown, stirring frequently, for 5 minutes. Remove the pan from the heat and stir the mixture into the casserole. Pour in the hot stock and cover. Transfer to a preheated oven and cook for 40 minutes, until the rice is tender and the stock absorbed. Serve with chutney and a minted cucumber yogurt salad.

■ COOK'S TIP

This is a good recipe for using up left-over turkey and stuffing. This one is easy on the cook and has a mildly exotic flavour.

100 TURKEY AND CHESTNUTS

Preparation time:	YOU WILL NEED:
40 minutes, plus	*marinade (see Cook's Tip)*
marinating	*1¼ kg/2½ lb boneless raw turkey*
	meat, skinned and cubed
Cooking time:	*2 tablespoons vegetable oil*
2 hours	*50 g/2 oz butter*
	1 medium onion, sliced
Oven temperature:	*1 garlic clove, chopped*
180C/350F/gas 4	*100 g/4 oz button mushrooms*
	40 g/1½ oz plain flour
Serves 4	*150 ml/¼ pint turkey stock*
	2 tablespoons cranberry jelly
Calories:	*freshly ground black pepper*
395 per portion	*225 g/8 oz cooked peeled chestnuts*

Put the marinade and turkey in a dish, cover and chill overnight. Lift the turkey from the marinade. and set aside. Strain the marinade and reserve. Heat the oil in a pan and brown the turkey. Place in a large flameproof casserole.

Melt the butter in the pan and cook the onion and garlic, stirring, 5 minutes. Add the mushrooms and cook 5 minutes. Blend the flour into the pan. Cook, stirring, for 2-3 minutes. Gradually whisk in the reserved marinade and stock. Bring to the boil, stirring constantly. Remove from the heat and add the cranberry jelly, salt and pepper. Pour the sauce over the turkey pieces, cover and cook in a preheated oven for 1 hour.

Transfer the turkey, mushrooms and onions to a dish and keep warm. Place the casserole on the stove, bring to the boil and reduce by a third. Add the chestnuts, simmer 5 minutes. Coat the turkey with the sauce; garnish with parsley, if liked.

■ COOK'S TIP

The casserole can be made earlier in the day, to the point where it has been cooked for one hour, covered and chilled. Reheat and simmer for 10 minutes *before proceeding with the recipe.*

101 MUGHLAI CHICKEN

Preparation time: 20 minutes	YOU WILL NEED: 1 x 1½ kg/3 lb chicken 25 g/1 oz butter
Cooking time: 1 hour 40 minutes	1 tablespoon oil 450 g/1 lb onions, chopped 1 garlic clove, crushed
Oven temperature: 190C/375F/gas 5	1 teaspoon ground coriander ½ teaspoon ground ginger pinch ground cloves
Serves 4	1 teaspoon ground chilli powder 1 teaspoon cardamom seeds

Calories:
575 per portion
	2 teaspoons ground cumin
	1 teaspoon ground turmeric
	150 ml/5 fl oz double cream
	150 ml/5 fl oz plain unsweetened
	   yogurt
	salt and pepper
	fresh coriander and raw onion
	   rings, to garnish

Skin the chicken and put into a casserole. Melt the butter and oil in a pan, add the onions and garlic and cook until softened. Mix the spices together, add to the pan and cook 1-2 minutes.

Put the cream and yogurt into a food processor, add the onion and spice mixture, salt and pepper, and blend to a pureé. Pour over the chicken, cover the casserole and cook in a preheated oven for 1½ hours, basting the chicken occasionally.

Remove the casserole from the oven, transfer the chicken to a serving dish and pour the sauce over. Garnish with fresh coriander and rings of raw onion.

■ COOK'S TIP

This spicy dish should be served with pilau rice and poppadums.

102 CHICKEN MARENGO

Preparation time: 20 minutes	YOU WILL NEED: 4 chicken pieces, skinned salt and pepper
Cooking time: about 50 minutes	50 g/2 oz butter 2 tablespoons brandy 1 onion, sliced
Oven temperature: 180C/350F/gas 4	1-2 garlic cloves, crushed 2 tablespoons flour 1 x 425 g/15 oz can tomatoes,
Serves 4	liquidized or finely chopped 150 ml/¼ pint dry white wine
Calories: 746 per portion	1 tablespoon tomato purée 100 g/4 oz button mushrooms 4 crayfish, shelled 25 g/1 oz butter 2 hard-boiled eggs, shelled and quartered few slices pickled walnut

Season the chicken. Melt half the butter in a pan and brown the chicken. Transfer to a casserole. Warm the brandy, pour over the chicken and ignite. When the flames have died down, add the remaining butter to the pan and fry the onion and garlic lightly. Add the flour and cook 1 minute. Gradually add the tomatoes, wine and purée and bring to the boil. Add the mushrooms and simmer 2 minutes. Pour over the chicken and cover the casserole. Cook in a preheated oven for 45-50 minutes, until tender. Lightly fry the crayfish in butter. Arrange the chicken pieces on a serving plate, spoon the sauce over and add the crayfish, egg quarters and slices of pickled walnut.

■ COOK'S TIP

This dramatic, highly flavoured dish should be served with plain boiled rice.

103 NIGERIAN CHICKEN AND PEANUT CASSEROLE

Preparation time:
15 minutes

Cooking time:
1 hour 20 minutes

Oven temperature:
180C/350F/gas 4

Serves 4

Calories:
624 per portion

YOU WILL NEED:
2 tablespoons oil
1 large onion, peeled and chopped
½ teaspoon chilli powder
1 teaspoon ground cumin
300 ml/½ pint chicken stock
100 g/4 oz crunchy peanut butter
salt and pepper
4 chicken joints, approx
    350 g/12 oz each
225 g/8 oz tomatoes, peeled,
    seeded and chopped
chilli powder and finely chopped
    parsley, to garnish

Heat the oil in a pan, add the onion and fry until it is soft. Add the chilli and cumin to the pan and cook for 1 minute. Add the stock, peanut butter, salt and pepper and bring to the boil, stirring well.

Skin the chicken joints and put into a casserole, add the tomatoes and cover with the peanut sauce. Cover the casserole and put into a preheated oven and cook for 1-1¼ hours until the chicken is very tender, turning the chicken from time to time.

Garnish with a little chilli powder and the finely chopped fresh parsley

104 POLYNESIAN POUSSIN

Preparation time:
15 minutes

Cooking time:
1 hour 10 minutes-1 hour 25 minutes

Oven temperature:
190C/375F/gas 5

Serves 4

Calories:
375 per portion

YOU WILL NEED:
3 tablespoons oil
4 x 450 g/1 lb poussins
1 x 450 g/1 lb can pineapple
    chunks in syrup
chicken stock
2 teaspoons cornflour
1 tablespoon tomato purée
1 onion, sliced
1 red pepper, cored, seeded and
    sliced
salt and pepper
50 g/2 oz macadamia nuts, chopped

Heat the oil in a frying pan and brown the poussins. Transfer to a casserole and reserve the oil in the pan.

Drain the syrup from the pineapple and make up to 300 ml/½ pint with chicken stock. Mix a little of this liquid with the cornflour and purée, put all the liquid into a small pan, bring to the boil and pour over the poussins. Cover the casserole, put into a preheated oven and cook 1-1¼ hours until the poussins are tender, basting occasionally.

Heat the reserved oil in the frying pan and lightly fry the onion and pepper. Strain the liquid from the casserole into the frying pan, add the pineapple and seasoning and boil until the mixture becomes syrupy. Put the poussins on a serving dish, pour the sauce over and sprinkle with the macadamia nuts.

■ COOK'S TIP

This recipe is best made with a standard peanut butter containing an emulsifier. If a peanut butter without emulsifier is used, 1 teaspoon of cornflour should be added to the stock with the peanut butter to prevent the oil in it separating.

■ COOK'S TIP

Macadamia nuts are natives of Australia. If they are not obtainable, use pecans or almonds instead.

105 ARTICHOKE CHICKEN

Preparation time:	YOU WILL NEED:
10 minutes	4 boneless chicken breasts
	salt and pepper
Cooking time:	40 g/1½ oz butter or margarine
about 1 hour	1 onion, sliced
	2 tablespoons flour
Oven temperature:	150 ml/¼ pint dry white wine
180C/350F/gas 4	150 ml/¼ pint chicken stock
	6 tablespoons single cream
Serves 4	1 x 425 g/15 oz can artichoke
	hearts, drained
Calories:	watercress, to garnish
402 per portion	

Trim the chicken, remove the skin if liked, and sprinkle lightly with salt and pepper. Heat the fat in a pan and fry the chicken until browned all over. Transfer to a casserole.

Fry the onion gently in the same fat until soft but only lightly coloured. Stir in the flour and cook for 1 minute. Gradually add the wine and stock and bring to the boil. Add the cream and plenty of salt and pepper and bring just back to the boil.

Cut each artichoke heart in half. Add to the pan, then pour over the chicken and cover the casserole. Cook in a preheated oven for 50-60 minutes or until the chicken is very tender. Garnish with watercress.

■ COOK'S TIP

Chicken portions or pieces of boneless chicken thigh meat may be used as well as boned breasts for this recipe.

106 TURKEY FRICASSEE

Preparation time:	YOU WILL NEED:
20 minutes	675 g/1½ lb boneless turkey
	breast, cubed
Cooking time:	2 onions, chopped
1¼ hours	3 carrots, sliced
	1 bay leaf
Oven temperature:	450 ml/¾ pint chicken stock
180C/350F/gas 4	salt and pepper
	50 g/2 oz butter or margarine
Serves 4	100 g/4 oz mushrooms, sliced
	50 g/1½ oz flour
Calories:	1 egg yolk
497 per portion	3 tablespoons double cream
	juice of ½ small lemon
	bacon rolls and watercress,
	to garnish

Place the turkey in a casserole with the onions, carrots, and bay leaf. Bring the stock to the boil, add salt and pepper and pour over the turkey just to cover. Cover and cook in a preheated oven for about 1 hour or until tender. Discard the bay leaf.

Strain the juices from the turkey and reserve 450 ml/¾ pint; keep the turkey warm. Melt the butter in a pan and fry the mushrooms for 1 minute. Stir in the flour and cook for 1 minute, then gradually add the reserved stock and bring to the boil until thickened, stirring frequently. Simmer for 2 minutes.

Blend the egg yolk with the cream, add a little sauce, then stir it all back into the sauce and reheat without boiling. Stir in the lemon juice. Pour the sauce over the turkey, mix well and serve garnished with grilled bacon rolls and watercress.

■ COOK'S TIP

This recipe can be made with veal or pork - use pie veal cut into cubes or any lean cut of pork, trimmed of fat and skin and cut into cubes. Cook as in the recipe but increase the initial cooking time to about 1½ hours or until the meat is tender. Replace 150 ml/¼ pint of the stock with white wine or cider.

107 CHICKEN VERONIQUE

Preparation time:	YOU WILL NEED:
15 minutes	4 *chicken breasts, partly boned*
	salt and pepper
Cooking time:	*25 g/1 oz butter*
55-60 minutes	*1 tablespoon oil*
	25 g/1 oz flour
Oven temperature:	*150 ml/¼ pint white wine*
180C/350F/gas 4	*150 ml/¼ pint chicken stock*
	grated rind of ½ lemon
Serves 4	*1 tablespoon lemon juice*
	1 bay leaf
Calories:	*150 ml/¼ pint single cream*
413 per portion	*1 egg yolk*
	100 g/4 oz green grapes, peeled,
	halved and seeded
	green grapes and watercress,
	to garnish

Skin the chicken, if liked, then sprinkle lightly with salt and pepper. Heat butter and oil in a pan and lightly brown the chicken. Transfer to a casserole. Stir the flour into the pan juices, then add the wine and stock and bring to the boil. Add the lemon rind and juice, season and pour over the chicken. Add the bay leaf. Cover the casserole and cook in a preheated oven for about 40 minutes.

Blend the cream with the egg yolk, add some of the sauce from the casserole, then stir back into the casserole with the grapes. Replace the lid and return to the oven for 15 minutes. Discard the bay leaf and serve garnished with small bunches of grapes and watercress.

■ COOK'S TIP

Turkey, pork or fish can also be used for this dish. For a fish Veronique, use either fillets of sole or plaice rolled up (allowing 2 per portion) and arranged in a *shallow ovenproof dish. Make the sauce using the butter, flour, wine and 4 tablespoons milk in place of the stock. Cook for 25 minutes.*

108 CHICKEN SMYRNA

Preparation time:	YOU WILL NEED:
20 minutes	4 *chicken joints, skinned*
	1 tablespoon lemon juice
Cooking time:	*pepper and salt*
1 hour	*40 g/1½ oz butter*
	1 medium onion, chopped
Serves 4	*2 teaspoons coriander seeds*
	200 ml/7 fl oz sweet cider
Calories:	*5 cm/2 inch piece cinnamon stick*
464 per portion	*2 tablespoons set honey*
	225 g/8 oz dried figs, soaked and
	drained
	2 tablespoons blanched almonds,
	toasted
	fresh coriander, to garnish

Brush the chicken joints with lemon juice and season with pepper. Melt 25 g/1 oz of the butter in a flameproof casserole and brown the chicken. Set aside.

Melt the remaining butter in the casserole and fry the onion and coriander seeds for about 3 minutes, stirring once or twice. Add the cider, cinnamon, honey and figs, stir well and season to taste with salt and pepper. Return the chicken joints to the casserole, bring the sauce to the boil, cover and simmer over low heat for 45 minutes, turning the chicken pieces once, until the chicken is tender.

Taste the sauce and adjust the seasoning, if necessary. Discard the cinnamon. Scatter the toasted almonds over the chicken, garnish with the sprigs of coriander leaves or parsley and serve with rice.

■ COOK'S TIP

If fresh figs are in season it would add to the exotic flavour to serve them, sliced, or quartered as a garnish.

109 CHICKEN WITH OLIVES

Preparation time: 30 minutes	YOU WILL NEED: *3 tablespoons olive oil* *8 chicken thighs*
Cooking time: 1¼ hours	*2 large onions, chopped* *1 garlic clove, finely chopped* *3 small red peppers, cored, seeded*
Serves 4	*and cut into strips* *6 medium tomatoes, peeled,*
Calories: 543 per portion	*seeded and chopped* *100 g/4 oz ham, diced* *75 g/3 oz stoned green olives* *salt and pepper* *300 ml/½ pint chicken stock*

Heat the oil in a large flameproof casserole over a medium-high heat. Add the chicken thighs and brown on all sides for 10 minutes, turning frequently. Using a pair of tongs, transfer the chicken to paper towels and drain. Set aside.

Pour off all but 1 tablespoon of the fat in the casserole. Add the onions and garlic, then cook over a moderate heat for 5 minutes, stirring frequently. Add the peppers and tomatoes. Cook for 10 minutes, stirring occasionally. Blend in the ham and olives. Place the chicken pieces on top of the vegetable mixture. Sprinkle with the salt and pepper, then pour in the stock. Cover and simmer for 40 minutes until the chicken is cooked through.

Transfer the chicken to a heated serving platter and keep warm. Cook the sauce in the casserole, uncovered, for 5 minutes to thicken. To serve, pour the sauce over the chicken. Garnish with watercress, if liked.

■ COOK'S TIP

*For a low-fat dish remove
the fat and skin from the
chicken before cooking.
You could also use skinned
chicken breast for this dish.*

110 TURKEY MEXICANA

Preparation time: 20 minutes	YOU WILL NEED: *50 g/2 oz seasoned flour* *4 turkey fillets*
Cooking time: 1 hour	*3 tablespoons oil* *1 medium onion, thinly sliced* *1 small red pepper, cored, seeded*
Oven temperature: 160C/325F/gas 3	*and sliced* *300 ml/½ pint chicken stock* *25 g/1 oz seedless raisins*
Serves 4	*pinch of ground cloves* *pinch of ground cumin*
Calories: 387 per portion	*½ teaspoon ground cinnamon* *3 tomatoes, skinned, seeded and* *sliced* *1 teaspoon chilli powder* *1 teaspoon sesame seeds* *25 g/1 oz plain dark chocolate,* *grated* *lime or lemon wedges, to garnish*

Use the seasoned flour to coat the turkey fillets. Heat the oil in a frying pan and brown the turkey. Transfer to a casserole.

Add the onion and red pepper to the frying pan and cook gently until softened. Sprinkle in any remaining seasoned flour and cook 2-3 minutes. Stir in the stock, raisins, cloves, cumin, cinnamon, tomatoes, chilli powder, sesame seeds and chocolate. Bring to the boil and simmer for 10 minutes.

Pour the sauce over the turkey. Cover the casserole and cook in a preheated oven for 50 minutes. Adjust the seasoning, then garnish with lime or lemon.

■ COOK'S TIP

*Chilli powder is very hot
and varies in strength
according to the brand
used, so use it cautiously.*

111 SMOKEY CHICKEN PARCELS

Preparation time:	YOU WILL NEED:
25 minutes	8 smoked streaky bacon rashers, rind removed
Cooking time:	50 g/2 oz mushrooms, finely chopped
1 hour	½ teaspoon dried basil
	salt and pepper
Oven temperature:	8 chicken drumsticks, skinned
180C/350F/gas 4	1 tablespoon oil
	1 x 425 g/15 oz can cream of
Serves 4	mushroom soup
	2 teaspoons cornflour
Calories:	1 tablespoon cold water
429 per portion	chopped fresh parsley, to garnish

Using a round-bladed knife spread and stretch the bacon rashers on a board until they are approximately doubled in size. Mix together the mushrooms, basil and salt and pepper to taste. Spread this over the bacon rashers, pressing down well.

Place a chicken drumstick at one end of a rasher of bacon and carefully roll up so that the drumstick is fully encased in bacon. Secure the end with a wooden cocktail stick. Heat the oil in a frying pan. Add the chicken parcels and cook until lightly browned on all sides. Transfer to a casserole.

Spread the soup evenly over the chicken. Cover and cook for 1 hour or until the chicken is tender.

Remove the chicken parcels. Remove the cocktail sticks, then set aside and keep hot. Dissolve the cornflour in the cold water and stir into the sauce until it has thickened. Taste and adjust the seasoning. Return the chicken to the sauce and reheat thoroughly. Serve sprinkled with a little chopped parsley.

■ COOK'S TIP

This can also be cooked in a slow cooker: cook on Low for 6-8 hours or High for 3 hours.

112 CHICKEN BREASTS IN QUINCE SAUCE

Preparation time:	YOU WILL NEED:
20 minutes	3 quinces, peeled, cored and sliced
	300 ml/½ pint water
Cooking time:	4 boneless chicken breasts
about 45 minutes	salt and pepper
	25 g/1 oz butter or margarine
Oven temperature:	1 tablespoon oil
180C/350F/gas 4	1 onion, chopped
	4 rashers streaky bacon, derinded
Serves 4	and chopped
	1 tablespoon flour
Calories:	1 chicken stock cube
357 per portion	sprigs of fresh herbs, to garnish

Cook the quinces in a covered small pan with the water for 15 minutes or until beginning to soften.

Trim the chicken and sprinkle well with salt and pepper. Heat the fat and oil in a pan and fry the chicken until browned all over. Remove to a casserole.

Fry the onion and bacon gently in the fat left in the pan, until lightly coloured. Stir the flour into the pan and cook for 1 minute. Drain the juice from the quinces and make up to 300 ml/1/2 pint with water. Add to the pan with the stock cube and bring to the boil. Stir the quinces into the sauce, add plenty of salt and pepper and pour over the chicken.

Cover the casserole and cook in a preheated oven for about 45 minutes or until tender. Garnish with sprigs of fresh herbs.

■ COOK'S TIP

Quinces have a very short season, but they do freeze well. Cut into chunks, unpeeled, and freeze as for apples.

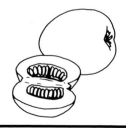

113 TURKEY ESCALOPES IN CREAMED CORN

Preparation time:
20 minutes

Cooking time:
about 40 minutes

Oven temperature:
180C/350F/gas 4

Serves 4

Calories:
459 per portion

YOU WILL NEED:
4 turkey escalopes
salt and pepper
stuffing (see Cook's Tip)
25 g/1 oz butter or margarine
1 onion, thinly sliced
1 garlic clove, crushed
about 150 ml/¼ pint chicken stock
2 teaspoons flour
1 x 275 g/10 oz can cream style sweetcorn
orange slices
stuffed green olives
watercress

Beat the turkey escalopes between 2 sheets of cling film until thin enough to roll up. Season lightly. Divide the stuffing between the pieces of turkey and roll up. Secure with cocktail sticks. Melt the butter in the pan and fry the turkey rolls until golden brown; transfer to a casserole. Fry the onion and garlic in the remaining fat in the pan until golden brown.

Make the orange juice up to 225 ml/8 fl oz with stock. Stir the flour into the pan and cook 1 minute, then gradually add the orange stock and bring to the boil. Stir in the remaining orange rind and creamed corn. Bring back to the boil. Season and pour over the turkey. Cover and cook in a preheated oven for about 40 minutes. Serve garnished with orange slices, stuffed olives and watercress.

▇ COOK'S TIP

When beating the escalopes be careful not to break the flesh.

114 CHICKEN IN EGG AND LEMON SAUCE

Preparation time:
20 minutes

Cooking time:
1¼ hours

Serves 4

Calories:
522 per portion

YOU WILL NEED:
50 g/2 oz butter
4 chicken quarters
2 medium onions, sliced
1 medium carrot, thinly sliced
2 tender celery sticks, sliced
1 teaspoon dried oregano
300 ml/½ pint water
salt and pepper
1 lemon, quartered
egg and lemon sauce (see Cook's Tip)

Melt the butter in a flameproof casserole and brown the chicken quarters lightly. Lift them out and set aside

Fry the onions, carrot and celery for 2-3 minutes, stirring once or twice. Return the chicken to the casserole, sprinkle with the oregano and pour on the water. Season and bring to the boil. Cover the dish and simmer gently over low heat for 45 minutes, or until the chicken is cooked. .

Make the sauce.

Gradually add the sauce to the casserole, a spoonful at a time, and stir it well. Reheat the sauce slowly over low heat, taking great care not to allow the sauce to boil, as this will curdle the mixture. Serve the chicken on a bed of boiled rice with the lemon wedges on top.

▇ COOK'S TIP

For the sauce, gradually stir 2 tablespoons water and 2 tablespoons cornflour together. Beat in 2 eggs and 4 tablespoons lemon juice. Pour a little hot chicken stock from the casserole into the mixture and beat thoroughly.

115 POULET VERSAILLES

Preparation time:	YOU WILL NEED:
15 minutes	1 tablespoon oil
	25 g/1 oz butter
Cooking time:	8 chicken thighs
about 1¼ hours	2 onions, chopped
	2 celery sticks, chopped
Oven temperature:	100 g/4 oz mushrooms, sliced
180C/350F/gas 4	25 g/1 oz plain flour
	300 ml/½ pint dry white wine
Serves 4	150 ml/¼ pint chicken stock
	1 tablespoon Worcestershire sauce
Calories:	salt and pepper
680 per portion	bouquet garni
	3-4 tablespoons double cream
	25 g/1 oz toasted flaked almonds
	1 tablespoon finely chopped parsley

Heat the oil and butter in a flameproof casserole and brown the chicken. Remove from the pan and set aside. Add the onion, celery and mushrooms to the pan and fry until soft. Sprinkle the flour into the onions and cook 1 minute, stirring.

Remove from the heat and gradually blend in the wine, chicken stock and Worcestershire sauce. Return to the heat, bring to the boil and simmer for 1 minute. Add salt and pepper. Return the chicken to the pan and add the bouquet garni. Cover and cook in a preheated oven for 50-60 minutes or until the chicken is very tender.

Stir the cream into the sauce just before serving. Transfer the chicken to a serving dish and coat with the sauce. Scatter toasted, flaked almonds and finely chopped parsley over.

▦ COOK'S TIP

For a less rich dish, cook the chicken in cider, not wine, and omit the cream in the sauce.

116 JUBILEE DUCKLING

Preparation time:	YOU WILL NEED:
30 minutes	25 g/1 oz butter
	2 x 1.5 kg/3 ½ lb ducklings,
Cooking time:	quartered
1 hour	1 onion, chopped
	2 tablespoons brandy
Oven temperature:	2 teaspoons lemon juice
180C/350F/gas 4	1 x 425 g/15 oz can Morello
	cherries, drained (juice
Serves 4	reserved) and stoned
	1 bay leaf
Calories:	150 ml/¼ pint red wine
464 per portion	salt and pepper
	1 tablespoon cornflour
	50 g/2 oz blanched almonds

Melt the butter in a pan and brown the duckling quarters. Transfer to a casserole. Drain surplus fat from the pan, leaving 1 tablespoon. Add the onion and cook until softened. Add the brandy, set alight and pour, flaming, over the duckling. Put the lemon juice, half the reserved cherry juice, bay leaf and wine into the pan. Bring to the boil, scraping the sediment from the bottom. Season. Pour into the casserole, cover and cook for 55 minutes, or until the duckling is tender. Skim off the fat.

Meanwhile, dissolve the cornflour in the remaining cherry juice. Put an almond into each cherry. Arrange the duckling on a serving dish. Keep hot. Pour the sauce into a pan and remove the bay leaf. Stir in the cornflour and bring to the boil. Simmer until thickened. Stir in the cherries, heat through and pour over the duckling. Garnish with olives and chives, if liked.

▦ COOK'S TIP

Black cherries can replace Morellos, but their flavour is sweeter and less distinctive.

117 CIRCASSIAN CHICKEN

Preparation time:
15 minutes, plus
cooling

Cooking time:
1-1 ¼ hours

Oven temperature:
180C/350F/gas 4

Serves 4

Calories:
664 per portion

YOU WILL NEED:
1 x 1 ½ kg/3 lb chicken, jointed
1 onion, chopped
1 carrot, chopped
1 celery stick, chopped
3 parsley stalks
salt and pepper
2 slices white bread, crusts removed
225 g/8 oz shelled walnuts
2 tablespoons oil (walnut if possible)
2 teaspoons paprika
*sprigs of fresh chervil and walnut
   pieces, to garnish*

Put the chicken into a casserole with the onion, carrot, celery, parsley stalks, salt and pepper. Cover with boiling water and cook in a preheated oven for 1-1¼ hours until the chicken is cooked.

Remove the casserole from the oven and leave it until the chicken is cool enough to handle. Strain the stock and reserve, discarding the vegetables. Skin and bone the chicken, then cut into small pieces. Place on a serving dish.

Put the bread, walnuts and 300 ml/½ pint of the reserved stock into a blender or food processor and blend into a thick sauce. Taste and adjust the seasoning, if necessary, and pour over the chicken. Mix together the oil and paprika and sprinkle over the chicken and sauce. Garnish with fresh chervil and walnut pieces and serve at room temperature.

■ COOK'S TIP

*The chicken can be cooked
up to one day in advance
and kept covered and
chilled until needed.
Proceed as above.*

118 MEXICAN CHICKEN IN GREEN ALMOND SAUCE

Preparation time:
15 minutes

Cooking time:
1¼ - 1½ hours

Oven temperature:
180C/350F/gas 4

Serves 4

Calories:
468 per portion

YOU WILL NEED:
*4 chicken joints, approx 350 g/12 oz
   each*
1 onion, chopped
1 garlic clove, crushed
1 green chilli, seeds removed
salt and pepper
300 ml/½ pint hot chicken stock
large bunch parsley, stalks removed
*large bunch fresh coriander, stalks
   removed*
50 g/2 oz ground almonds
25 g/1 oz flaked almonds

Skin the chicken joints and put them in an even layer in a casserole, add the onion, garlic, green chilli, salt and pepper and pour the stock over. Cover the casserole and cook in a preheated oven for 1 - 1¼ hours until the chicken is cooked.

Remove the casserole from the oven, put the stock, onion, garlic and green chilli into a blender or food processor then add the parsley, fresh coriander and ground almonds Blend to a thick sauce. Taste and adjust the seasoning, if necessary.

Sprinkle the flaked almonds over the chicken and pour the sauce over. Recover the casserole and return to the oven for a further 15 minutes to heat through. Serve the casserole with a watercress and cherry tomato salad, if liked.

■ COOK'S TIP

*This will freeze for up to 3
months. Defrost overnight
in the refrigerator or for 4-6
hours at room temperature.
Reheat at 180C/350F/gas 4
for about 40 minutes.*

119 TURKEY HASH

Preparation time:
25 minutes

Cooking time:
50 minutes

Oven temperature:
180C/350F/gas 4

Serves 6

Calories:
563 per portion

YOU WILL NEED:
40 g/1 1/2 oz butter
1 medium onion, finely chopped
1 red pepper, cored, seeded and
    diced
225 g/8 oz mushrooms, sliced
450 g/1 lb cooked turkey meat, cubed
275 g/10 oz leftover turkey
    stuffing, cubed
300 ml/½ pint double cream
250 ml/8 fl oz turkey or chicken stock
120 ml/4 fl oz leftover turkey gravy
2 tablespoons cornflour
15 g/½ oz chopped parsley
⅛ teaspoon ground nutmeg
salt and pepper
25 g/1 oz Gruyère cheese, grated

Melt the butter in a flameproof casserole. Add the onion and cook, stirring, 5 minutes. Add the pepper and mushrooms and cook 3 minutes, until the mushrooms soften. Add the turkey and stuffing and cook 5 minutes, stirring. Take off the heat.

Mix the cream, 175 ml/6 fl oz of the stock and the gravy in a pan. Bring to the boil over a high heat. Mix the cornflour and the remaining stock in a cup until smooth and whisk into the sauce. Simmer 2-3 minutes, stirring, until thick. Remove from the heat and add the parsley, nutmeg, salt and pepper. Blend the sauce into the casserole, then sprinkle over the cheese. Cover the casserole, place in a preheated oven and cook for 25 minutes until heated through.

■ COOK'S TIP

The casserole can be prepared in the morning, covered and kept chilled. Cook for 30 minutes until heated through.

120 STUFFED CHICKEN ROLLS WITH TARRAGON SAUCE

Preparation time:
35 minutes

Cooking time:
1 hour

Oven temperature:
180C/350F/gas 4

Serves 6

Calories:
585 per portion

YOU WILL NEED:
tarragon sauce (see Cook's Tip)
15 g/½ oz butter
2 medium carrots, cut into fine
    julienne strips
1 medium leek, cut into fine
    julienne strips
6 large chicken breasts, halved,
    skinned, boned and flattened to
    an even thickness
1 litre/1¼ pints hot chicken stock
freshly ground black pepper

Make the tarragon sauce. Melt the butter in a frying pan. Add the carrots and leek, then cook for 1 minute, stirring constantly. Remove from the heat and set aside.

Place the chicken breasts, skinned side down, on a working surface. Season with salt and pepper. Divide the carrot and leek mixture between them, roll the chicken pieces up tightly to enclose the vegetables, then tie with string to secure. Transfer the chicken rolls to a casserole. Add the stock. Cover and cook in a preheated oven for 25 minutes until firm. While the rolls are cooking, reheat the sauce over a gentle heat. Stir frequently.

Remove the casserole from the oven and transfer the rolls to a working surface. Cut the string off the rolls. Cut each roll into 4 . Pour the sauce on to 6 plates, just coating the bottom. Arrange 1 cut roll on each plate.

■ COOK'S TIP

Sauce: cook 2 chopped shallots in 15 g/½ oz butter until soft. Add 250 ml/8fl oz white wine, and boil until reduced to 2 tablespoons. Stir in 475 ml/16 fl oz chicken stock. Boil until reduced to 120 ml/4 fl oz. Add 475 ml/16 fl oz double cream and 2 tablespoons chopped tarragon and boil till thickened. Season.

GAME

Low in fat, game is becoming an increasingly popular option, especially now it is widely available all year round. The variety is surprising, from venison, rabbit and hare to grouse, quail, pheasant and partridge. Casseroled, game is tender, moist and full of flavour. It is a rich meat, so most of the dishes need little in the way of an accompaniment.

121 ELIZABETHAN RABBIT

Preparation time:	YOU WILL NEED:
20 minutes	1 rabbit, approx 1¼ kg/2½ lb, jointed
Cooking time:	1 tablespoon seasoned flour
2 hours 10 minutes	2-3 tablespoons oil
	1 dessert apple, peeled, cored and
Oven temperature:	sliced
160C/325F/gas 3	100 g/4 oz seedless green grapes
	50 g/2¼ oz raisins
Serves 4	1 orange, segmented
	grated rind and juice of 1 orange
Calories:	1 bouquet garni
442 per portion	1 onion, chopped
	2 sticks celery, sliced
	150 ml/¼ pint red wine
	85 ml/3 fl oz chicken stock
	salt and pepper
	fine strips of orange rind, to garnish

Coat the rabbit with the seasoned flour. Heat the oil in a frying pan and fry the rabbit joints until browned. Transfer to a casserole, then put the apple, grapes, raisins, orange segments, orange rind and juice and bouquet garni into the casserole.

Add the onion and celery to the frying pan with a little extra oil, if necessary, and cook for 2-3 minutes. Add the wine and stock to the pan, bring to the boil and pour over the rabbit. Cover the casserole, put into a preheated oven and cook for 2 hours until the rabbit is very tender.

Remove the bouquet garni before serving garnished with strips of orange rind.

■ COOK'S TIP

A basic bouquet garni consists of fresh parsley, thyme and a bay leaf tied together. Fresh herbs give the best flavour, but purchased muslin bags of *dried bouquet garni give acceptable flavours in long-cooked casseroles.*

122 QUAIL CASSEROLE

Preparation time:	YOU WILL NEED:
20 minutes, plus 30	225 g/8 oz bacon, rinded and cut
minutes	into strips
reconstitution	75 g/3 oz butter
	8 quail, about 100 g/4 oz each
Cooking time:	475 ml/16 fl oz chicken stock
1¼ hours	250 ml/8 fl oz Madeira wine
	salt and pepper
Serves 4	275 g/10 oz button mushrooms
	15 g/½ oz porcini mushrooms,
Calories:	reconstituted (see Cook's Tip)
730 per portion	3 tablespoons cornflour
	120 ml/4 fl oz double cream

Melt 50 g/2 oz of the butter in a flameproof casserole over a medium heat. Add the bacon and cook 10 minutes. Add the quail and brown on all sides. Drain off excess fat and discard. Blend in the stock, 120 ml/4 fl oz of the Madeira, salt and pepper. Cover and cook over medium-low heat for 30 minutes.

Melt the remaining butter in a frying pan, add the quartered button and reconstituted porcini mushrooms. Cover and cook for 10 minutes. Remove from the heat and set aside. When the quail have cooked for 30 minutes, add the mushrooms to the casserole. Cover and continue cooking for another 20 minutes.

Transfer the quail to a serving platter. Increase the heat under the casserole to high. Blend the cornflour and remaining Madeira in a cup until smooth. Stir into the casserole. Add the cream and let the mixture come to the boil. Boil for 2-3 minutes. To serve, pour the sauce over the quail.

■ COOK'S TIP

To reconstitute porcini mushrooms, soak them in 250 ml/8 fl oz warm water for 30 minutes, then drain well and chop coarsely.

123 BRAISED GUINEA FOUL

Preparation time:	YOU WILL NEED:
20 minutes	1 large oven-ready guinea fowl, about 1.5 kg/3 lb
Cooking time:	salt and pepper
1¼ hours	4 slices streaky bacon, rinded
	50 g/2 oz butter
Serves 4	1 large onion, chopped
	100 g/4 oz ham, chopped
Calories:	450 g/1 lb chicory, trimmed
676 per portion	2 tablespoons orange juice
	3 tablespoons sweet sherry
	1 tablespoon plain flour
	2 tablespoons blanched almonds, toasted

Season the guinea fowl with salt and pepper. Cover the breast and legs with bacon slices and tie the bird round with twine.

Melt 25 g/1 oz of the butter in a flameproof casserole and fry the bird until the underside is lightly browned. Remove the bird. Add the onion and ham to the casserole and fry gently, stirring, for 5 minutes. Lower the heat, add the chicory heads and fry until they begin to soften. Stir in the orange juice and bring to the boil. Return the bird to the casserole, breast side down. Cover and simmer for 50 minutes-1 hour, until the bird is tender. Discard the bacon, cut the guinea fowl into 4 portions and arrange on a serving dish. Lift out the chicken and arrange around the game portions.

Stir the sherry into the casserole and bring to simmering point. Mix together the remaining butter and the flour and add a little at the time to the sauce. Pour over the quail.

▨ COOK'S TIP

Guinea fowl can be cooked in ways suitable for chicken and pheasant -braised, casseroled and roast. For extra piquancy, add 12 garlic cloves to this dish.

124 PHEASANT CASSEROLE

Preparation time:	YOU WILL NEED
25 minutes, plus marinating	marinade (see Cook's Tip)
	2 pheasants, about 1¼ kg/2½ lb each, skinned and jointed
Cooking time:	75 g/3 oz butter
1½ hours	15 g/½ oz porcini mushrooms, reconstituted (see recipe 122)
Oven temperature:	225 g/8 oz field mushrooms, sliced
180C/350F/gas 4	25 g/1 oz plain flour
	300 ml/½ pint pheasant or
Serves 6	chicken stock
	150 ml/¼ pint double cream
Calories:	
801 per portion	

Add the pheasant pieces to the marinade. Cover and chill overnight. Next day, take the pheasant from the marinade . Strain and reserve the marinade. Melt 50 g/2 oz butter in a frying pan. Brown the pheasant pieces, turning occasionally, for 10 minutes, then transfer to a flameproof casserole. Set aside.

Melt the remaining butter in the frying pan. Add the porcini and field mushrooms. Cook for 5 minutes. Blend in the flour and, stirring continuously, cook for 2-3 minutes. Lower the heat. Gradually add the stock and reserved marinade. Cook, whisking continuously, until the sauce comes to the boil and has slightly thickened. Pour over the pheasant. Cover and cook in a preheated oven for 1 hour.

Transfer the pheasant to a serving dish. Keep warm. Pour the sauce from the casserole into a saucepan. Bring to the boil. Add the cream, simmer 2-3 minutes. Pour over the pheasant.

▨ COOK'S TIP

For the marinade, mix together 450 ml/¾ pint port, 1 sliced onion,1 sliced carrot, 2 chopped sticks celery, 1 chopped garlic clove,1 tablespoon fresh chopped thyme, 4 crushed juniper berries, a bay leaf and salt and pepper to taste.

125 GASCONY RABBIT

Preparation time:	YOU WILL NEED:
30 minutes, plus	*marinade (see Cook's Tip)*
marinating	*1 young rabbit, jointed*
	225 g/8 oz dried apricots
Cooking time:	*450 ml/¾ pint strained tea*
2¼ hours	*40 g/1½ oz butter*
	100 g/4 oz streaky bacon, diced
Oven temperature:	*2 tablespoons plain flour*
180C/350F/gas 4	*150 ml/¼ pint chicken stock*
	150 ml/¼ pint red wine
Serves 4	*2 medium carrots, thinly sliced*
	2 celery sticks, sliced
Calories:	*salt and pepper*
677 per portion	*2 tablespoons crème fraîche*

Make the marinade. Add the rabbit to it, cover and chill for 8 hours, or overnight. Soak the apricots in the tea for 8 hours or overnight. Strain and reserve the liquid. Lift out the rabbit from the marinade. Strain and reserve the marinade.

Melt the butter in a flameproof casserole and fry the bacon for 3-4 minutes. Remove the bacon and set aside. Sauté the rabbit joints in two batches, turning them to brown evenly, then take out of the casserole. Stir in the flour and gradually pour on the reserved marinade and apricot soaking liquid, stirring constantly. Add the chicken stock and wine. Bring the sauce to the boil for 3 minutes, stirring constantly.

Add the rabbit, apricots, bacon, carrots and celery and salt and pepper. Bring to the boil, cover and cook in a preheated oven for 1¼ hours. Swirl the crème fraîche over the rabbit immediately before serving.

■ COOK'S TIP

For the marinade, mix 150 ml/¼ pint red wine, 1 chopped onion, 1 sliced celery stick, 1 tablespoon chopped celery leaves, 2 crumbled bay leaves, 12 crushed juniper berries, 6 crushed black peppercorns and 3 tablespoons oil.

126 KONIGSBERG HARE

Preparation time:	YOU WILL NEED:
15 minutes, plus	*6 hare joints*
marinating	*marinade (see Cook's Tip)*
	2 tablespoons plain flour
Cooking time:	*50 g/2 oz butter*
3 hours	*4 rashers streaky bacon, diced*
	1 tablespoon Dijon mustard
Oven temperature:	*2 tablespoons tomato purée*
160C/325F/gas 3	*1 x 450 g/1 lb can red plums*
	18 button onions, peeled and
Serves 6	*blanched in boiling water for*
	2 minutes
Calories:	*100 g/4 oz button mushrooms*
624 per portion	*chopped parsley, to garnish*

Place the wiped hare joints in the marinade. Leave to stand for 3-4 hours. Drain the joints thoroughly, pat dry, coat with flour. Reserve the marinade. Heat the butter in a flameproof casserole and fry the joints of hare until well browned. Drain over the pan and set aside. Add the bacon to the casserole together with the remaining flour and fry, stirring, for 1 minute.

Remove from the heat and blend in the mustard, tomato purée, strained marinade and the syrup drained from the plums. Return to the heat and simmer for 1 minute, stirring.

Return the joints of hare to the pan together with the button onions and coat with the sauce. Cover closely with a lid or foil and cook in a preheated oven for 2½ hours.

Add the mushrooms and the plums and cook, uncovered, for 15 minutes or until the hare is tender. Skim the fat from the surface, then sprinkle liberally with chopped parsley.

■ COOK'S TIP

For the marinade: 1 peeled onion, 1 garlic clove, bouquet garni, 300 ml/½ pint red wine, 2 tablespoons tarragon vinegar and salt and pepper.

127 WILD DUCK IN CUMBERLAND SAUCE

Preparation time:
about 15 minutes

Cooking time:
about 1¼ hours

Oven temperature:
220C/425F/gas 7;
180C/350F/gas 4

Serves 4

Calories:
410 per portion

YOU WILL NEED:
2 wild duck
salt and pepper
25 g/1 oz melted butter
finely pared rind of 1 orange and 1
*   lemon, in julienne strips*
juice of 2 oranges
juice of ½-1 lemon
4 tablespoons port
3 tablespoons redcurrant,
*   cranberry or bramble jelly*
1 tablespoon cornflour
orange slices and watercress,
*   to garnish*

Season the ducks well, brush with melted butter and cook uncovered in a preheated oven for 20 minutes, basting once.

Cook the strips of fruit rind in boiling water for 5 minutes; drain. Heat the fruit juices, port and redcurrant jelly until the jelly melts. Add most of the fruit rinds and salt and pepper.

Spoon off any fat from the ducks, leaving just the pan juices, and pour over the orange mixture. Cover the casserole with a lid or foil. Reduce the oven temperature and cook the ducks for about 45 minutes, basting once or twice, until tender.

Strain the juices from the ducks into a pan and add the cornflour, blended in a little cold water. Bring to the boil to thickened. Serve in a jug. Serve the ducks sprinkled with the strips of fruit rind and with orange slices and watercress.

■ COOK'S TIP

The easiest way to remove rind without the white pith from citrus fruit is with a potato peeler; otherwise cut the rind as thinly as possible with a sharp knife, *then place on a flat surface, rind side downwards, and cut off all the white pith. Julienne strips are very narrow strips cut with a large heavy sharp knife.*

128 PHEASANTS WITH BRANDY

Preparation time:
30 minutes

Cooking time:
about 2 hours

Oven temperature:
180C/350F/gas 4

Serves 6-8

Calories:
821-616 per portion

YOU WILL NEED:
1 brace pheasants, with giblets
salt and pepper
bouquet garni
40 g/1½ oz seasoned flour
2 thick rashers streaky bacon,
*   rinded and diced (save rinds)*
100 g/4 oz butter or margarine
18 shallots, peeled
100 g/4 oz small button mushrooms
2-3 tablespoons brandy
3 tablespoons double cream
75 g/3 oz coarse soft breadcrumbs

Joint each pheasant. Put the backbones and giblets into a saucepan with water to cover (about 900 ml/1¼ pints), seasoning and bouquet garni. Simmer for 1 hour, strain and put 600 ml/1 pint on one side.

Coat the pheasant joints in the flour. Heat the bacon rinds with half the butter in a frying pan. Add the pheasant joints and fry gently until golden brown. Transfer to a casserole.

Discard the bacon rinds. Fry the diced bacon and shallots in the pan for 5 minutes. Add to the pheasants. Gradually blend the reserved stock into any fat and flour in the pan. Bring to the boil, stirring. Simmer 5 minutes. Add the mushrooms and brandy. Pour over the pheasant, cover and cook in a preheated oven for 1¼ hours. Stir in the cream and cook for a further 10-20 minutes. Meanwhile, heat the remaining butter in a pan, add the breadcrumbs and fry until brown and crisp. Top each portion of pheasant with crumbs.

■ COOK'S TIP

If you prefer a thicker sauce, blend an extra 1½ tablespoons flour into the residue fat in the pan before adding the pheasant stock or use a beurre manié.

129 ST MELLONS RABBIT

Preparation time:	YOU WILL NEED:
20 minutes	675 g/1½lb rabbit joints
	25 g/1 oz seasoned flour
Cooking time:	175 g/6 oz piece salt belly pork
about 2 hours	2 tablespoons oil or dripping
	2 onions, cut into wedges
Oven temperature:	300 ml/½ pint pale ale
180C/350F/gas 4;	150 ml/¼ pint beef stock
200C/400F/gas 6	1 tablespoon French mustard
	1 tablespoon wine vinegar
Serves 4	2 teaspoons brown sugar
	salt and pepper
Calories:	2 carrots, sliced
354 per portion	2 slices bread, crusts removed
	1 egg, beaten
	2 tablespoons milk
	100 g/4 oz button mushrooms,
	trimmed and halved

Coat the rabbit in the flour. Skin and dice the pork. Heat the oil and fry the rabbit and pork until brown. Transfer to a casserole.

Fry the onions in the same fat until browned, then sprinkle on any remaining flour. Add the ale and stock and bring to the boil. Stir in the mustard, vinegar, sugar, seasoning and carrots. Pour over the rabbit. Cover and cook for 1 ½ hours.

Cut the bread into squares. Whisk the egg and milk together and dip the bread into it. Add the mushrooms to the casserole then lay the bread on top. Return the casserole to the oven, uncovered, for 20-30 minutes or until crisp.

■ COOK'S TIP

If using frozen rabbit make sure it is completely thawed before cooking. The casserole may be frozen for up to 2 months; it makes no difference if the dish is *made with frozen or fresh rabbit, it can be frozen a second time once it has been cooked, although refreezing may affect the eating quality and texture.*

130 VINEYARD PIGEON

Preparation time:	YOU WILL NEED:
20 minutes	75 g/3 oz butter, softened
	salt and pepper
Cooking time:	4 young, oven-ready pigeons
1¼ hours	8 slices streaky bacon, rinded
	225 g/8 oz button onions, peeled
Oven temperature:	1 garlic clove, peeled and chopped
180C/350F/gas 4	1 tablespoon plain flour
	150 ml/¼ pint white wine
Serves 4	150 ml/¼ pint chicken stock
	225 g/8 oz seedless grapes
Calories:	150 ml/¼ pint single cream
700 per portion	sprigs of mint, to garnish

Season the butter with salt and pepper. Set aside 25 g/1 oz and divide the remainder into 4 pieces. Lift up the skin of each pigeon from the neck end and rub the butter under the skin on to the breast. Season the birds with salt and pepper inside and out, wrap each one in 2 slices of bacon and secure with twine.

Melt the remaining butter in a flameproof casserole. Fry the pigeons, two at a time, over moderate heat for 5-6 minutes. Remove the pigeons and add the onions and garlic. Fry for 3-4 minutes. Sprinkle on the flour and stir until it forms a paste with the fat in the casserole. Gradually pour on the wine and stock, stirring. Bring to the boil. Return the pigeons to the casserole. Cover the casserole and cook in a preheated oven for 1 hour. Stir in the grapes, reserving a few for garnish. Cover and continue cooking for 15 minutes, or until the pigeons are tender. (Pierce a thigh with a fine skewer to test.) Stir in the cream. Garnish with mint sprigs and the reserved grapes.

■ COOK'S TIP

Be sure not to omit the bacon - pigeon, like all game, is a dry meat and the bacon helps to keep it moist during cooking.

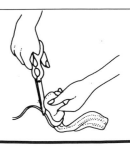

131 PARTRIDGE PUDDING

Preparation time:
1 hour

Cooking time:
2½ hours

Serves 4

Calories:
1261 per portion

YOU WILL NEED:
2 partridges or 2 pigeons
450 g/1 lb braising steak
2 tablespoons plain flour
½ teaspoon salt
¼ teaspoon black pepper
¼ teaspoon dried thyme
¼ teaspoon dried marjoram
750 g/1½ lb suet crust
   (see Cook's Tip)
1 large onion, finely sliced
100 g/4 oz mushrooms, finely sliced
900 ml/1½ pints brown stock

Cut the birds in half through the breast bone, using a heavy knife. Trim the steak and divide into 4 pieces. Season the flour with salt, pepper and herbs, and roll the game and steak in it.

Roll out the suet crust to 5 mm/¼ inch thickness and line a 1.5 litre/2½ pint pudding basin. Roll out a separate circle for the lid. Put the steak in the lined basin and pack the game on top. Tuck slices of onion and mushroom into all the spaces and sprinkle the remainder over the top. Pour in the stock to about 1 cm/½ inch below the top of the bowl. Brush the top edge of the crust with milk and put on the lid, pinching the edges well together. Cover with foil and put a plate on top.

Stand the basin in a large saucepan and pour in boiling water halfway up the sides. Simmer gently for 2½ hours, adding more boiling water, if necessary.

To serve, cut off the top crust and set on one side, so that the meat and game can easily be lifted out.

▓ COOK'S TIP

For suet crust dough: mix
225 g/8 oz shredded suet,
450 g/1 lb flour, 50 g/2 oz
fresh white breadcrumbs,
pinch of salt with 300 ml/½
pint cold water.

132 RABBIT WITH PRUNES

Preparation time:
15 minutes, plus
marinating

Cooking time:
2¼ hours

Oven temperature:
180C/350F/gas 4

Serves 4

Calories:
522 per portion

YOU WILL NEED:
marinade (see Cook's Tip)
1 kg/2 lb rabbit joints
25 g/1 oz butter
100 g/4 oz streaky bacon, rinded
   and cut into 2.5 cm/1 inch squares
4 teaspoons plain flour
300 ml/½ pint chicken stock
225 g/8 oz stoned prunes, soaked
   (if necessary) and drained
225 g/8 oz carrots, thinly sliced
salt and pepper

Mix together the marinade ingredients. Put the rabbit joints into a strong polythene bag, pour on the marinade and close the bag. Shake well and set aside for 2-3 hours or overnight.

Remove the rabbit from the marinade. Dry the rabbit pieces. Strain and reserve the marinade. Melt the butter in a flameproof casserole and fry the bacon over moderate heat for 2-3 minutes. Remove the bacon and set aside. Fry the rabbit to brown it on all sides, then remove it.

Stir in the flour and gradually pour on the marinade and the chicken stock, stirring. Bring to the boil and simmer for 2-3 minutes. Add the bacon, rabbit, prunes and carrots. Taste the stock and season with salt and pepper. Return the stock to the boil and cover the casserole. Cook in a preheated oven for 2 hours, until the rabbit is tender.

▓ COOK'S TIP

For the marinade, mix
together 2 tablespoons oil, 2
tablespoons orange juice,
150 ml/¼ pint sweet cider, 2
crumbled bay leaves, strip
of thinly pared orange rind,

1 teaspoon dried thyme, 1
sliced onion and salt and
pepper.

133 PHEASANT IN RED WINE

Preparation time:	YOU WILL NEED:
30 minutes, plus	½ bottle dry red wine
cooking the	40 g/1½ oz butter
chestnuts	1 x 1½ kg/3 lb young pheasant,
	jointed, liver reserved
Cooking time:	1 onion, sliced
1 hour	1 carrot, sliced
	1 garlic clove, crushed
Oven temperature:	25 g/1 oz plain flour
180C/350F/gas 4	sprig of fresh rosemary
	150 ml/¼ pint giblet stock
Serves 4	salt and pepper
	225 g/8 oz chestnuts, peeled and
Calories:	cooked
815 per portion	4 x 5 cm/2 inch rounds fried bread

Pour the wine into a small saucepan, bring to the boil and simmer until reduced by half. Remove from the heat and reserve. Melt 25 g/1 oz butter in a frying pan, add the pheasant and brown on all sides. Transfer to a casserole. Add the onion and carrot to the frying pan and cook gently for 5 minutes. Add to the casserole with the garlic.

Stir the flour into the fat in the frying pan and cook for 2 minutes. Stir in the reserved reduced wine, rosemary and stock and bring to the boil, stirring. Season to taste. Pour the sauce over the pheasant, cover and cook in a preheated oven for 45 minutes. Add the chestnuts and cook for a further 15 minutes.

Slice the reserved liver. Melt the remaining butter, add the liver and cook 4 minutes. Pound to a cream. Season and spread on the bread. Garnish the pheasant with the bread rounds.

▇ COOK'S TIP

If you dislike the gamey taste of pheasant liver, omit it and serve the pheasant with plain croûtons, instead. Garnish with parsley, if liked.

134 CASSEROLE OF HARE

Preparation time:	YOU WILL NEED:
30 minutes	3 tablespoons oil
	1 small hare, jointed
Cooking time:	2 onions, sliced
1½ hours	2 carrots, sliced
	2 garlic cloves, crushed
Oven temperature:	450 ml/¼ pint stock
180C/350F/gas 4	150 ml/¼ pint port
	juice of 1 lemon
Serves 4	1 bouquet garni
	salt and pepper
Calories:	bacon topping (see Cook's Tip)
584 per portion	beurre manié (see Cook's Tip)

Heat the oil in a large frying pan, add the hare joints and brown on all sides. Transfer to a casserole.

Add the onions and carrots to the pan and cook gently until the onions begin to brown. Pour off the surplus oil. Add the garlic, stock, port, lemon juice and bouquet garni. Season to taste. Bring to the boil, then pour over the hare in the casserole. Tuck a piece of greaseproof paper over the stew. Cover and cook for 1 ¼ hours or until the hare is very tender.

Meanwhile, make the bacon topping and set aside. Add the mushrooms to the pan and cook for 5 minutes. Drain. Keep the topping and mushrooms hot on separate plates.

Arrange the hare in a serving dish and keep hot. Strain the sauce into a pan and bring slowly to the boil. Make the beurre manié (see Cook's Tip), whisk into the sauce in small pieces and simmer, stirring, until it thickens. Pour the sauce over the hare, and top with the bacon, mushrooms and parsley, if liked.

▇ COOK'S TIP

For the bacon topping, melt 25 g/1 oz butter in a pan and add 100 g/4 oz of rinded and cubed streaky bacon. Cook gently for five minutes. For beurre manié, *mix 25 g/1oz each of butter and plain flour together to make a paste.*

135 GROUSE WITH RED CABBAGE

Preparation time:	YOU WILL NEED:
20 minutes	*2 grouse, prepared*
	12 rashers streaky bacon, derinded
Cooking time:	*salt and pepper*
about 1½ hours	*40 g/1½ oz butter or margarine*
	2 onions, sliced
Oven temperature:	*225 g/8 oz chipolata sausages, halved*
180C/350F/gas 4	*1 small red cabbage, about 1 kg/2 lb,*
	finely shredded
Serves 4	*bouquet garni*
	150 ml/¼ pint red wine
Calories:	*150 ml/¼ pint game or beef stock*
845 per portion	*2 tablespoons vinegar*
	parsley sprigs
	lemon wedges, to garnish

Halve the grouse and wrap 2 rashers of bacon around each half, securing with wooden cocktail sticks. Season the birds lightly. Melt the fat in a pan and fry the birds to brown all over, then remove from the pan. Add the remainder of the bacon, cut into strips, the onions and chipolatas to the pan and fry until browned.

Place about two-thirds of the cabbage in a casserole and arrange the grouse, bacon, onions, chipolatas and bouquet garni on top. Cover with the remaining cabbage.

Bring the wine, stock and vinegar to the boil, season, and add to the casserole. Cover and cook for about 1½ hours, until tender. Discard the bouquet garni and cocktail sticks.

To serve, arrange the cabbage mixture in a dish with the grouse on top. Garnish with parsley and lemon.

■ COOK'S TIP

If the grouse are very small allow 1 bird per person and either cut in half or leave whole.

136 ORCHARD GROUSE

Preparation time:	YOU WILL NEED:
30 minutes	*50 g/2 oz butter*
	2 tablespoons oil
Cooking time:	*2 oven-ready grouse or pheasants*
2 hours	*1 medium onion, finely chopped*
	225 g/8 oz pie veal, finely minced
Oven temperature:	*2 small cooking apples*
160C/325F/gas 3	*150 ml/¼ pint chicken stock*
	salt and pepper
Serves 4	*2 bay leaves*
	2 teaspoons lemon juice
Calories:	*4 tablespoons double cream*
792 per portion	*2 tablespoons Calvados or brandy*
	mustard and cress

Melt 25 g/1 oz butter with the oil in a flameproof casserole and fry the grouse over moderate heat for 8-10 minutes, turning them to brown evenly. Remove and keep warm.

Add the onion and veal to the casserole. Peel, core and chop one apple, stir it into the casserole and cook gently for 5 minutes, stirring. Pour on the stock, season and add the bay leaves and juice. Bring to the boil and add the grouse, breast sides down. Cover the casserole and cook for 1¼ hours. Discard the bay leaves. Stir in the cream and liqueur, cover and continue cooking for 20 minutes, until the birds are tender.

Peel and core the second apple and slice it into rings. Fry the rings in the remaining butter until golden.

Skim the fat off the sauce and spoon on to a serving dish. Place the birds on top, arrange the apple slices round them, and sprinkle with mustard and cress (and parsley, if liked).

■ COOK'S TIP

All game should be hung for a few days, to tenderize the meat and allow the flavour to develop, so it is not advisable to rush out and buy grouse at the very beginning of the sporting season in August, on the 'Glorious Twelfth'.

137 PIGEON WITH RAISIN SAUCE

Preparation time:	YOU WILL NEED:
15 minutes, plus	50 g/2 oz butter
soaking	2 pigeons, drawn and trussed
	4 rashers streaky bacon, diced
Cooking time:	1 small onion, finely chopped
about 1¼-2 hours	1 celery stick, trimmed and chopped
	1 tablespoon plain flour
Oven temperature:	150 ml/¼ pint red wine
150C/300F/gas 2	150 ml/¼ pint chicken stock
	8 juniper berries, crushed
Serves 4	8 coriander seeds, crushed
	salt and pepper
Calories:	50 g/2 oz raisins, soaked in 4
555 per portion	tablespoons port for 3-4 hours
	1 tablespoon redcurrant jelly
	4 rounds fried bread, cut into
	triangles

Heat the butter in a flameproof casserole and fry the pigeons until lightly browned, then drain, cut in half and trim away the backbone. Add the bacon to the casserole, cook until the fat begins to flow, then add the onion and celery and cook for 4-5 minutes until soft. Sprinkle in the flour and stir over moderate heat for 1 minute. Remove from the heat and blend in the red wine and stock. Return to the heat, bring to the boil and simmer for 1 minute, stirring. Add the juniper berries and coriander seeds and seasoning. Return the pigeons to the pan and coat with the sauce. Cover closely and cook for 1 hour. Stir in the raisins and port and return to the oven for a further 30 minutes or until very tender. To serve, see Cook's Tip.

■ COOK'S TIP

To serve the pigeons, transfer them to a warmed serving dish. Skim any fat from the sauce and stir in the redcurrant jelly, reheating if necessary. Pour *some sauce over the pigeons and garnish with the fried bread and bay leaves and fresh juniper berries, if liked. Serve the remaining sauce separately.*

138 COTSWOLD PHEASANT

Preparation time:	YOU WILL NEED:
20 minutes	1 cock pheasant, 750 g/1½ lb, cut
	into 8 pieces
Cooking time:	2 tablespoons plain flour
about 1¼ hours	25-50 g/1-2 oz butter
	50 g/2 oz cooked ham, finely chopped
Oven temperature:	2 celery sticks, trimmed and chopped
180C/350F/gas 4	1 small onion, finely chopped
	225 g/8 oz Cox's apples, peeled,
Serves 4	cored and thinly sliced
	salt and pepper
Calories:	1 tablespoon sweet sherry
360 per portion	150 ml/¼ pint medium cider
	150 ml/¼ pint chicken stock
	4 tablespoons whipping cream

Coat the pheasant with flour. Heat 25 g/1 oz butter in a flameproof casserole and fry the the pheasant gently until golden brown all over. Remove from the pan and set aside. Add a little extra butter to the pan and fry the ham, celery, onion and apples for 4-5 minutes or until tender. Season, stir in the sherry, cider and stock and bring to the boil. Return the pheasant pieces to the casserole, skin side up, and coat with the sauce. Cover and cook in a preheated oven for 45 minutes.

Uncover the casserole and continue cooking for 15 minutes or until the pheasant is quite tender. Transfer the pheasant to a serving dish and keep hot. Skim any fat from the sauce, then liquidize until smooth. Stir in the cream, return to the pan, and reheat without boiling. Pour over the pheasant and serve.

■ COOK'S TIP

Choose a young bird for this dish. Fried bacon rolls and apple slices make good garnishes for it.

139 PARTRIDGE WITH RED CABBAGE

Preparation time:	YOU WILL NEED:
15 minutes	2 oven- ready partridges
	salt and pepper
Cooking time:	1 tablespoon lemon juice
about 2 hours	50 g/2 oz butter
	1 small red cabbage, finely shredded
Oven temperature:	1 onion, sliced
180C/350F/gas 4	300 ml/½ pint cider
	1 tablespoon brown sugar
Serves 4	1 tablespoon vinegar
	pinch of ground mace
Calories:	2 rashers streaky bacon
458 per portion	parsley sprigs, to garnish

Season the partridges inside with salt and pepper and sprinkle with lemon juice. Melt the butter in a flameproof casserole and fry the partridges until golden brown all over. Drain well over the casserole and keep on one side.

Add the shredded red cabbage, onion, cider, sugar, vinegar and mace to the fat remaining in the casserole and season well with salt and pepper.

Cover closely with a lid or foil and cook in the centre of a preheated oven for 30 minutes.

Wrap each partridge in a bacon rasher and place on top of the cabbage in the casserole. Cover, return to the oven and cook for a further 1-1½ hours or until the partridges are tender. Garnish with parsley sprigs.

140 SPICED VENISON

Preparation time:	YOU WILL NEED:
15 minutes, plus	750 g/1¾-2 lb joint of boneless
marinating	venison, neatly tied if necessary
	marinade (see Cook's Tip)
Cooking time:	50 g/2 oz butter
about 2¼ hours	4 rashers streaky bacon, rinded
	2 large leeks, thinly sliced
Oven temperature:	1 large carrot, peeled and diced
160C/325F/gas 3	1 tablespoon tomato purée
	finely grated rind of ½ orange
Serves 4	4 tablespoons orange juice
	235 g/1 oz plain flour
Calories:	finely shredded rind of ½ orange,
624 per portion	to garnish

Marinate the venison in the marinade for 1-2 days, turning.

Drain the venison well and pat dry. Keep the marinade on one side. Heat half the butter in a pan and brown the venison. Transfer to a large casserole. Brown the bacon and arrange on top of the venison. Add the leek and carrot to the fat remaining in the pan and fry for 2-3 minutes. Stir in the tomato purée, orange rind and juice and the strained marinade. Bring to the boil and pour into the casserole around the venison. Cover closely and cook in a preheated oven for about 2 hours or until the venison is very tender.

Transfer the venison to a serving dish and keep hot. Skim any fat from the sauce. Blend the remaining butter and flour and stir into the sauce in small pieces until thickened. Pour a little sauce around the venison. Sprinkle over the orange rind.

▧ COOK'S TIP

Line a casserole with foil so that you can lift out the package when it is frozen. This way, your casserole dishes are not lost for months in the freezer.

▧ COOK'S TIP

For the marinade, mix together 2 tablespoons oil, 1 small sliced onion, ½ teaspoon ground allspice, a 2.5 cm/1 inch piece cinnamon stick, ½ teaspoon shredded fresh ginger, 300 ml/1/2 pint red wine and salt and pepper to taste.

PASTA, RICE & PULSES

Looking for a nourishing dish packed with protein? All the grains and pulses are represented here - bulgur wheat, couscous, lentils, buckwheat, beans, rice - in hearty and flavoursome casseroles that look and taste delicious. Pasta is well represented, too, from noodles and macaroni to classic lasagne.

141 ITALIAN MARKET DAY

Preparation time:	YOU WILL NEED:
about 20 minutes,	450 g/1 lb aubergines, trimmed
plus soaking the	and cut into 1 cm/½ inch cubes
aubergines	salt and pepper
	225 g/8 oz wholewheat pasta shapes
Cooking time:	6 tablespoons olive oil
30 minutes	1 each red, green and yellow peppers,
	cored, seeded and sliced
Serves 4	1 large onion, sliced
	1 x 400 g/14 oz can tomatoes
Calories:	1 teaspoon dried oregano
444 per portion	2 tablespoons chopped fresh parsley
	2 tablespoons black olives

Sprinkle the aubergine cubes with salt. Set aside for about 1 hour, then rinse under cold water, drain and dry thoroughly.

Cook the pasta in a large pan of boiling salted water for 10 minutes. Drain.

Heat 4 tablespoons of the oil in a flameproof casserole over moderate heat and fry the aubergine cubes for 3-4 minutes until they are light brown. Remove and set aside. Add the remaining oil and fry the peppers and onions for 3 minutes.

Return the aubergine to the casserole, add the tomatoes and oregano and season with salt and pepper. Cover the casserole, lower the heat and simmer for 15 minutes.

Add the pasta shapes, stir lightly and taste the sauce. Adjust the seasoning if necessary. Cover and simmer for 5 minutes.

Stir in half the parsley. Sprinkle the remainder on top and scatter with the olives. Serve with crusty wholewheat rolls and a bowl of shelled nuts.

■ COOK'S TIP

If you cannot buy an assortment of peppers, substitute a courgette for one of the peppers.

142 NOODLES PAPRIKA

Preparation time:	YOU WILL NEED:
10 minutes	175 g/6 oz noodles
	salt and pepper
Cooking time:	15 g/½ oz butter
40 minutes	1 medium onion, finely chopped
	1 garlic clove, crushed
Oven temperature:	2 teaspoons paprika
180C/350F/gas 4	225 g/8 oz cottage cheese
	300 ml/½ pint fresh sour cream
Serves 4-6	few drops of Tabasco sauce
	1 teaspoon caraway seeds (optional)
Calories:	paprika, to garnish
356-237 per portion	

Cook the noodles in boiling salted water until just tender. Drain well. Melt the butter in a frying pan, add the onion and garlic and fry until softened. Stir in the paprika. Cook, stirring, for 1 minute.

Remove from the heat and stir in the cottage cheese, sour cream. Tabasco and salt and pepper to taste. Add the caraway seeds (if using). Fold in the noodles.

Turn into a greased casserole and cook in a preheated moderate oven, for 30 minutes. Sprinkle with paprika to garnish.

■ COOK'S TIP

For variety, use pasta quills (penne) or macaroni in this recipe.

143 MUSHROOM CASSEROLE

Preparation time:
15 minutes

Cooking time:
55 minutes

Oven temperature:
200C/400F/gas 6

Serves 8

Calories:
516 per portion

YOU WILL NEED:
350 g/12 oz fettucine noodles
75 g/3 oz butter
1 small onion, finely chopped
450 g/1 lb button mushrooms,
   cleaned
salt and pepper
2 tablespoons plain flour
350 ml/12 fl oz double cream
120 ml/4 fl oz dry white wine
2 eggs, beaten
50 ml/2 fl oz milk
50 g/2 oz grated Parmesan cheese
1 tablespoon chopped fresh chives

Cook the noodles in boiling salted water until almost tender. Drain well in a colander under warm water. Put the noodles in a bowl. Add 2 tablespoons of the butter, toss the noodles to coat. Set aside.

Melt the remaining butter in a saucepan over moderate heat. Add the onion and cook for 5 minutes, stirring. Add the mushrooms, salt and pepper. Cook for 5 minutes. Sprinkle the flour on the vegetable mixture. Cook for 2-3 minutes, stirring constantly. Gradually whisk in the cream and wine. Cook for 2-3 minutes, stirring. Remove the saucepan from the heat.

Mix the eggs and milk and slowly stir into the creamed mushroom mixture. Put the noodles in a large casserole and pour over the creamed mushroom mixture, stirring to combine. Sprinkle with the cheese and cook in a preheated oven for 20 minutes. Garnish with chives.

■ COOK'S TIP

*This is a rich dish, but good
for quick entertaining. If
you like, 225 g/8 oz of
cubed, cooked chicken can
be added to the casserole
with the noodles.*

144 BLACK-EYE BEAN STROGANOFF

Preparation time:
15 minutes, plus
soaking

Cooking time:
1¼ hours

Oven temperature:
180C/350F/gas 4

Serves 4

Calories:
444 per portion

YOU WILL NEED:
350 g/12 oz black-eye beans,
   soaked overnight
2 tablespoons oil
1 large onion, sliced
1 garlic clove, crushed
350 g/12 oz mushrooms, peeled
   and sliced
2 teaspoons paprika
1 tablespoon tomato purée
150 ml/¼ pint vegetable stock
salt and pepper
150 ml/5 fl oz soured cream
paprika, to garnish

Put the beans into a pan of cold water, bring to the boil and boil rapidly for 10 minutes. Reduce the heat and simmer for 20-30 minutes. The beans should be cooked but still firm.

While the beans are cooking, heat the oil in a pan, then fry the onion, garlic and mushrooms for 2-3 minutes. Add the paprika to the pan and cook for a further minute.

Drain the beans and put into a casserole. Add the onion, garlic and mushrooms, the tomato purée, stock, salt and pepper to the casserole. Stir well, cover the casserole, put into a preheated oven and cook for 40 minutes. Remove the casserole from the oven. Swirl in the soured cream and sprinkle with the paprika before serving.

■ COOK'S TIP

*This could be made with
red kidney beans or any
other pulses. If short of
time, use canned beans.*

145 LASAGNE

Preparation time:	YOU WILL NEED:
10 minutes	2 tablespoons olive oil
	2 onions, chopped
Cooking time:	1 garlic clove, crushed
2 hours 45 minutes	750 g/1½ lb minced beef
	2 x 397 g/14 oz cans tomatoes
Oven temperature:	2 tablespoons tomato purée
180C/350F/gas 4	150 ml/¼ pint water
	1½ teaspoons sugar
Serves 8-10	2 teaspoons dried mixed herbs
	1 bay leaf
Calories:	salt and pepper
895-716 per portion	225 g/8 oz mushrooms, sliced
	450 g/1 lb lasagne
	450 g/1 lb Ricotta or curd cheese
	450 g/1 lb Mozzarella cheese,
	sliced
	225 g/8 oz Parmesan cheese, grated

Heat the oil in a frying pan, add the onions and garlic and fry until softened. Add the beef and fry until browned, then stir in the tomatoes with their juice, tomato purée, water, sugar, herbs and salt and pepper. Bring to the boil and simmer for 1¼ hours. Stir in the mushrooms and simmer for 20 minutes. Discard the bay leaf. Just before the sauce is ready, cook the lasagne, in batches, in boiling salted water. Drain well.

Spoon sauce over the bottom of a baking dish. Cover with a layer of lasagne, then a layer each of Ricotta, Mozzarella and Parmesan cheeses. Continue making layers, ending with lasagne sprinkled with Parmesan. Cook in a preheated oven for 1 hour.

■ COOK'S TIP

As an alternative spread the top layer of lasagne with plain yogurt before sprinkling with Parmesan.

146 SOUTHERNER'S RICE

Preparation time:	YOU WILL NEED:
5-10 minutes	225 g/8 oz brown rice, washed
	and well drained
Cooking time:	2 carrots, finely grated
about 55 minutes	1 teaspoon curry powder
	finely grated rind of ½ orange
Oven temperature:	1 tablespoon finely chopped parsley
180C/350F/gas 4	25 g/1 oz butter
	2 teaspoons instant minced onion
Serves 4	150 ml/¼ pint chicken stock, boiling
	150 ml/¼ pint orange juice
Calories:	50 g/2 oz flaked almonds, toasted
370 per portion	and orange slices, to garnish

Mix the rice in a bowl with the carrots, curry powder, orange rind and parsley and transfer to a shallow, lightly buttered casserole. Add the butter and onion to the boiling stock and leave to stand for 1 minute, then pour into the casserole together with the orange juice. Stir well, then cover closely with a lid or foil and cook in a preheated oven for 45 minutes or until all the stock has been absorbed.

Leave the lid on and stand the casserole in a warm place for 5-10 minutes. Garnish with toasted almonds and orange slices before serving.

■ COOK'S TIP

Flameproof casseroles can be used on top of the cooker as well as in the oven, but ovenproof casseroles should never be used on a hob.

147 CRAB AND SPAGHETTI BAKE

Preparation time:
15 minutes

Cooking time:
40 minutes

Oven temperature:
190C/375F/gas 5

Serves 4-6

Calories:
644-430 per portion

YOU WILL NEED:
175 g/6 oz spaghetti
salt and pepper
25 g/1 oz butter
1 large onion, chopped
1 medium red pepper, cored,
   seeded and diced
25 g/1 oz plain flour
300 ml/½ pint milk
150 ml/¼ pint single cream
2 teaspoons French mustard
1 tablespoon Worcestershire sauce
225 g/8 oz cooked fresh, or canned
   crabmeat, drained and flaked
4 hard-boiled eggs, sliced
100 g/4 oz mature Cheddar
   cheese, grated

Break the spaghetti into short lengths and cook in boiling salted water until just tender. Meanwhile, melt the butter in a saucepan, add the onion and red pepper and sauté until softened. Stir in the flour and cook, stirring, for 1 minute, then gradually stir in the milk and cream. Bring to the boil and simmer, stirring, until thickened. Stir in the mustard, Worcestershire sauce and salt and pepper to taste.

Drain the spaghetti and fold into the sauce. Spread half this mixture in a greased shallow casserole dish. Cover with the crabmeat, then the sliced eggs and top with the remaining spaghetti sauce. Sprinkle the cheese over the top. Cook in a preheated oven for 25 minutes or until heated through.

■ COOK'S TIP

This dish would be equally good with macaroni or other short pasta, such as quills (penne) or tubes.

148 LENTIL COBBLER

Preparation time:
40 minutes, plus
soaking

Cooking time:
2 ½ hours

Oven temperature:
180C/350F/gas 4;
200C/400F/gas 6

Serves 4

Calories:
412 per portion

YOU WILL NEED:
225 g/8 oz brown lentils, soaked
   and drained
1 bay leaf
25 g/1 oz soft margarine
1 large onion, thinly sliced
2 medium leeks, trimmed and
   thinly sliced
4 celery sticks, thinly sliced
4 medium carrots, trimmed and diced
1 small white turnip, trimmed and
   diced
2 medium potatoes, peeled and diced
600 ml/1 pint vegetable stock
scone topping (see Cook's Tip)

Partly cook the lentils in boiling, unsalted water with the bay leaf for 45 minutes. Drain them.

Melt the margarine in a flameproof casserole and fry the onion over moderate heat for 2 minutes. Add the leeks and celery, stir well and fry for 2 minutes more. Stir in the carrots, turnip, potatoes and lentils. Pour on the stock, bring to the boil and season. Cover and cook in a preheated oven for 1 hour.

Meanwhile, make the scone topping. Divide the dough into about 16 small pieces. Roll each one into a ball.

Increase the oven temperature. Check the sauce: the potatoes should have disintegrated and thickened it. Place the dough balls on the vegetables, brush with any leftover egg and milk and sprinkle on fennel seeds. Return to the oven and cook, uncovered, for 20-25 minutes, until the topping is risen.

■ COOK'S TIP

Scone topping: sift together 175 g/6 oz wholemeal flour, 1 teaspoon baking powder and a pinch of salt. Rub in 25 g/ 1 oz hard margarine. Stir in ½ teaspoon fennel seeds. Beat together one small egg and 2 tablespoons milk and mix in enough to make a soft dough. Knead until smooth and free of cracks.

149 CRACKED WHEAT AND SPINACH PILAFF

Preparation time:	YOU WILL NEED:
15 minutes	*3 tablespoons oil*
	1 large onion, finely chopped
Cooking time:	*1 garlic clove, finely chopped*
30 minutes	*225 g/8 oz cracked wheat, washed*
	and drained (see Cook's Tip)
Serves 4	*450 ml/¾ pint vegetable stock*
	4 tablespoons seedless raisins
Calories:	*½ small cauliflower, cut into florets*
407 per portion	*175 g/6 oz spinach leaves, stalks*
	removed
	salt and pepper
	2 tablespoons snipped chives
	4 tablespoons blanched almonds,
	toasted

Heat the oil in a flameproof casserole and fry the onion over moderate heat for 3 minutes, stirring once or twice. Stir in the garlic and fry for 1 minute. Stir in the cracked wheat, cook for 1 minute, then pour on the vegetable stock. Stir in the raisins and cauliflower florets, season with salt and pepper and bring to the boil. Cover the casserole and simmer for 20 minutes, until the wheat and cauliflower are almost tender.

Add the spinach leaves, increase the heat and stir to distribute them well. Serve as soon as the spinach is just tender and the liquid has evaporated. The dish should be just moist. Stir in the chives and almonds, and turn the pilaff on to a serving dish. Garnish with tomato wedges, if liked.

■ COOK'S TIP

Cracked wheat, also known as burghal and bulgar, looks somewhat like a large-grain semolina. It contains the whole wheat grain and is partly pre-cooked, and therefore cuts down considerably on the cooking time. It is obtainable from health-food shops and supermarket counters.

150 MACARONI CHEESE WITH SOUR CREAM

Preparation time:	YOU WILL NEED:
5 minutes	*225 g/8 oz macaroni*
	salt and pepper
Cooking time:	*25 g/1 oz butter, melted*
35 minutes	*100 g/4 oz mature Cheddar*
	cheese, grated
Oven temperature:	*150 ml/¼ pint fresh sour cream*
200C/400F/gas 6	*4 tablespoons milk*
	1 egg, beaten
Serves 4	*pinch of paprika*
Calories:	
483 per portion	

Cook the macaroni in boiling salted water until tender. Drain well, then mix with the butter and salt and pepper to taste. Make alternate layers of macaroni and cheese in a casserole, reserving about 2 tablespoons of the cheese for the topping.

Mix together the sour cream, milk, egg, paprika and salt and pepper to taste. Pour over the macaroni and scatter the remaining cheese on top. Cook in a preheated moderate oven for about 20 minutes or until the top is golden brown.

■ COOK'S TIP

If preferred, you could use plain, unsweetened yogurt instead of the sour cream.

151 COURGETTE RISOTTO

Preparation time:
20 minutes

Cooking time:
50 minutes

Serves 4

Calories:
586 per portion

YOU WILL NEED:
25 g/1 oz soft margarine
3 tablespoons oil
1 medium onion, chopped
225 g/8 oz small courgettes,
   trimmed and thickly sliced
8 spring onions, trimmed and sliced
225 g/8 oz brown rice, washed
   and drained
600 ml/1 pint vegetable stock, hot
salt and pepper
225 g/8 oz frozen peas, thawed
2 tablespoons pumpkin seeds
1 tablespoon sunflower seeds
100 g/4 oz Cheshire cheese, finely diced
1 egg, lightly beaten
4 tablespoons Greek yogurt
3 tablespoons cashew nuts, lightly
   toasted

Heat the margarine and oil in a flameproof casserole and fry the onion over moderate heat for 2 minutes, stirring once or twice. Stir in the courgettes and spring onions, cook for 1 minute, then stir in the rice. Cook for 1 minute, stirring to coat the rice with the oil. Pour on the hot stock, bring to the boil and season well. Cover the dish and simmer for 30 minutes.

Stir in the peas, forking over the rice to separate the grains. Cover the dish and cook for a further 15 minutes. Stir in the seeds and the cheese cubes, and fork in the beaten egg. Swirl the yogurt over and scatter the nuts on top. Serve at once.

■ COOK'S TIP

You can substitute other vegetables, cooked in a similar way, when courgettes are not available. For example, use one medium aubergine, thickly diced, salted and rinsed and drained, or ½ small cauliflower, cut into florets and blanched in salted water for 3 minutes.

152 KITCHIRI

Preparation time:
40 minutes, plus
soaking the lentils

Cooking time:
1¼ hours

Oven temperature:
180C/350F/gas 4

Serves 6

Calories:
406 per portion

YOU WILL NEED:
3 tablespoons oil
2 large onions, chopped
1 teaspoon crushed coriander seeds
1 teaspoon ground turmeric
1 medium potato, diced
2 large tomatoes, peeled and sliced
2 tablespoons chopped mint
350 g/12 oz mixed fresh vegetables
salt and pepper
225 g/8 oz brown lentils, soaked
   and drained
4 tablespoons chopped fresh parsley
900 ml/1¼ pints vegetable stock
2 tablespoons lemon juice

Heat the oil and fry the onions over moderate heat for 3 minutes, stirring. Add the coriander and turmeric and cook for 1 minute. Stir in the potato, tomatoes and mint and cook for 2 minutes, stirring. Remove the pan from the heat and set aside.

Blanch the mixed vegetables in boiling, salted water for 3 minutes, then drain them.

Grease a large casserole and make layers of the rice, tomato mixture, lentils and fresh vegetable mixture, beginning and ending with rice and sprinkling parsley between each layer. Season the stock and stir in the lemon juice. Pour the hot stock over the rice and cover the dish with a layer of foil pressed around the rim. Stand the dish in a roasting pan half filled with water and cook in a preheated oven for 50-55 minutes, until the rice is just tender and the stock has been absorbed.

■ COOK'S TIP

Suitable mixed vegetables for this dish include diced carrot, cauliflower florets and sliced green beans. Garnish the dish with mint and desiccated coconut.

153 OKRA AND PASTA CASSEROLE NICOISE

Preparation time:
15 minutes

Cooking time:
1 hour

Oven temperature:
180C/350F/gas 4

Serves 4

Calories:
434 per portion

YOU WILL NEED:
2 tablespoons oil
1 onion, chopped
1 garlic clove, crushed
1 x 400 g/14 oz can chopped tomatoes
300 ml/½ pint vegetable stock
450 g/1 lb okra, stalk end removed
1 teaspoon dried marjoram
salt and pepper
350 g/12 oz pasta bows
50 g/2 oz black olives

Heat the oil in a flameproof casserole, add the onion and garlic and cook for 2-3 minutes, add the tomatoes and their juice, stock, okra, marjoram, salt and pepper and bring to the boil. Cover the casserole, put into a preheated oven and cook for 40 minutes.

While the okra is cooking, put the pasta into a pan of boiling salted water and cook for 5 minutes. Drain well and rinse with cold water.

After the casserole has been in the oven for 40 minutes, add the pasta and olives, mix well, cover the casserole again and cook for a further 15 minutes.

154 MANDARIN RISOTTO

Preparation time:
15 minutes

Cooking time:
35 minutes

Serves 4

Calories:
568 per portion

YOU WILL NEED:
3 tablespoons oil
3 tablespoons cashew nuts
1 medium onion, chopped
225 g/8 oz long-grain rice
600 ml/1 pint chicken stock
100 g/4 oz canned water chestnuts
350 g/12 oz cooked boned
*   chicken, diced*
150 g/6 oz peeled prawns
2 tablespoons soy sauce
3 tablespoons orange juice
freshly ground black pepper
2 tablespoons slivered blanched
*   almonds*
2 tablespoons seedless raisins

Heat the oil in a flameproof casserole and sauté the cashew nuts over moderate heat for 3-4 minutes, stirring to brown them. Remove the nuts with a draining spoon and set aside.

Fry the onion for 3-4 minutes in the remaining oil. Add the rice, stir well and cook for 1-2 minutes. Pour on the stock, bring to the boil, cover and simmer for 20 minutes until the rice begins to soften and has absorbed most of the stock.

Drain, rinse and thinly slice the water chestnuts, then stir into the rice with the chicken and prawns. Mix together the soy sauce and orange juice, pour over the rice, season and cover. Cook for 5 minutes, or until the rice is tender. Turn the rice into a serving dish, scatter over the almonds and raisins.

■ COOK'S TIP

Okra tend to become slimy if cut up. Choose small ones so that you can leave them whole.

■ COOK'S TIP

With its colourful medley of crisp and contrasting ingredients, this Oriental-style risotto looks appetizing and impressive. It is a good choice for an *informal buffet party or a late supper. The dish looks good garnished with wedges of orange.*

155 SAG DHAL

Preparation time:
15 minutes, plus
soaking

Cooking time:
1 hour 10 minutes

Oven temperature:
160C/325F/gas 3

Serves 4

Calories:
256 per portion

YOU WILL NEED:
2 tablespoons oil
1 onion, chopped
1 garlic clove, crushed
1 teaspoon grated fresh ginger
½ teaspoon ground turmeric
1 teaspoon ground cumin
1 teaspoon mustard seeds
½ teaspoon cayenne pepper
175 g/6 oz whole green lentils,
  soaked overnight
600 ml/1 pint water
450 g/1 lb spinach, washed and
  shredded, or 225 g/8 oz frozen
  leaf spinach, thawed
salt
150 ml/5 fl oz plain unsweetened
  yogurt

Heat the oil in a flameproof casserole, add the onion, garlic and ginger and cook for 2 minutes, then add the turmeric, cumin, mustard seeds and cayenne and cook for a further minute. Add the drained lentils to the casserole, add the water and bring to the boil, then add the spinach and salt.

Cover the casserole, put into a preheated oven and cook for 1 hour, stirring gently from time to time. Spoon the yogurt over the casserole before serving.

156 BOSTON BAKED BEANS

Preparation time:
10 minutes, plus
soaking

Cooking time:
4¾ hours

Oven temperature:
140C/275F/gas 1

Serves 4

Calories:
362 per portion

YOU WILL NEED:
350 g/12 oz haricot beans, soaked
  overnight
3 tablespoons oil
1 onion, chopped
1 garlic clove, crushed
1 tablespoon wholegrain mustard
1 tablespoon molasses or black treacle
1 x 150 g/5 oz can tomato purée
1 tablespoon soft brown sugar
salt and pepper

Put the beans into a pan, cover with cold water, bring to the boil and boil rapidly for 10 minutes. Reduce the heat and simmer the beans for a further 30 minutes. Drain the beans, reserving 600 ml/1 pint of the cooking liquid.

Heat the oil in a pan, add the onion and garlic and cook until lightly browned.

Put the beans into a casserole, add the onion and garlic and any remaining oil, then add the mustard, molasses or treacle, tomato purée, sugar, salt and pepper. Mix in the reserved cooking liquid. Cover the casserole with foil and a lid, place in a preheated oven and cook for 4 hours, stirring gently from time to time.

■ COOK'S TIP

Freeze for up to 3 months.
Defrost overnight in the
refrigerator or for 4-6 hours
at room temperature.
Reheat at 180C/350F/gas 4
for 20-25 minutes.

■ COOK'S TIP

Freeze for up to 3 months.
Defrost or 4-6 hours at
room temperature or
overnight in a refrigerator.
Reheat for 30 minutes at
180C/350F/gas 4.

157 CHICK PEA RATATOUILLE

Preparation time:	YOU WILL NEED:
30 minutes, plus	2 medium aubergines, diced
soaking the	salt and pepper
aubergines	8 tablespoons olive oil
	1 large onion, sliced
Cooking time:	2 garlic cloves, finely chopped
45 minutes	2 red peppers, cored, seeded and sliced
	4 medium courgettes, sliced
Serves 4	225 g/8 oz tomatoes, skinned and
	sliced
Calories:	2 tablespoons tomato purée
342 per portion	1 teaspoon dried oregano
	3 tablespoons chopped fresh parsley
	100 g/4 oz cooked dried chick peas

Sprinkle the aubergines with salt and leave for 30 minutes. Wash, drain and dry the aubergines. Heat 2 tablespoons of the oil in a frying pan and fry the onion and garlic for 3 minutes, stirring. Add the peppers and fry for a further 3 minutes. Transfer the vegetables to a flameproof casserole.

Add more oil to the pan and fry the aubergines, in batches, until brown. Add the aubergines to the casserole. Add the remaining oil to the pan and fry the courgettes for 3-4 minutes, stirring once or twice, then add them to the other vegetables.

Stir the tomatoes, purée, oregano and 2 tablespoons chopped parsley into the vegetables and season. Cover and simmer for 15-20 minutes, until the vegetables are just tender. Stir in the chick peas and simmer for 5 minutes to heat through. Sprinkle over the remaining parsley to garnish. Serve with brown rice

■ COOK'S TIP

*If short of time use canned,
ready-cooked chick peas.*

158 GOULASH WITH DUMPLINGS

Preparation time:	YOU WILL NEED:
40 minutes, plus	225 g/8 oz soya beans, soaked
soaking overnight	overnight and drained
	3 tablespoons oil
Cooking time:	2 medium onions, sliced
3½-4 hours, or 2-2½	4 celery sticks, thinly sliced
hours if using a	1 garlic clove, crushed (optional)
pressure cooker	1 tablespoon paprika
	2 tablespoons tomato purée
Serves 4	2 medium carrots, trimmed and diced
	1 x 425 g/15 oz can tomatoes
Calories:	150 ml/¼ pint vegetable stock
545 per portion	1 bay leaf
	salt and pepper
	carraway dumplings (Cook's Tip)

Cook the soya beans in boiling, unsalted water for 2-2½ hours, until they are tender. Drain.

Heat the oil in a flameproof casserole and fry the onion, celery and garlic, if using, over moderate heat for 3-4 minutes. Stir in the paprika and cook for 1 minute. Stir in the tomato purée and then the carrots, tomatoes and soya beans. Pour on the stock, add the bay leaf and seasoning. Bring to the boil. Cover the casserole and simmer gently for 1 hour.

Meanwhile, make the dumpling dough and shape it into a round. Divide the dough into 8 pieces and shape into balls.

Taste the sauce and adjust the seasoning, if necessary. Discard the bay leaf. Place the dumplings on top of the vegetables and cook for a further 20-25 minutes until they are risen. Garnish with the celery leaves, if liked.

■ COOK'S TIP

Carraway dumplings: mix together 75 g/3 oz wholemeal flour, 2 tablespoons wholemeal breadcrumbs and salt and pepper. Rub in 50 g/2 oz hard margarine. Stir in 1 teaspoon carraway seeds and about 4 tablespoons milk (enough to make a soft dough). Knead until smooth.

159 NEAPOLITAN PASTA CASSEROLE

Preparation time:
10 minutes

Cooking time:
about 1 hour

Oven temperature:
200C/400F/gas 6

Serves 4

Calories:
257 per portion

YOU WILL NEED:
175 g/6 oz wholewheat pasta spirals
50 g/2 oz butter
1 large onion, finely chopped
1 garlic clove, crushed (optional)
3 tablespoons tomato purée
1 teaspoon dried oregano or basil
150 ml/¼ pint wine
300 ml/½ pint chicken stock
salt and pepper
450 g/1 lb courgettes, trimmed
   and thinly sliced
25 g/1 oz finely grated Parmesan
   cheese

Cook the pasta in boiling salted water for 10 minutes or until just tender. Drain well.

Meanwhile, heat the butter in a pan and fry the onion and garlic for 4-5 minutes until tender and browned. Blend in the tomato purée and oregano or basil, then stir in the wine and stock. Season well with salt and pepper.

Arrange alternate layers of cooked pasta and courgettes in a buttered casserole, finishing with a layer of courgettes, then spoon the onion and wine mixture over the top.

Cover with a lid or foil and cook in a preheated oven for 30 minutes. Remove the cover, sprinkle the top with cheese, and return to the oven for 20 minutes or until the top is golden brown and crisp and the courgettes are tender.

■ COOK'S TIP

Rather than always serving pasta with a sauce poured over the top, try cooking it in a casserole in lots of sauce. In this way the flavours have time to blend and there is the added bonus of a bubbly cheese topping.

160 VEGETARIAN HOT POT

Preparation time:
20 minutes

Cooking time:
about 3 hours

Oven temperature:
180C/350F/gas 4

Serves 4

Calories:
885 per portion

YOU WILL NEED:
175 g/6 oz lentils
salt and pepper
50 g/2 oz butter
225 g/8 oz carrots, thinly sliced
225 g/8 oz potatoes, thinly sliced
350 g/12 oz leeks, trimmed and sliced
100 g/4 oz mushrooms, sliced
3-4 tablespoons chopped parsley
1 tablespoon tomato purée
150 ml/¼ pint red wine
150 ml/¼ pint chicken stock
nut topping (see Cook's Tip)
parsley, to garnish

Place the lentils in a pan, cover with salted water, bring to the boil and simmer for 45 minutes or until tender. Drain well.

Heat the butter in a pan, add the carrots, potatoes and leeks and fry gently for 10 minutes until lightly browned. Arrange layers of the fried vegetables, mushrooms and lentils in a well-greased, deep casserole, sprinkling each layer with salt, pepper and chopped parsley, reserving a few mushrooms for garnish. Blend the tomato purée, wine and stock and add to the casserole.Cover closely with a lid or foil and cook in a preheated oven for 1 hour or until the vegetables are tender.

Make the nut topping Remove the casserole from the oven, spoon the nut topping over the top so that the surface is covered completely and return to the oven for 30 minutes or until the top is golden. Garnish with mushrooms and parsley.

■ COOK'S TIP

For the nut topping, blend together 100 g/4 oz butter, 50 g/2 oz wholewheat flour, 50g/2 oz chopped mix nuts and 50 g/2 oz finely grated Cheddar.

161 MUSHROOM AND RAISIN PILAFF

Preparation time: 10 minutes	YOU WILL NEED: 25 g/1 oz butter
	1 tablespoon oil
Cooking time: about 55 minutes	1 large onion, finely chopped
	1 garlic clove, crushed
	225 g/8 oz brown rice, washed
Oven temperature: 180C/350F/gas 4	and well drained
	100 g/4 oz button mushrooms,
	wiped and thinly sliced
Serves 4	½ teaspoon dried dill
	½ teaspoon turmeric
Calories: 357 per portion	450 ml/¾ pint chicken stock
	salt and pepper
	50 g/2 oz seedless raisins
	small baked tomatoes and
	broccoli spears, to garnish

Heat the butter and oil in a shallow, flameproof casserole and gently fry the onion and garlic for 3-4 minutes until tender and lightly browned. Add the rice, mushrooms, dill and turmeric and continue cooking for 1-2 minutes, stirring all the time.

Pour in the stock and season lightly. Cover and cook in a preheated oven for 35 minutes. Stir in the raisins, cover the casserole and return to the oven for 10 minutes or until all the stock has been absorbed. Leave the lid on and stand the casserole in a warm place for 5-10 minutes to complete the cooking, then transfer the pilaff to a serving dish, forking the grains to separate. Garnish with tomatoes and broccoli.

■ COOK'S TIP

The final 5-10 minutes cooking of the rice takes place in the heat left in the pan after it has been removed from the oven. In this way the grains remain separate and the texture of the rice retains a slight 'bite'.

162 CHICORY CASSEROLE WITH TOASTED WALNUTS

Preparation time: 15 minutes	YOU WILL NEED: 8 small, even-sized heads of
	chicory, approx 100 g/4 oz each
Cooking time: 1 hour-1 hour 10 minutes	1 tablespoon lemon juice
	salt and pepper
	25 g/1 oz butter
	1 small onion, finely chopped
Oven temperature: 180C/350F/gas 4	1 tablespoon plain flour
	85 ml/3 fl oz milk
	150 ml/5 fl oz vegetable stock
Serves 4	1 tablespoon lemon juice
	50 g/2 oz chopped walnuts
Calories: 180 per portion	

Remove the core from the base of each chicory head and discard. Put the chicory in a pan of boiling salted water with the lemon juice and cook for 5 minutes. Drain well, then put into a shallow casserole.

Melt the butter in a pan, add the onion and cook for 2 minutes. Stir in the flour and cook for a further minute. Add the milk and vegetable stock to the pan, bring to the boil and cook for 2-3 minutes. Add pepper and the lemon juice, then pour over the chicory. Cover the casserole and cook for 30-40 minutes, until the chicory is tender.

Toast the walnuts on a baking sheet at the same time as the chicory, taking them out again after about 10 minutes. Serve the chicory sprinkled with the toasted walnuts.

■ COOK'S TIP

Don't omit the lemon juice when cooking the chicory - the lemon juice prevents the heads from turning brown when cooked.

163 COURGETTE AND BROWN RICE LAYERED CASSEROLE

Preparation time:
20 minutes

Cooking time:
50 minutes

Oven temperature:
180C/350F/gas 4

Serves 4

Calories:
821 per portion

YOU WILL NEED:
2 tablespoons oil
1 onion, chopped
1 garlic clove, crushed
225 g/8 oz tomatoes, peeled,
   seeded and chopped
450 g/1 lb courgettes, topped,
   tailed and thinly sliced
½ teaspoon dried tarragon
salt and pepper
450 g/1 lb cooked brown rice
2 eggs, beaten
150 ml/5 fl oz double or whipping
   cream
100 g/4 oz grated Cheddar cheese

Heat the oil in a pan, add the onion and garlic and cook until soft. Add the tomatoes, courgettes, tarragon, salt and pepper and cook for a further 3-4 minutes.

Mix together the rice, eggs, cream, most of the cheese and a little salt and pepper.

Put a third of the rice mixture into a casserole followed by half the courgette mixture. Repeat the layers, then finish with a layer of rice. Sprinkle the remaining cheese over the top. Put into a preheated oven and cook for 40 minutes.

164 GREEK BAKER'S POT

Preparation time:
30 minutes, plus
soaking overnight

Cooking time:
4¼ hours

Oven temperature:
140C/275F/gas 1

Serves 4

Calories:
415 per portion

YOU WILL NEED:
2 tablespoons olive oil
2 medium onions, sliced
2 garlic cloves, crushed (optional)
4 celery sticks, sliced
1 each green and red pepper,
   cored, seeded and chopped
2 teaspoons chopped basil, or 1
   teaspoon dried oregano
pinch of dried thyme
3 tablespoons chopped fresh parsley
1 x 400 g/14 oz can chick peas
1 x 200 g/7 oz can tomatoes
salt and pepper
½ teaspoon sugar
225 g/8 oz potatoes, peeled and
   thinly sliced

Heat the oil in a flameproof casserole and fry the onion over moderate heat for 2 minutes, stirring once or twice. Add the garlic, if using, the celery and green and red peppers and fry, stirring once or twice, for 3 minutes.

Stir in the herbs, reserving 1 tablespoon of the parsley for garnish, add the drained chick peas and the tomatoes, and season with salt and pepper. Stir in the sugar and bring the sauce to the boil. Arrange the potato rings on top.

Cover the casserole and cook in a preheated oven for 2½ hours, removing the lid for the last 30 minutes to brown the potato topping. Sprinkle the dish with the remaining parsley.

■ COOK'S TIP

The courgettes and rice can
be prepared up to 8 hours
in advance, then proceed
with the recipe.

■ COOK'S TIP

When cooking pulses,
remember that any left-over
chick peas, kidney beans,
lentils and so on can be
stirred into vegetable
casseroles, rice dishes and
soups to add protein,
dietary fibre and texture.

165 MUSHROOM AND GREEN BEAN PILAFF

Preparation time: 15 minutes	YOU WILL NEED: 4 tablespoons oil 1 medium onion, finely chopped
Cooking time: 1 hour	1 garlic clove, finely chopped 225 g/8 oz brown rice, washed and drained
Oven temperature: 180C/350F/gas 4	175 g/6 oz button mushrooms, trimmed and sliced 450 ml/¾ pint vegetable stock
Serves 4	2 tablespoons orange juice salt and pepper
Calories: 385 per portion	225 g/8 oz frozen green beans, thawed 2 large, ripe tomatoes, skinned and sliced 2 tablespoons chopped fresh coriander

Heat the oil in a shallow flameproof casserole and fry the onion and garlic over moderate heat for 3 minutes, stirring once or twice.

Stir in the rice and cook for 1 minute, then stir in the mushrooms and cook for 2 minutes, stirring once or twice. Pour on the vegetable stock and orange juice, season with salt and pepper and bring to the boil. Cover the casserole and cook in a preheated oven for 20 minutes. Add the green beans and tomatoes, fork over the rice, cover and cook for a further 15 minutes. Stir in the chopped herb and serve with hot orange herb bread (see Cook's Tip) and a green salad.

166 SPANISH RICE CASSEROLE

Preparation time: 15 minutes	YOU WILL NEED: 5 tablespoons olive oil 1 onion, finely chopped
Cooking time: 40 minutes	1 garlic clove, crushed 225 g/8 oz long-grain rice 1 tablespoon chilli powder
Oven temperature: 180C/350F/gas 4	(or to taste) salt and pepper 100 g/4 oz chorizo or garlic
Serves 4	sausage, diced 100 g/4 oz small button mushrooms
Calories: 514 per portion	450 ml/¾ pint boiling stock (approximately)

Heat the oil in a flameproof casserole, add the onion and garlic and fry until softened. Stir in the rice, chilli powder and salt and pepper to taste. Cook, stirring, until the rice is golden. Add the chorizo or garlic sausage and mushrooms and mix well. Add enough stock to come about 2.5 cm/1 inch above the level of the rice; stir thoroughly.

Cover tightly and cook in a preheated moderate oven for 30 minutes or until the rice is tender and the liquid absorbed.

■ COOK'S TIP

Orange herb bread: beat 2 teaspoons grated orange rind and 2 teaspoons chopped parsley into 100 g/4 oz softened unsalted butter. Make diagonal slits in a French loaf without slicing right through it. Spread flavoured butter into each slit, wrap the loaf tightly in foil and heat in the oven.

■ COOK'S TIP

For a vegetarian version of this dish leave out the sausage and instead add 2 diced peppers, one red, one green.

167 VEGETABLE GOULASH

Preparation time:
20 minutes

Cooking time:
1 hour 10 minutes-1
hour 25 minutes

Oven temperature:
180C/350F/gas 4

Serves 4

Calories:
243 per portion

YOU WILL NEED:
2 tablespoons oil
1 large onion, chopped
1 tablespoon paprika
1 x 400 g/14 oz can tomatoes
1 large green pepper, cored,
    seeded and chopped
225 g/8 oz peeled weight carrots,
    sliced
225 g/8 oz peeled weight potatoes,
    diced
225 g/8 oz peeled weight
    pumpkins or squash, diced
salt and pepper
150 ml/5 fl oz soured cream

Heat the oil in a flameproof casserole, add the onion and cook until soft, then add the paprika and cook for 1 minute. Add the tomatoes and their juice, then bring to the boil.

Add the green pepper, carrots, potatoes and pumpkin to the casserole and season with the salt and pepper. Cover the casserole, put into a preheated oven and cook for 1-1¼ hours, stirring from time to time.

Remove the casserole from the oven and put back on to the heat. Stir in most of the soured cream and reheat gently without boiling. Put the remaining soured cream on top of the casserole before serving.

168 ADUKI BEAN AND BULGAR CASSEROLE

Preparation time:
20 minutes, plus
soaking

Cooking time:
1½ hours

Oven temperature:
180C/350F/gas 4

Serves 4

Calories:
543 per portion

YOU WILL NEED:
225 g/8 oz aduki beans, soaked
    overnight
2 tablespoons oil
1 onion, chopped
1 garlic clove, crushed
225 g/8 oz carrots, peeled and diced
1 green pepper, cored, seeded and
    diced
1 tablespoon tomato purée
300 ml/½ pint vegetable stock
175 g/6 oz bulgar, soaked for
    30 minutes
salt and pepper
50 g/2 oz melted butter
3 tablespoons boiling water

Put the beans into a pan of cold water, bring to the boil, boil rapidly for 10 minutes, then reduce the heat and cook for a further 15 minutes or until soft. Drain the beans and set aside.

Heat the oil in a pan, add the onion, garlic, carrots and green pepper and cook for 3 minutes.

Put the drained beans into a casserole, add the vegetables, tomato purée, stock, half the bulgar, salt and pepper and mix well. Mix the remaining bulgar with the melted butter and water and put in an even layer over the beans and vegetables. Cook the casserole, uncovered, in a preheated oven for 1 hour.

■ COOK'S TIP

You can freeze this
casserole for up to 3
months. Do not add cream.
Defrost for 4-6 hours at
room temperature or
overnight in a refrigerator.

Reheat for 30 minutes at
180C/350F/gas 4, then add
the soured cream.

■ COOK'S TIP

The beans can be cooked
up to 1 day in advance.
Keep covered and chilled.

169 VEGETABLE DHANSAK

Preparation time:	YOU WILL NEED:
20 minutes	*100 g/4 oz red lentils*
	2 tablespoons oil
Cooking time:	*1 onion, chopped*
1¼ hours	*1 garlic clove, crushed*
	1 teaspoon ground cumin
Oven temperature:	*½ teaspoon ground coriander*
180C/350F/gas 4	*1 teaspoon cardamom seeds*
	pinch ground cinnamon
Serves 4	*2 teaspoons white wine vinegar*
	1 tablespoon mild lime pickle
Calories:	*450 ml/¾ pint water*
226 per portion	*225 g/8 oz aubergine, stalk*
	removed and diced
	225 g/8 oz sweet potato, peeled
	and diced
	225 g/8 oz potato, peeled and diced
	salt and pepper
	sprig of fresh coriander, to garnish

Put the lentils into a pan of cold water, bring to the boil and simmer for 10 minutes. Drain well.

Heat the oil in a pan, add the onion and garlic and cook until soft. Add the spices to the pan, cook for 1 minute, then add the vinegar, pickle and water and bring to the boil.

Put the lentils into a casserole, add the contents of the pan, season with salt and pepper and mix well. Cover the casserole and put into preheated oven and cook for 1 hour, stirring gently from time to time. Serve garnished with fresh coriander.

■ COOK'S TIP

The lentils can be cooked up to 1 day in advance. Keep covered and chilled.

170 FETTUCINE CASSEROLE

Preparation time:	YOU WILL NEED:
10 minutes	*225 g/8 oz green noodles*
	(fettucine verde)
Cooking time:	*salt and pepper*
about 1 hour	*2 tablespoons olive oil*
	1 onion, chopped
Oven temperature:	*1 clove garlic, crushed (optional)*
160C/325F/gas 3	*100 g/4 oz mushrooms, sliced*
	25 g/8 oz Italian garlic sausage,
Serves 4	*finely chopped*
	25 g/8 oz Ricotta or curd cheese
Calories:	*1 egg*
672 per portion	*100 g/4 oz Mozzarella or Gruyère*
	cheese, shredded

Cook the noodles in boiling salted water until just tender.

Meanwhile, heat the oil in a frying pan, add the onion and garlic (if using) and fry until softened. Add the mushrooms and fry for a further 3 minutes, then stir in the sausage. Remove from the heat.

Drain the noodles and fold into the sausage mixture. Beat the Ricotta cheese and egg together and stir into the sausage mixture with salt and pepper to taste. Turn into a casserole and top with the Mozzarella or Gruyère cheese. Bake in a preheated moderate oven for 35 minutes.

■ COOK'S TIP

For a vegetarian version, increase mushrooms to 225 g/8 oz and add one diced green pepper.

171 ITALIAN BEAN CASSEROLE

Preparation time:
15 minutes, plus
soaking

Cooking time:
1¼ hours

Oven temperature:
160C/325F/gas 3

Serves 4

Calories:
353 per portion

YOU WILL NEED:
100 g/4 oz red kidney beans,
  soaked overnight
100 g/4 oz cannellini beans,
  soaked overnight
100 g/4 oz flageolet beans, soaked
  overnight
2 tablespoons olive oil
1 onion, chopped
1 green pepper, cored, seeded and
  chopped
1 teaspoon dried oregano
1 x 150 g/5 oz can tomato purée
300 ml/½ pint water
1 teaspoon caster sugar
salt and pepper
sprig of fresh oregano, to garnish

Cook the beans separately, to avoid the red beans colouring the others. Cover with cold water, bring to the boil, boil rapidly for 10 minutes, then reduce the heat and cook until the beans are just cooked.

Heat the oil in a pan, add the onion and green pepper and cook until soft. Add the oregano, tomato purée, water, sugar, salt and pepper to the pan and bring to the boil.

Drain the beans, put into a casserole, pour the onion and pepper sauce over them, then put into a preheated oven uncovered and cook for 1 hour, stirring frequently but gently until most of the liquid has been absorbed. Serve the casserole garnished with fresh oregano.

■ COOK'S TIP

These beans can all be bought canned, if you are short of time. Drain and rinse before using.

172 SPEEDY MIXED BEAN GOULASH

Preparation time:
5-10 minutes

Cooking time:
35-40 minutes

Oven temperature:
190C/375F/gas 5

Serves 4

Calories:
334 per portion

YOU WILL NEED:
50 g/2 oz butter
225 g/8 oz onions, chopped
1 garlic clove, crushed
2 tablespoons tomato purée
1 tablespoon mild paprika pepper
½ teaspoon caraway seeds (optional)
1 x 225 g/8 oz can butter beans,
  drained and rinsed
1 x 210 g/7½ oz can red kidney
  beans, drained and rinsed
1 x 225 g/8 oz can baked beans
1 x 425 g/15 oz can peeled tomatoes
185 g/6½ oz can pimientos,
  drained and roughly chopped
1 tablespoon lemon juice
salt and pepper
4-6 tablespoons soured cream and
  paprika pepper, to garnish

Heat the butter in a flameproof casserole and fry the onions and garlic for 4-5 minutes until tender and lightly browned. Stir in the tomato purée, paprika pepper, and, if liked, the caraway seeds. Continue cooking for 1 minute. Add the remaining ingredients, stir well together and season with salt and pepper.

Cover closely with a lid or foil and cook in a preheated oven for 30 minutes to heat through. Spoon the soured cream over the top and sprinkle with paprika pepper.

■ COOK'S TIP

With these ingredients in your store cupboard, you will never be short of a tasty and colourful supper dish. For variety, use different kinds of beans.

Haricot and cannellini beans are also available canned.

VEGETABLES

Whether you are looking for a main dish or an accompaniment, there is plenty of choice here. The humble potato and cabbage appear in many new guises while more exotic vegetables such as okra and aubergines lend excitement. Some come with dumplings and a cheesy topping for an extra-filling meal.

173 BAKED RATATOUILLE

Preparation time:	YOU WILL NEED:
20 minutes	2 tablespoons olive oil
	1 large onion, sliced
Cooking time:	2 garlic cloves, crushed
1 hour 20 minutes	1 each red and green pepper,
	cored, seeded and sliced
Oven temperature:	225 g/8 oz aubergine, stalks
180C/350F/gas 4	removed and chopped
	225 g/8 oz courgettes, sliced
Serves 4	1 x 400 g/14 oz can chopped
	tomatoes
Calories:	2 teaspoons Herbes de Provence
417 per portion	salt and pepper
	1 small French loaf
	2-3 tablespoons oil
	175-225 g/6-8 oz goat's cheese

Heat the oil in a flameproof casserole, add the onion and garlic and cook until soft. Add peppers, aubergine and courgettes and mix well, then add the tomatoes and juice, Herbes de Provence, salt and pepper. Bring to the boil, cover the casserole and cook in a preheated oven for 1 hour.

After the casserole has been in the oven 45 minutes, cut the French loaf into 8 slices, discarding the ends. Dip each slice into the oil, place on a baking sheet and put into the oven above the casserole for 15 minutes, until crisp.

Take the casserole from the oven, remove the lid, stir the vegetables, then put the slices of bread on top of the vegetables. Put a piece of goat's cheese on top of each piece of French bread. Put under a hot grill until the cheese is bubbling.

■ COOK'S TIP

The ratatouille can be prepared 1 day in advance. Keep covered and chilled, then proceed with the recipe.

174 SPANISH GREEN BEAN CASSEROLE

Preparation time:	YOU WILL NEED:
15 minutes	350 g/12 oz French beans, topped
	and tailed
Cooking time:	salt and pepper
35 minutes	25 g/1 oz butter
	1 small onion, finely chopped
Oven temperature:	1 small green pepper, cored,
180C/350F/gas 4	seeded and finely chopped
	15 g/½ oz plain flour
Serves 4	175 ml/6 fl oz tomato juice
	50 g/2 oz brown breadcrumbs
Calories:	25 g/1 oz grated Cheddar cheese
147 per portion	

Put the beans into a pan of boiling salted water and cook for 5 minutes. Drain well then put into a shallow casserole.

Melt the butter in a pan, add the onion and pepper and cook until soft. Stir in the flour and cook for 1 minute, then add the tomato juice and pepper and bring to the boil. Pour the sauce over the beans in the casserole and mix well.

Mix together the breadcrumbs and cheese and spread in an even layer over the beans. Put the uncovered casserole into a preheated oven and cook for 25 minutes.

■ COOK'S TIP

To accentuate the Continental flavour add 1 crushed garlic clove to the sauce. Alternatively, stir in one teaspoonful of pesto.

175 LEEK AND JERUSALEM ARTICHOKE CASSEROLE

Preparation time:
15 minutes

Cooking time:
45-50 minutes

Oven temperature:
180C/350F/gas 4

Serves 4 - 6

Calories:
176-117 per portion

YOU WILL NEED:
450 g/1 lb Jerusalem artichokes,
    peeled and cut into bite-size
    pieces
1 teaspoon lemon juice
salt and pepper
25 g/1 oz butter
450 g/1 lb leeks, washed and sliced
1 tablespoon plain flour
150 ml/5 fl oz single cream
50 g/2 oz flaked almonds
1 teaspoon coriander seeds

Put the artichokes into a pan of cold water with the lemon juice and a little salt. Bring to the boil, reduce the heat and simmer for 2 minutes. Drain, reserving 150 ml/¼ pint of the water.

Melt the butter in a pan, add the leeks and cook for 2-3 minutes. Add the flour to the pan, cook for 1 minute, then add the artichoke water and cream. Add the artichokes, almonds and coriander seeds. Taste and adjust the seasoning, if necessary. Transfer the mixture to a casserole, cover and cook for 30-35 minutes, until the vegetables are tender.

■ COOK'S TIP

The lemon juice is essential to this recipe to prevent the artichokes from becoming discoloured.

176 KITCHEN GARDEN POTTAGE

Preparation time:
30 minutes

Cooking time:
45 minutes

Serves 4

Calories:
491 per portion

YOU WILL NEED:
40 g/1½ oz soft margarine
6 small onions, peeled
450 g/1 lb potatoes, diced
225 g/8 oz carrots, thinly sliced
225 g/8 oz celeriac, diced
100 g/4 oz sweetcorn kernels
900 ml/1½ pints vegetable stock
2 bay leaves
salt and pepper
100 g/4 oz Wensleydale or feta
    cheese, diced
2 tablespoons chopped parsley
FOR THE CROUTONS
4 x 1 cm/½ inch thick slices cut
    from a small wholemeal loaf
40 g/1½ oz soft margarine
25 g/1 oz grated Parmesan cheese

Melt the margarine in a flameproof casserole and fry the onions 3 minutes. Stir in the potatoes, carrots and celeriac, cover and cook over low heat 10 minutes. Stir in the sweetcorn, pour on the stock, add the bay leaves and salt and pepper. Bring to the boil, cover and simmer 20 minutes. Discard the bay leaves.

Cut the crusts from the bread and cut into cubes. Melt the margarine in a pan and fry the bread until it is crisp. Drain.

Liquidize half the stock and vegetables. Stir this purée into the stock in the casserole, then the cheese and parsley, scatter over the croûtons and sprinkle with the Parmesan.

■ COOK'S TIP

Celeriac discolours quickly once it has been peeled and is exposed to the air. If you are not going to cook the vegetable straightaway it is a good idea to drop each
slice as you cut it into a bowl of cold water acidulated with 1 tablespoon lemon juice or vinegar.

177 VEGETABLE CURRY

Preparation time:	YOU WILL NEED:
30 minutes	225 g/8 oz carrots, diced
	225 g/8 oz shelled broad beans
Cooking time:	225 g/8 oz shelled peas
30 minutes	1 small cauliflower, cut into florets
	salt
Serves 4	3 tablespoons oil
	1 medium onion, sliced
Calories:	1 teaspoon paprika
354 per portion	1 teaspoon Madras curry powder
	1 teaspoon curry paste
	1 tablespoon wholewheat flour
	5 tablespoons double cream
	1 teaspoon lemon juice
	2 tablespoons chopped fresh
	coriander
	4 tablespoons cashew nuts, toasted

Steam the carrots, broad beans, peas and cauliflower over boiling, salted water until barely tender - they will cook a little more in the sauce. Reserve 300 ml/½ pint of the liquid.

Heat the oil in a flameproof casserole and fry the onion over moderate heat for 3 minutes. Stir in the paprika and curry powder and cook for 1 minute. Stir in the curry paste and flour. Pour the reserved liquid into the casserole, stirring until the sauce thickens. Stir in the cream and lemon juice.

Add all the vegetables to the sauce, cover and simmer over low heat for 5 minutes. Stir in 1 tablespoon of the herb and 2 tablespoons cashews. Sprinkle the remaining herb over the vegetables and scatter on the remaining nuts.

■ COOK'S TIP

This is a perfect dish to serve on a busy day. You can prepare and cook the vegetables in advance, ready to blend in the delicately spiced, creamy sauce, or completely cook and cook the dish, to be gently reheated on serving.

178 STUFFED CABBAGE LEAVES

Preparation time:	YOU WILL NEED:
30 minutes	8 large cabbage leaves
	100 g/4 oz cooked rice
Cooking time:	100 g/4 oz cooked chicken meat
35 minutes	1 tablespoon cooked sweetcorn
	1 small onion, finely diced
Oven temperature:	few drops Tabasco sauce
180C/350F/gas 4	salt and pepper
	FOR THE TOMATO SAUCE
Serves 4	1 tablespoon oil
	1 onion, finely diced
Calories:	1 x 396 g/14 oz can tomatoes
127 per portion	150 ml/¼ pint chicken stock
	2 teaspoons oregano
	few drops Tabasco sauce
	1 tablespoon tomato purée
	1 teaspoon lemon juice
	salt and pepper

Blanch the cabbage leaves. Mix all other ingredients well and spoon out into portions on to cabbage leaves. Tie the leaves up into 'parcels' with fine string or fasten with cocktail sticks. Place in casserole dish.

To make the tomato sauce, sauté the onion in the oil for 4-5 minutes. Add all other ingredients and bring to the boil. Taste and adjust the seasoning. Now pour the sauce mixture through a sieve over the stuffed cabbage leaves. Cover and cook in the oven for 25 minutes.

■ COOK'S TIP

Any cabbage leaves are suitable. Try dark green Savoy cabbage for a dramatic colour contrast with the tomato sauce.

179 ARTICHOKES AU GRATIN

Preparation time:	YOU WILL NEED:
10 minutes	450 g/1 lb Jerusalem artichokes
	300 ml/½ pint milk
Cooking time:	300 ml/¼ pint water
40 minutes	1/2 teaspoon salt
	100 g/4 oz mushrooms, washed
Oven temperature:	and chopped
180C/350F/gas 4	1 onion, diced
	25 g/1 oz butter
Serves 4	25 g/1 oz flour
	salt and pepper
Calories:	2 tablespoons single cream
226 per portion	25 g/1 oz fresh breadcrumbs
	254 g/1 oz cheese, grated

Peel the artichokes and place in a saucepan with the milk, water and salt. Bring to the boil slowly and simmer for 10 minutes or until tender. Arrange in a casserole, cover with the mushrooms and onions. Melt the butter in a saucepan, add flour to make a roux, then pour in 450 ml/¾ pint of the artichoke liquid, stir well until you have a thin sauce, season well. Pour into the casserole and cook in the oven, covered, for 15 minutes. Remove the lid, sprinkle with the cream, breadcrumbs and grated cheese, return to the oven for a further 15 minutes.

180 AUBERGINES TAVERNA

Preparation time:	YOU WILL NEED:
5-10 minutes	450-750 g/1-1½ lb aubergines,
	trimmed and sliced
Cooking time:	25 g/1 oz butter
40-45 minutes	garlic salt
	freshly ground black pepper
Oven temperature:	1 teaspoon dried thyme
190C/375F/gas 5	1 x 425 g/15 oz can chopped
	tomatoes
Serves 4-6	1 tablespoon honey
	2 tablespoons finely grated
Calories:	Parmesan cheese
195-130 per portion	25 g/1 oz pine kernels

Put the aubergine slices into boiling salted water, bring back to the boil and simmer for 5 minutes. Drain well, then arrange in a well-buttered shallow casserole, dot with butter and sprinkle with the garlic salt, black pepper and thyme. Pour the tomatoes over the top to cover the aubergines, then drizzle the honey over the surface. Add more salt and pepper. Cover closely with a lid or foil and cook in the centre of a preheated oven for 20 minutes.

Remove the cover, sprinkle with Parmesan cheese and scatter the pine kernels over the top. Return to the oven for a further 15-20 minutes or until the cheese and nuts are browned.

■ COOK'S TIP

Look out for the new variety of Jerusalem artichoke which is smooth-skinned - they are much easier to peel that the usual knobbly variety.

■ COOK'S TIP

Roasting tins can be used as casseroles by using aluminium foil as a lid. Cut a generous square of foil and tie it around the top of the container or tuck it in firmly at the edges of the roasting tin.

181 POTATO AND TOMATO CASSEROLE

Preparation time: 20 minutes	YOU WILL NEED: 25 g/1 oz butter
	2 large onions, thinly sliced
Cooking time: 1 ¼ hours	1 garlic clove, crushed (optional)
	450 g/1 lb potatoes, peeled and thinly sliced
Oven temperature: 160C/325F/gas 3	salt and pepper
	300 ml/½ pint stock
	FOR THE TOPPING
Serves 4	2 tomatoes, thinly sliced
	50 g/2 oz cheese, grated
Calories: 263 per portion	1 teaspoon chopped chives

Melt the butter in a frying pan and gently sauté the sliced onion and crushed garlic. Place a layer of onion and garlic alternately in a casserole with thinly sliced potatoes, seasoning well between each layer. Pour over the hot stock and cover the casserole. Put into the oven and cook until the vegetables are tender and the stock is absorbed. Top with sliced tomatoes and grated cheese. Brown under the grill before serving and sprinkle with chopped chives. Cut into portions to serve with chops, steak or beefburgers although it is delicious on its own.

182 COUNTRY VEGETABLE CASSEROLE

Preparation time: 20 minutes	YOU WILL NEED: 50 g/2 oz butter
	2 large onions, thinly sliced
Cooking time: 1 hour	4 new carrots, thinly sliced
	1 new turnip, thinly sliced
	1 leek, sliced
Oven temperature: 180C/350F/gas 4	2 potatoes, thinly sliced
	225 g/8 oz pkt frozen corn and sweet peppers
Serves 4	salt and pepper
	300 ml/½ pint stock
Calories: 287 per portion	50 g/2 oz cheese, grated

Melt the butter in an ovenproof casserole. Toss in the sliced onions and leave on a low heat for about 5 minutes. Add the thinly sliced vegetables and the corn and sweet peppers, with seasoning between each layer. Pour over the stock, cover the casserole and cook in the oven for 45 minutes or until the vegetables have absorbed the stock. Sprinkle with the grated cheese and brown under the grill.

■ COOK'S TIP

For a more Continental flavour use Parmesan cheese for the topping and sprinkle with 1 tablespoon olive oil before browning.

■ COOK'S TIP

Use whatever vegetables are in season. Other suitable ones include parsnips, swedes and French beans.

183 CHINESE VEGETABLE CASSEROLE

Preparation time:
15 minutes, plus soaking

Cooking time:
40 minutes

Oven temperature:
180C/350F/gas 4

Serves 4

Calories:
137 per portion

YOU WILL NEED:
25 g/1 oz dried Chinese
   mushrooms, soaked for 15
   minutes in boiling water
2 tablespoons oil
1 onion, sliced
2 teaspoons cornflour
1 tablespoon light soy sauce
300 ml/½ pint vegetable stock
½ teaspoon five spice powder
225 g/8 oz whole baby sweetcorn
100 g/4 oz bean sprouts
1 x 225 g/8 oz can bamboo shoots,
   drained
salt and pepper
100 g/4 oz mangetout, topped and
   tailed

Drain the Chinese mushrooms, discard the stalks, then chop roughly. Heat the oil in a flameproof casserole, add the onion and cook until soft.

Mix together the cornflour, soy sauce, stock and five spice powder then add to the casserole. Add the mushrooms, sweetcorn, bean sprouts and bamboo shoots. Bring to the boil, taste and adjust the seasoning, if necessary, then cover the casserole, put into a preheated oven and cook for 10 minutes. Add the mangetout to the casserole and cook for a further 10 minutes.

■ COOK'S TIP

*Serve this casserole with
Chinese egg noodles or egg-
fried rice for a complete
Chinese meal.*

184 TOMATO, SPINACH AND RICOTTA CASSEROLE

Preparation time:
15 minutes

Cooking time:
50 minutes

Oven temperature:
180C/350F/gas 4

Serves 4

Calories:
296 per portion

YOU WILL NEED:
750 g/1½ lb spinach, washed
   and shredded
1 tablespoon water
salt
25 g/1 oz butter
1 onion, peeled and chopped
1 garlic clove, peeled and crushed
4 large tomatoes, peeled and sliced
350 g/12 oz ricotta cheese
freshly ground black pepper
1 tablespoon grated Parmesan
   cheese

Put the spinach in a pan with the water and a little salt. Cook for 2-3 minutes until soft, then drain well.

Use a little of the butter to grease a casserole. Melt the remaining butter in a pan, add the onion and garlic and cook until soft, stir into the spinach and mix well. Put half the spinach, two of the tomatoes and half the ricotta cheese in layers in the casserole. Repeat the layers, seasoning between each layer. Sprinkle with the Parmesan cheese. Cover the casserole and put into a preheated oven. Cook for 30 minutes, uncover the casserole and cook for a further 10 minutes to brown the top.

■ COOK'S TIP

*If short of time use canned
tomatoes instead of fresh
ones.*

185 HOT LEEKS VINAIGRETTE

Preparation time:	YOU WILL NEED:
10 minutes	8 leeks, about 750 g/1½ lb,
	trimmed
Cooking time:	4 tablespoons oil
45-50 minutes	1 tablespoon lemon juice
	1 tablespoon wine or cider vinegar
Oven temperature:	1 small garlic clove, crushed
160C/325F/gas 3	(optional)
	good pinch of dry mustard
Serves 4	good pinch of salt
	good pinch of freshly ground
Calories:	black pepper
183 per portion	good pinch of sugar
	16 coriander seeds
	lemon slices and parsley sprigs, to
	garnish

Clean the leeks, then place them in a pan of boiling, salted water to cover, bring back to the boil and boil for 5 minutes. Drain thoroughly.

Place the oil together with the remaining ingredients in a screw-top jar. Fit the lid on firmly and shake thoroughly until they are well blended.

Arrange the leeks in a shallow casserole and pour the dressing over the top. Cover closely with a lid or foil and cook in a preheated oven for 40-45 minutes or until the leeks are tender. Carefully drain the juices then serve the leeks straight from the casserole, garnished with lemon slices and fresh parsley sprigs.

186 BRAISED RED CABBAGE

Preparation time:	YOU WILL NEED:
15 minutes	1 small red cabbage, about
	1 kg/2 lb
Cooking time:	1 large onion, sliced
2¼-2½ hours	2 cooking apples, peeled, cored
	and sliced
Oven temperature:	salt and pepper
150C/300F/gas 2	2 tablespoons soft brown sugar
	5 tablespoons wine vinegar
Serves 6	1 bay leaf
	3-4 tablespoons redcurrant jelly
Calories:	chopped parsley, to garnish
91 per portion	

Finely shred the red cabbage, discarding the stalk and coarse outer leaves. Arrange it in layers in a deep casserole with the onion, reserving a few slices for garnish, and the apples, seasoning well between each layer with salt, pepper and sugar. Pour in the vinegar and tuck the bay leaf down the side of the casserole.

Cover closely with a lid or foil and cook in the centre of a preheated oven for 2-2½ hours or until the cabbage is soft and tender. Adjust the seasoning if necessary, stir in the redcurrant jelly and return to the oven for a further 5-10 minutes or until heated through. Garnish with onion rings and chopped parsley.

■ COOK'S TIP

Leeks cooked in this way
are also delicious served as
a cold starter. The slow
cooking allows the dressing
to flavour the leeks right
through.

■ COOK'S TIP

If preferred, use dry white
wine or cider instead of the
wine vinegar.

187 FENNEL WITH MUSHROOMS

Preparation time:	YOU WILL NEED:
5-10 minutes	*2 heads fennel, each about*
	275 g/10 oz, trimmed and cut
Cooking time:	*into quarters lengthways*
about 35 minutes	*100 g/4 oz button mushrooms,*
	wiped and sliced
Oven temperature:	*salt and pepper*
180C/350F/gas 4	*1 tablespoon lemon juice*
	2 tablespoons water
Serves 4	*1 teaspoon sugar*
	1 tablespoon finely chopped parsley
Calories:	*25 g/1 oz butter, melted*
90 per portion	*fennel leaves, to garnish*

Cook the fennel in boiling, salted water to cover for 5-6 minutes until tender. Drain well. Arrange the pieces of fennel in a well-buttered shallow casserole. Scatter the mushrooms over them and sprinkle with salt and pepper. Mix together the lemon juice, water, sugar and parsley and pour into the casserole. Dot with small pieces of butter.

Cover and cook near the top of a preheated oven for 20 minutes. Remove the cover, baste with the juices, cover and cook for 10 minutes. Garnish with fennel leaves.

188 GRUYERE POTATOES

Preparation time:	YOU WILL NEED:
15 minutes	*750 g-1 kg/1¾-2 lb evenly*
	shaped potatoes, about
Cooking time:	*6 cm/2½ inches long, peeled*
1¼-1½ hours	*300 ml/½ pint double cream*
	2 teaspoons chopped chives
Oven temperature:	*salt and pepper*
190C/375F/gas 5	*¼ teaspoon paprika pepper*
	2 teaspoons finely chopped parsley
Serves 4	*75 g/3 oz Gruyère cheese, grated*
Calories:	
507 per portion	

Trim the potatoes so that they are all the same size, then place in a pan and cover with cold water. Add a little salt to taste. Bring to the boil and simmer for 5 minutes. Drain thoroughly.

Butter a round casserole or soufflé dish, 18 cm/7 inch diameter by about 7.5 cm/3 inches deep. Arrange the potatoes so that they are standing upright and packed in so firmly that they cannot move.

Mix together the cream, chives, salt, black pepper, paprika pepper and parsley and pour over the potatoes. Sprinkle the cheese over the surface so that the potatoes are covered completely. Cook, uncovered, in the centre of a preheated oven for about 1-1¼ hours or until the potatoes are cooked through and the cheese is crusty and golden brown.

■ COOK'S TIP

Buy fennel with fresh featherlike leaves and crisp firm stalks. The bulb should be pearly white. With its slightly aniseed flavour, fennel makes an excellent accompaniment to game or poultry.

■ COOK'S TIP

This dish needs no last-minute attention and looks and tastes marvellous. If liked, rub a cut clove of garlic around the casserole before it is buttered.

189 AUBERGINES STUFFED WITH PINE NUTS

Preparation time:
20 minutes, plus
salting

Cooking time:
1 hour-1 hour 10
minutes

Oven temperature:
180C/350F/gas 4

Serves 4

Calories:
223 per portion

YOU WILL NEED:
2 large aubergines, about
350 g/12 oz each
salt and pepper
25 g/1 oz butter
1 large onion, chopped
1 garlic clove, crushed
50 g/2 oz pine nuts
4 large tomatoes, peeled, seeded
and chopped
1 tablespoon tomato purée
1 teaspoon dried oregano
2 teaspoons paprika
vegetable or olive oil for frying
50 ml/¼ pint vegetable stock

Remove the stalks from the aubergines, cut in half lengthways, then cut each half into three slices, lengthways. Sprinkle the slices with salt and leave for 30 minutes to drain. Meanwhile, make the filling. Melt the butter, add the onion and garlic and cook until soft. Add the pine nuts and stir until browned. Add the tomatoes, purée, oregano, paprika and pepper. Stir well and cook until a thick purée is formed.

Rinse the aubergine slices and dry. Heat the oil and fry the slices in batches. Drain. Reassemble the aubergine halves by spreading 1 tablespoon of the filling between each slice and pressing the slices together. Put in a casserole, pour the stock over, cover and cook for 45-50 minutes.

■ COOK'S TIP

The aubergines can be
prepared up to 1 day in
advance. Keep covered and
chilled.

190 CHICK PEA CURRY

Preparation time:
20 minutes, plus
soaking

Cooking time:
2 hours

Oven temperature:
180C/350F/gas 4

Serves 4

Calories:
204 per portion

YOU WILL NEED:
175 g/6 oz chick peas, soaked
overnight
3-4 tablespoons oil
1 onion, chopped
1 garlic clove, crushed
175 g/6 oz carrots, diced
225 g/8 oz cauliflower florets
2 teaspoons ground turmeric
1 teaspoon ground cumin
½ teaspoon ground coriander
½ teaspoon ground ginger
½ teaspoon garam masala
1/2 teaspoon ground chilli
salt and pepper
1 large potato, peeled and diced

Put the chick peas in a pan, cover with cold water, bring to the boil and boil rapidly for 10 minutes. Reduce the heat and cook for 30-40 minutes, until tender. Drain, reserving 350 ml/12 fl oz of the cooking water. Put the chick peas into a casserole.

Heat the oil in a pan, add the onion and garlic and cook until soft, then put in the casserole. Add the carrots and cauliflower to the pan, cook until browned then transfer to the casserole. Put the spices into the pan, adding a little extra oil, if necessary. Cook the spices gently for 1 minute, then add the reserved liquid, salt, pepper and potato. Bring to the boil, pour into the casserole, cover and cook in a pre-heated oven for 1-1¼ hours, stirring from time to time.

■ COOK'S TIP

Freeze for up to 3 months.
Defrost 4-6 hours at room
temperature or overnight in
the refrigerator. Reheat for
30 minutes at
180C/350F/Gas 4.

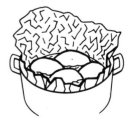

191 VEGETABLE HOT POT WITH ORANGE DUMPLINGS

Preparation time:
30 minutes, plus
soaking overnight

Cooking time:
2½ hours

Serves 4

Calories:
476 per portion

YOU WILL NEED:
225 g/8 oz dried white haricot
  beans, soaked overnight
1 bouquet garni
3 celery sticks, sliced
25 g/1 oz soft margarine
2 medium onions, sliced
225 g/8 oz carrots, thinly sliced
225 g/8 oz parsnips, diced
300 ml/½ pint vegetable stock
1 x 200 g/7 oz can tomatoes
1 teaspoon tomato purée
salt and pepper
2 tablespoons chopped fresh parsley
orange dumplings (Cook's Tip)

Drain the beans and cook in unsalted boiling water flavoured with the bouquet garni and 1 celery stick for 1 hour, or until they are tender. Drain the beans and discard the flavourings.

Melt the margarine in a flameproof casserole and fry the remaining celery and the onions over moderate heat for 4-5 minutes. Add the carrots, parsnips, stock, tomatoes and purée, season and stir in the beans and the parsley. Bring the sauce to the boil. Cover the casserole and simmer gently for 1 hour.

Make the dumpling dough. Shape the dough into a round and knead it in the bowl until smooth. Divide the dough into 8 and roll each piece into a ball. Place in the casserole, cover and simmer for 20 minutes, until the dumplings are light and fluffy.

■ COOK'S TIP

1Orange dumplings: sift together 100 g/4 oz wholewheat self-raising flour, salt and pepper. Stir in 1 teaspoon mixed dried herbs, 50 g/2 oz grated hard margarine and 2 tablespoons coarsely grated orange rind. Mix to a firm dough with 4 tablespoons orange juice.

192 BROCCOLI LORRAINE

Preparation time:
10 minutes

Cooking time:
40 minutes

Oven temperature:
180C/350F/gas 4

Serves 4 to 6

Calories:
352-235 per portion

YOU WILL NEED:
750 g/1½lb broccoli, cut into
  5 cm/2 inch pieces
15 g/½ oz butter
4 back bacon rashers, derinded
  and diced
1 onion, thinly sliced
300 ml/½ pint milk
150 ml/¼ pint single cream
4 eggs, beaten
25 g/1 oz Gruyère cheese, grated
salt and pepper

Arrange the broccoli in a greased casserole. Melt the butter in a frying pan, add the bacon and fry until crisp. Remove the bacon with a slotted soon and sprinkle on top of the broccoli.

Fry the onion in the fat remaining in the pan until golden, then remove with a slotted spoon and scatter over the broccoli.

Mix together the milk, cream, eggs, cheese and salt and pepper to taste, then pour into the casserole.

Place the casserole in a roasting pan, containing about 2.5 cm/1 inch of boiling water. cook in a preheated oven for 30 minutes or until just set.

■ COOK'S TIP

This recipe could also be used for cauliflower, though the colour contrast is not so dramatic.

193 SPICED RED CABBAGE AND BEETROOT CASSEROLE

Preparation time: 20 minutes	YOU WILL NEED: 50 g/2 oz butter
	1 large onion, sliced
Cooking time: 1 hour 20 minutes	450 g/1 lb red cabbage, washed, quartered and shredded
	225 g/8 oz cooking apple, peeled, cored and chopped
Oven temperature: 180C/350F/gas 4	350 g/12 oz peeled weight chestnuts or 275 g/10 oz canned whole chestnuts
Serves 4	2 tablespoons soft brown sugar
	1 tablespoon red wine vinegar
Calories: 324 per portion	½ teaspoon ground cinnamon
	300 ml/½ pint water
	salt and pepper
	225 g/8 oz fresh cooked beetroot, peeled and chopped

Melt the butter in a flameproof casserole, add the onion and cook until soft. Add the red cabbage and apple and stir well together until the cabbage is coated with the butter. Add the chestnuts, brown sugar, vinegar, spices, water, salt and pepper to the casserole and stir well. Bring to the boil, cover the casserole, put into a preheated oven and cook for 1 hour until the chestnuts are cooked.

Add the beetroot to the casserole and cook for a further 15 minutes.

194 CABBAGE AND CELERY CASSEROLE

Preparation time: 15 minutes	YOU WILL NEED: 50 g/2 oz butter
	1 small onion, sliced
Cooking time: 30 minutes	1 small head celery, washed and sliced
	½ small white cabbage, washed and shredded
Oven temperature: 180C/350F/gas 4	25 g/1 oz butter
	25 g/1 oz flour
Serves 4	300 ml/½ pint milk
	salt and pepper
Calories: 197 per portion	25 g/1 oz fresh white breadcrumbs
	25 g/1 oz butter

Melt the butter in a frying pan, add the onion and celery and cook gently for 5 minutes, stirring from time to time. Add the cabbage and allow to simmer on a gentle heat for a further 5 minutes. Melt the butter in a saucepan and add the flour to make a roux. Add the milk gradually, stirring with a wooden spoon until a smooth sauce is formed. Season well. Turn the vegetables into a 1 litre/2 pint casserole and season well. Pour the sauce over the vegetables and sprinkle with breadcrumbs dotted with butter. Cover and cook in the oven for 20 minutes until the crumb topping is golden brown.

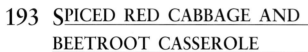

■ COOK'S TIP

You can freeze this for up to 3 months. Defrost for 4-6 hours at room temperature or overnight in a refrigerator. Reheat for 30 minutes at 180C/350F, gas 4.

■ COOK'S TIP

This would work equally well with a Savoy cabbage, or with cauliflower.

195 BUTTER BEANS BRETON

Preparation time:
20 minutes

Cooking time:
1½-2 hours

Oven temperature:
180C/350F/gas 4

Serves 4

Calories:
362 per portion

YOU WILL NEED:
50 g/2 oz butter
2 onions, finely chopped
225 g/8 oz dried butter beans,
    soaked in water overnight and
    drained
2 sprigs fresh savory, or 1 teaspoon
    dried savory
600 ml/1 pint chicken or vegetable
    stock
1 teaspoon ground nutmeg
salt and pepper
150 ml/¼ pint double cream
cooked green beans, to garnish

Melt the butter in a flameproof casserole, add the onions and cook until softened. Stir in the beans

Mix in the savory, stock and nutmeg and season to taste with salt and pepper. Cover the casserole and transfer to a preheated oven. Cook for 1½ hours or until the beans are tender and the stock has been absorbed.

Stir in the cream, adjust the seasoning, cover and return to the oven for 10 minutes. Garnish with green beans and serve with pork or bacon dishes.

196 POMMES DAUPHINOISES

Preparation time:
10 minutes

Cooking time:
1 hour 35 minutes

Oven temperature:
160C/325F/gas 3

Serves 4

Calories:
356 per portion

YOU WILL NEED:
40 g/1½ oz butter
1 garlic clove, crushed
500 g/1¼ lb white potatoes,
    peeled and thinly sliced
salt and pepper
300 ml/½ pint single cream
chopped fresh parsley, to garnish

Butter a shallow casserole well. Melt the remaining butter in a small pan, then add the crushed garlic. Layer the potatoes in the casserole, brushing each layer with the garlic butter and seasoning with salt and pepper.

Pour the cream over the potatoes. Cover the casserole, put into a preheated oven and cook for 1 hour. Uncover the casserole and cook for a further 30 minutes, until the potatoes are browned on top. Serve garnished with fresh parsley.

■ COOK'S TIP

This nutritious dish could be served as part of a vegetarian meal. Other dishes could include rice, pasta and mixed vegetable salads.

■ COOK'S TIP

This classic potato recipe makes a very good lunch dish. Serve it with a green salad and French bread.

197 BAKED COLCANNON

Preparation time:	YOU WILL NEED:
15 minutes	*450 g/1 lb potatoes, peeled*
	salt and pepper
Cooking time:	*225 g/8 oz curly kale*
45 minutes	*50 g/8 oz butter*
	1 bunch spring onions, chopped
Oven temperature:	*2 tablespoons single cream or top*
200C/400F/gas 6	*of the milk*
	50 g/2 oz grated Cheddar cheese
Serves 4	
Calories:	
613 per portion	

Put the potatoes in to a pan of salted water, bring to the boil, cover and simmer for 10 minutes. Add the kale to the pan and cook for a further 10 minutes. Drain well. Use a little of the butter to grease a shallow casserole. Melt the remaining butter in a pan, add the spring onions and cook for 2-3 minutes. Add the potatoes and kale, cream and pepper and mash well.

Transfer the mixture to the casserole, sprinkle with grated cheese, put uncovered into a preheated oven and cook for 20 minutes.

198 PEPPERONATA

Preparation time:	YOU WILL NEED:
15 minutes	*225 g/8 oz green peppers, cored*
	and seeded
Cooking time:	*225 g/8 oz red peppers, cored and*
30-40 minutes	*seeded*
	225 g/8 oz yellow peppers, cored
Oven temperature:	*and seeded*
180C/350F/gas 4	*2 tablespoons olive oil*
	1 large onion
Serves 4	*(Spanish for preference), sliced*
	350 g/12 oz tomatoes, skinned,
Calories:	*seeded and chopped*
103 per portion	*salt and pepper*

Cut the peppers into even-sized pieces. Heat the oil in a flameproof casserole, add the onion and cook until soft. Add the peppers, tomatoes, salt and pepper to the casserole and cook until the tomatoes become a thick purée.

Cover the casserole, put into a preheated oven and cook for 20-30 minutes, until the peppers are soft.

■ COOK'S TIP

The potatoes and kale can be prepared up to 1 day in advance. Keep covered and chilled.

■ COOK'S TIP

This colourful dish would go well with a rice or pasta dish as part of a buffet lunch.

199 MIXED GREEN VEGETABLES WITH COCONUT SAUCE

Preparation time:	YOU WILL NEED:
20 minutes	*100 g/4 oz French beans, trimmed*
	225 g/8 oz broccoli, cut into small
Cooking time:	*florets*
50 minutes	*salt and pepper*
	175 g/6 oz courgettes, topped and
Oven temperature:	*tailed and cut into thick sticks*
180C/350F/gas 4	*1 green pepper, cored, seeded and*
	cut into strips
Serves 4	*300 ml/½ pint plain unsweetened*
	yogurt
Calories:	*150 ml/¼ pint water*
140 per portion	*2 teaspoons cornflour*
	4 tablespoons desiccated coconut
	2 garlic cloves, peeled
	1 fresh green chilli, seeded and
	chopped
	1 teaspoon cumin seeds

Cook the beans and broccoli in boiling salted water for 2 minutes. Add the courgettes and green pepper and cook for 2 minutes. Drain the vegetables and put in a flameproof casserole.

Blend the yogurt, water, cornflour, coconut, garlic, chilli and cumin together to a smooth paste. Add to the vegetables, stir and bring slowly to the boil, stirring all the time. Check the seasoning, cover the casserole, put into a preheated oven and cook for about 40 minutes, until the vegetables are tender.

■ COOK'S TIP

Originally the milk from fresh coconuts would have been used in this dish, but desiccated coconut blended with water makes a good substitute.

200 BRUSSELS SPROUTS AND MUSHROOM CASSEROLE

Preparation time:	YOU WILL NEED:
25 minutes	*450 g/1 lb trimmed weight*
	Brussels sprouts
Cooking time:	*salt and pepper*
50 minutes	*25 g/1 oz butter*
	1 onion, chopped
Oven temperature:	*225 g/8 oz button mushrooms,*
200C/400F/gas 6	*wiped*
	15 g/½ oz plain flour
Serves 4	FOR THE TOPPING
	100 g/4 oz self-raising flour
Calories:	*2 eggs, beaten*
338 per portion	*150 ml/¼ pint milk*
	75 g/3 oz Cheddar cheese, grated

Cook the Brussels sprouts in boiling salted water for 5 minutes then drain, reserving 150 ml/¼ pint of the cooking liquid. Put the Brussels sprouts into a shallow casserole.

Melt the butter in a pan, add the onion and cook until soft, then add the mushrooms and cook for a further minute. Add the plain flour to the pan, cook for 1 minute, then add the reserved liquid. Bring to the boil, taste and adjust the seasoning, if necessary, and pour over the Brussels sprouts, mixing well.

For the topping, sift the flour into a bowl, add the eggs, milk and all but 1 tablespoon of the cheese. Season and pour over the vegetables in the casserole. Sprinkle with the remaining cheese and cook, uncovered, in a preheated oven for 40 minutes.

■ COOK'S TIP

The vegetables can be prepared up to 8 hours in advance. Cover and keep cool until required.

201 WINTER VEGETABLE HOT POT

Preparation time:	YOU WILL NEED:
20 minutes	*2 tablespoons oil*
	1 large onion, chopped
Cooking time:	*1 large leek, sliced*
1 hour 50 minutes-2	*225 g/8 oz carrots, diced*
hours	*225 g/8 oz swede, diced*
	100 g/4 oz parsnips, diced
Oven temperature:	*50 g/2 oz pearl barley*
190C/375F/gas 5;	*600 ml/1 pint vegetable stock*
then 220C/425F/gas 7	*salt and pepper*
	450 g/1 lb potatoes, thinly sliced
Serves 4	*15 g/½ oz melted butter*

Calories:
395 per portion

Heat the oil in a pan, add the onion and leeks and cook until soft. Put the carrots, swede and parsnips into the pan, add the pearl barley, 450 ml/¾ pint of the stock, salt and pepper. Bring to the boil then transfer the contents of the pan to a casserole.

Layer the potatoes over the vegetables in the casserole. Pour over the remaining stock and brush the potatoes with the melted butter. Cover the casserole, put into a preheated oven and cook for 1½ hours. Uncover the casserole, increase the heat and cook for a further 15 minutes to brown the potatoes.

202 CHINESE CABBAGE WITH TOMATO AND GINGER

Preparation time:	YOU WILL NEED:
10 minutes	*1 head of chinese cabbage,*
	approx. 750 g-1 kg/1½-2 lbs
Cooking time:	*2 tablespoons oil*
30 minutes	*1 large onion, sliced*
	2 tablespoons tomato purée
Oven temperature:	*200 ml/7 fl oz water*
180C/350F/gas 4	*1 teaspoon caster sugar*
	2 teaspoons grated root ginger
Serves 4	*salt and pepper*

Calories:
111 per portion

Cut the chinese cabbage into thick slices, removing and discarding the core. Heat the oil in a flameproof casserole, add the onion and cabbage and stir around until the vegetables are coated with the oil.

Add the tomato purée, water, sugar, ginger, salt and pepper and bring to the boil. Cover the casserole, put into a preheated oven and cook for 25 minutes.

■ COOK'S TIP

Serve with crusty brown bread to mop up the juice: this will make a filling supper dish.

■ COOK'S TIP

If Chinese cabbage is not available, this dish can be made with celery. Either cut the celery into thick chunks or use celery hearts which are often available in packs.

If celery hearts are used, the cooking time should be increased to 40-45 minutes.

203 BROCCOLI IN WHOLEGRAIN MUSTARD SAUCE

Preparation time:	YOU WILL NEED:
10 minutes	*450 g/1 lb broccoli, cut into florets*
	salt
Cooking time:	*15 g/½ oz butter*
30-40 minutes	*15 g/½ oz plain flour*
	200 ml/7 fl oz milk
Oven temperature:	*2 teaspoons wholegrain mustard*
180C/350F/gas 4	*½ teaspoon lemon juice*
	freshly ground black pepper
Serves 4	*15 g/½ oz toasted flaked almonds,*
	to garnish
Calories:	
73 per portion	

Put the broccoli into a pan of boiling salted water, bring to the boil and simmer for 3 minutes. Drain well, then put the broccoli into a casserole.

Melt the butter in a pan, add the flour and cook for 1 minute. Add the milk, bring to the boil and simmer for 2-3 minutes. Add the mustard, lemon juice and pepper then pour over the broccoli. Cover the casserole, put into a preheated oven and cook for 20-30 minutes until the broccoli is tender.

Serve the casserole garnished with toasted flaked almonds.

204 SAUERKRAUT WITH ORANGE AND RAISINS

Preparation time:	YOU WILL NEED:
15 minutes	*500 g/1¼ lb sauerkraut*
	1 onion, sliced
Cooking time:	*grated rind and juice of 1 orange*
1 hour 10 minutes	*50 g/2 oz raisins*
	pepper
Oven temperature:	*150 ml/¼ pint water*
180C/350F/gas 4	*1 orange, segmented*
	25 g/1 oz melted butter
Serves 4	
Calories:	
138 per portion	

Mix together the sauerkraut, onion, orange rind and juice, raisins, pepper and water in a casserole. Cover the casserole and put into a preheated oven. Cook for 1 hour, stirring from time to time and adding a little extra water if it appears to be drying out.

Remove the casserole from the oven and uncover. Put the orange segments on top of the sauerkraut and brush with the melted butter. Return to the oven uncovered and cook for a further 10 minutes.

■ COOK'S TIP

This would work equally well will cauliflower. To provide some colour, sprinkle with finely chopped parsley before garnishing with the almonds.

■ COOK'S TIP

For a delicious variation on this recipe substitute 425g/15 oz can pineapple chunks in syrup for the orange and raisins. Use the syrup from the can instead *of the orange juice, then stir the pineapple chunks into the casserole for the last 15 minutes of cooking time.*

SPECIAL OCCASIONS

A truly eclectic collection of dishes from around the world. The classics are well represented here - beef, veal, salmon, game - but so, too, are more unusual choices, such as oysters or scallops. They are all designed to please and impress.

205 JAMBALAYA

Preparation time:	YOU WILL NEED:
20 minutes	2 tablespoons oil
	25 g/1 oz butter or margarine
Cooking time:	450 g/1 lb lean pork, cut into
1 hour	narrow strips
	1 large onion, chopped
Oven temperature:	1 green pepper, deseeded and sliced
180C/350F/gas 4	1 red pepper, deseeded and sliced
	100 g/4 oz mushrooms, thickly sliced
Serves 4	150 g/5 oz long-grain rice
	450 ml/¾ pint beef stock
Calories:	¼ teaspoon ground allspice
509 per portion	salt and pepper
	100 g/4 oz smoked sausage, sliced
	100 g/4 oz peeled prawns
	prawns and tomato wedges

Heat the oil and butter in a pan and fry the pieces of pork until well browned. Transfer to a large casserole.

Fry the onion gently in the same fat until soft. Add the peppers and continue cooking for 3-4 minutes, stirring frequently. Add the mushrooms and continue cooking for a further 1 minute, then stir in the rice followed by the stock and bring to the boil. Add the allspice, salt and pepper and the smoked sausage. Pour over the pork, mix well and cover tightly. Cook in a preheated oven for 45 minutes.

Stir well, add the prawns and a little more boiling stock if necessary. Cover again and return to the oven for about 15 minutes or until the liquid has been absorbed and the meat is tender. Garnish with whole prawns and tomato wedges

■ COOK'S TIP

When using whole prawns for garnish, check to see if there is any roe present. Remove legs and any roe before placing in the finished dish.

206 SOLE PAUPIETTES

Preparation time:	YOU WILL NEED:
15 minutes	8 lemon sole fillets, skinned
	2 tablespoons lemon juice
Cooking time:	175 g/6 oz cooked, peeled prawns
30 minutes	salt and pepper
	150 ml/¼ pint milk
Oven temperature:	150 ml/¼ pint fish stock
180C/350F/gas 4	1 bay leaf
	2 sprigs fresh parsley
Serves 4	1 teaspoon butter, for greasing
	anchovy sauce (Cook's Tip)
Calories:	4 sprigs fresh parsley, to garnish
323 per portion	

Lay the sole fillets, skinned side up, on a working surface. Sprinkle with lemon juice. Set aside 8 of the prawns for the garnish and chop the remainder. Put a little of the chopped prawns on each sole fillet. Season with salt and pepper. Roll up tightly from the tail end and secure with a wooden cocktail stock. Place the fillets in a small casserole.

Combine the milk and fish stock in a small bowl. Pour over the fillets, then add the bay leaf and parsley sprigs. Cover the casserole with greaseproof paper, greased with the teaspoon of butter, and the lid. Place in a preheated oven and cook for 15-20 minutes until the paupiettes are firm to the touch.

Remove the casserole from the oven. Transfer the fillets to a heated serving plater and keep warm. Strain the cooking liquid, discarding the bay leaf and parsley, and reserve.Make the sauce. To serve, pour the sauce over the sole and garnish with the parsley and reserved prawns.

■ COOK'S TIP

For anchovy sauce: melt 25 g/1 oz butter in a pan, blend in 25 g/1 oz flour and cook 2 minutes. Gradually add reserved cooking liquid, 300 ml/¼ pint milk and 2 teaspoons anchovy essence. Bring to boil, stirring, and simmer 2 minutes until thick. Check taste and add salt and pepper, if necessary.

207 CORFIOT FISH STEAKS

Preparation time:
15 minutes

Cooking time:
30 minutes

Serves 4

Calories:
340 per portion

YOU WILL NEED:
4 cod steaks, each 175-200 g/6-7 oz
1 tablespoon plain flour
salt
½ teaspoon turmeric
15 g/½ oz butter
3 tablespoons oil
1 x 2.5 cm/1 inch piece fresh root
   ginger, peeled and finely chopped
1 medium onion, finely chopped
1 red pepper, cored, seeded and
   chopped
¼ teaspoon cardamom seeds,
   crushed
2 teaspoons plain flour
1 tablespoon lemon juice
300 g/11 oz Greek yogurt
1 teaspoon clear honey
lemon slices, to garnish

Dry the cod steaks. Mix the flour, salt and turmeric and rub evenly over the steaks. Melt the butter in a flameproof casserole and fry the steaks over moderate heat for 2-3 minutes on each side, until golden. Remove the fish and keep warm.

Heat the oil in the casserole and stir-fry the ginger, onion, pepper and cardamom for 2 minutes. Stir in the flour. Lower the heat and add the lemon juice, yogurt and honey. Heat the yogurt gently, stirring it in one direction until it bubbles.

Return the fish steaks to the casserole, cover and simmer gently for 10 minutes. Garnish with the lemon slices.

■ COOK'S TIP

You could, in advance, heat the yogurt slowly with the flour to stabilize it, and prevent it separating. Mix the 2 teaspoons flour to a thick paste with 2 teaspoons water. Stir in a little of the yogurt and pour the rest into a small pan. Whisk in the flour paste and stir over low heat until bubbles appear.

208 CASSEROLE OF SCALLOPS

Preparation time:
20 minutes

Cooking time:
30 minutes

Oven temperature:
160C/325F/gas 3

Serves 4

Calories:
520 per portion

YOU WILL NEED:
8 large scallops,
50 g/2 oz butter
25 g/1 oz shallots, peeled and sliced
225 g/8 oz mushrooms, sliced
2 garlic cloves, crushed
2 teaspoons tomato purée
4-6 tablespoons sherry
salt and pepper
250 ml/8 fl oz double cream
2 egg yolks, beaten
2 teaspoons lemon juice
2 tablespoons chopped fresh parsley

Detach the coral from the scallops, and slice them in half into two rounds. Melt the butter in a flameproof casserole, add the scallops and coral and cook very gently for 5 minutes. Lift them on to a plate.

Cook the shallots, mushrooms and garlic gently in the casserole for 2 minutes, turning the vegetables in the butter. Mix the tomato purée into the sherry and stir into the vegetables. Heat gently, then remove from the stove. Replace the scallops and coral in the casserole and season to taste. Cover and cook in a preheated oven for 20 minutes.

Transfer the scallops, coral and vegetables to a serving dish and keep hot. Stir the cream and egg yolks together and add to the casserole. Stirring constantly over gentle heat, cook until the sauce thickens. Do not let it boil. Stir in the lemon juice and half the parsley. Pour the sauce over the scallops, and garnish with the remaining parsley.

■ COOK'S TIP

Scallops need careful handling and cooking. Oven-cooking, on too high a heat, can make them dry and unappetising.

209 SQUID PROVENCAL

Preparation time:	YOU WILL NEED:
20-25 minutes	1.5 kg/3 lb fresh squid
	2 tablespoons olive oil
Cooking time:	2 onions, sliced
about 45 minutes	1 garlic clove, crushed
	2 tablespoons flour
Oven temperature:	1 tablespoon tomato purée
160C/325F/gas 3	200 ml/7 fl oz dry white wine or
	vermouth
Serves 4	150 ml/¼ pint stock
	1 tablespoon lemon juice
Calories:	350 g/12 oz tomatoes, peeled and
394 per portion	sliced
	salt and pepper
	½ teaspoon paprika
	pinch of cayenne
	pinch of sugar
	1 bay leaf
	chopped fresh parsley, to garnish

Heat the oil in a flameproof casserole and fry the onions and garlic until lightly browned. Add the squid and cook until lightly coloured.

Stir in the flour followed by the tomato purée, wine or vermouth, stock and lemon juice. Bring to the boil and add the tomatoes, salt and pepper, paprika, cayenne and sugar to taste. Add the bay leaf and cover.

Cook in a preheated oven for about 45 minutes or until tender. Discard the bay leaf and adjust the seasoning. Serve garnished with chopped parsley.

■ COOK'S TIP

To prepare squid: pull head away from body and remove 'nib'. Wash body and cut into rings. Cut the tentacles into pieces. Discard head and entrails.

210 TURKEY TERRINE

Preparation time:	YOU WILL NEED:
45 minutes, plus	1 kg/2 lb cooked boneless turkey
marinating time	salt and pepper
	50 g/2 oz butter
Cooking time:	450 g/1 lb chicken livers, trimmed
1½ hours	225 g/8 oz salt pork
	1 onion, peeled
Oven temperature:	2 sprigs fresh parsley
180C/350F/gas 4	3 tablespoons milk
	1 thick slice of bread, crust removed
Serves 10	1 egg, beaten
	pinch of mixed spice
Calories:	1 teaspoon tomato purée
424 per portion	450 g/1 lb streaky bacon, rinded
	1 bay leaf

Marinate 450 g/1 lb of the turkey meat (see Cook's Tip).

Melt the butter and cook the livers for 3-4 minutes. Drain, slice and reserve. Mince together the remaining 450 g/1 lb turkey, pork, onion and parsley. Soak the bread in the milk for a few minutes. Squeeze dry and mix with the minced ingredients. Add the egg, spice and purée, and season with pepper. Strain the turkey strips and reserve the brandy.

Line a casserole with three-quarters of the bacon and the liver. Layer the minced ingredients and turkey strips finishing with the mince. Pour in the reserved brandy. Press the contents well down in the dish. Cover with the remaining bacon and top with the bay leaf. Cover closely with foil, then the casserole lid. Place the casserole in a roasting tin half filled with hot water and cook in a preheated oven for 1½ hours. Leave until cold.

■ COOK'S TIP

To marinate the turkey, slice it into matchstick-size pieces, put in a bowl, and pour over 150 ml/¼ pint brandy. Leave for several hours, stirring occasionally.

To serve the terrine, remove it from the casserole, scrape off surplus fat, turn back on to a serving dish and garnish with watercress and chopped walnuts.

211 CHICKEN MARSALA

Preparation time:	YOU WILL NEED:
20 minutes	8 thin slices chicken breast, about
	75 g/3 oz each
Cooking time:	100 g/4 oz thinly sliced ham,
30 minutes	trimmed of fat
	¼ teaspoon dried sage
Serves 4	freshly ground black pepper
	25 g/1 oz butter
Calories:	1 small onion, finely chopped
458 per portion	1 garlic clove, crushed
	2 teaspoons plain flour
	100 ml/3½ fl oz chicken stock
	1 bay leaf
	4 tablespoons Marsala
	croutons, to garnish

Flatten the chicken breast, using a meat bat or rolling pin. Cut the ham and arrange it neatly to cover each chicken slice. Sprinkle on the dried sage and season with pepper. Roll up the slices to enclose the ham and secure with cocktail sticks.

Melt the butter in a flameproof casserole and sauté the onion for 2-3 minutes. Add the garlic and fry gently for 1 minute. Add the chicken rolls and fry them for 4-5 minutes, turning to brown on all sides. Stir in the flour and pour on the stock, stirring constantly. Add the bay leaf. Cover and simmer over low heat for 5 minutes. Pour on the Marsala, stir well, cover and simmer for 10 minutes more, stirring and turning the chicken once or twice. Discard the bay leaf from the casserole. Taste the sauce and adjust the seasoning, if necessary. Remove the cocktail sticks. Scatter the croûtons over the chicken pieces.

■ COOK'S TIP

You can buy Marsala, a relatively inexpensive wine, in most supermarkets and wine merchants. If you cannot obtain it, use a sweet 'brown' sherry.

212 DUCK WITH ORANGE SAUCE

Preparation time:	YOU WILL NEED:
25-30 minutes	4 duck portions, about
	300-425 g/11-15 oz each, trimmed
Cooking time:	salt and pepper
50-60 minutes	2 oranges
	1 tablespoon oil or dripping
Oven temperature:	1 tablespoon flour
180C/350F/gas 4	1 meat stock cube
	150 ml/¼ pint boiling water
Serves 4	juice of ½ lemon
	4 tablespoons port
Calories:	2 tablespoons redcurrant or
512 per portion	bramble jelly
	orange segments and watercress,

Prick the skin of the duck all over with a fork. Sprinkle with salt and pepper. Pare the rind from the oranges and cut into julienne strips; alternatively, grate the rind coarsely from the fruit. Squeeze out the juice. Heat the oil or dripping in a pan and fry the duck until browned all over. Transfer to a casserole. Pour off all but 1 tablespoon of the fat from the pan.

Stir the flour into the pan and cook for 1 minute. Dissolve the stock cube in the water and add to the pan with the orange juice, rind, lemon juice, port and redcurrant jelly.

Bring to the boil and simmer until the jelly has dissolved, then add salt and pepper and pour over the duck. Cover the casserole tightly. Cook in a preheated oven for 50-60 minutes or until the duck is tender. Arrange the duck portions in a deep serving dish, spoon the sauce over and garnish with orange segments and watercress.

■ COOK'S TIP

To cut a duck into four portions, first cut in two, breast side up. Cut out the backbone and remove, then cut each half in two.

213 MONKFISH GRATIN

Preparation time: 15 minutes	YOU WILL NEED: 750 g/1½ lb boneless monkfish, skinned and cut into cubes
Cooking time: about 40 minutes	1-2 slices lemon 1 very small onion, halved 1 small bay leaf
Oven temperature: 180C/360F/gas 4; then 200C/400F/gas 6	150 ml/¼ pint dry white wine salt and pepper 25 g/1 oz butter 2 tablespoons plain flour
Serves 4	150 ml/¼ pint milk 50 g/2 oz cucumber, coarsely grated
Calories: 329 per portion	1 teaspoon made mustard 75 g/3 oz Cheddar cheese, grated 25 g/1 oz fresh white breadcrumbs

Put the monkfish, lemon, onion, bay leaf, wine and seasoning in a buttered casserole. Cover and cook in a preheated oven for 20 minutes. Strain the juices from the casserole and keep on one side. Discard the lemon, onion and bay leaf.

Melt the butter, sprinkle in the flour and cook for 1 minute. Remove from the heat and gradually blend in the reserved fish liquid and milk. Bring to the boil and simmer for 1 minute, stirring. Remove from the heat. Pat the cucumber dry and stir into the sauce with the mustard and 50 g/2 oz of the cheese. Pour the sauce into the casserole. Sprinkle with a mixture of the remaining cheese and the breadcrumbs. Increase the oven temperature. Return the uncovered casserole to the oven for a further 15 minutes or until crisp and golden.

■ COOK'S TIP

An attractive garnish for this dish can be made from slices of lemon and cucumber, arranged on the casserole or on individual servings.

214 NEW ENGLAND OYSTERS

Preparation time: 20 minutes	YOU WILL NEED: 450 g/1 lb freshly shelled oysters, with 120 m/4 fl oz of the oyster
Cooking time: 30 minutes	liquor reserved 40 g/1½ oz melted butter 100 g/4 oz salted cracker crumbs
Oven temperature: 200C/400F/gas 6	freshly ground black pepper Tabasco sauce 120 ml/4 fl oz double or whipping
Serves 4	cream
Calories: 362 per portion	

Place a sieve lined with a double thickness of muslin cloth over a medium bowl. Drain the oyster liquor in the sieve and reserve. Remove any pieces of shell or grit from the oysters. Rinse briefly, then drain well in the sieve. Combine the reserved oyster liquor with the cream. Set aside.

Grease a medium casserole with 1 tablespoon of the melted butter. Place a third of the crumbs on the bottom of the dish. Arrange half of the drained oysters over the crumbs. Season with the pepper and Tabasco sauce. Pour half of the oyster liquor mixture over the oysters. Top evenly with another third of the crumbs. Arrange the remaining oysters evenly over the crumbs. Season with the pepper and Tabasco sauce. Pour the remaining oyster liquor over the oysters. Top with the remaining crumbs and dot with the remaining butter.

Cook the casserole uncovered in a preheated oven for 30 minutes, until the cream is bubbly and the crumbs golden.

■ COOK'S TIP

To open oysters, wrap a tea-towel round your left hand and hold the oyster in the palm. Slip a short, wide-bladed knife under the hinge and push into the oyster. Twist the knife and prise the two parts of the shell apart.

215 COQ AU VIN ROSE

Preparation time:
20 minutes

Cooking time:
about 1¼ hours

Oven temperature:
180C/350F/gas 4

Serves 4

Calories:
596 per portion

YOU WILL NEED:
1 x 175 g/4 lb chicken
salt and pepper
25 g/1 oz butter
1 tablespoon oil
2 tablespoons brandy
4 rashers streaky bacon, rinded
  and diced
225 g/8 oz button onions, peeled
1 garlic clove, crushed
300 ml/½ pint dry rosé wine
300 ml/½ pint chicken stock
2 teaspoons tomato purée
225 g/8 oz button mushrooms
bouquet garni
1 x 150 g/5 oz can pimientos,
  drained and cut into strips
paprika pepper

Cut the chicken into 8 pieces, remove the skin and season. Melt the butter and oil in a pan and brown the chicken. Drain well and transfer to a casserole. Warm the brandy, pour over the chicken and carefully set alight.

Cook the bacon in the fat in the pan for 1 minute. Add the onions and garlic and cook 4-5 minutes until browned. Stir in the wine, stock, purée, mushrooms and salt and pepper. Pour the sauce over the chicken. Add the bouquet garni. Cover and cook in a preheated oven for 45 minutes. Uncover the casserole, add the pimiento, cover again and cook for a further 15 minutes or until the chicken is tender. Garnish with paprika.

■ COOK'S TIP

The sauce here could be thickened with a beurre manié: blend 15 g/½ oz butter with enough flour to make a smooth paste. Add to the sauce in small pieces.

216 STUFFED VEAL ROLLS

Preparation time:
30 minutes

Cooking time:
1¼ hours

Oven temperature:
180C/350F/gas 4

Serves 4

Calories:
468 per portion

YOU WILL NEED:
65 g/2½ oz butter
450 g/1 lb lean minced pork
1 small onion, finely chopped
1 celery stalk, finely chopped
75 g/3 oz field mushrooms,
  cleaned and chopped
1 garlic clove, finely chopped
2 tablespoons chopped parsley
salt and pepper
8 veal escalopes, about 50 g/2 oz
  each and 15 cm/6 inches wide
wine sauce (see Cook's Tip)

Melt 15 g/½ oz of the butter in a pan and brown the pork. Remove the pork and set aside. Melt 25 g/1 oz butter in the pan, add the onion, celery, mushrooms and garlic and cook for 10 minutes. Mix into the cooked pork. Stir in the parsley, salt and pepper. Put 2 tablespoons of this stuffing on one end of each escalope. Roll up and tie securely with string.

Melt 25 g/1 oz butter in a large flameproof casserole. Add the veal rolls and cook for 5 minutes, browning on all sides. Remove the casserole from the heat and set aside.

Make the wine sauce and pour over the veal rolls. Cover the casserole and cook in a preheated oven for 20-30 minutes.

Transfer the veal rolls to a serving dish. Remove the strings. Place the casserole over a medium-high heat. Mix the cornflour and a little stock until smooth. Gradually stir into the casserole. Bring to the boil and simmer until thick. Coat the veal rolls with the sauce and garnish with parsley.

■ COOK'S TIP

Wine sauce: cook 2 finely sliced onions in 25 g/1oz butteruntil soft. Add a chopped garlic clove and cook 1 minute. Pour in 250 ml/8 fl oz dry white wine and 275 ml/9 fl oz beef stock and cook 2-3 minutes, stirring. Season to taste with salt and pepper.

217 TURKEY BREASTS WITH AVOCADO

Preparation time:	YOU WILL NEED:
10 minutes	*4 turkey breast fillets, each about*
	150 g/5 oz
Cooking time:	*salt and pepper*
1 hour	*½ teaspoon finely grated lemon rind*
	2 tablespoons chopped onion
Oven temperature:	*½ teaspoon dried tarragon*
180C/350F/gas 4	*½ teaspoon dried basil*
	2 tablespoons medium sherry
Serves 4	*1 tablespoon lemon juice*
	150 ml/¼ pint tomato juice
Calories:	*25 g/1 oz butter*
387 per portion	*1 avocado pear*
	2 tomatoes, cut into wedges
	2-3 tablespoons finely grated
	Cheddar cheese

Arrange the turkey breasts in a greased shallow casserole and sprinkle with salt, pepper, lemon rind, chopped onion, tarragon and basil. Mix together the sherry and juices and pour over the turkey fillets. Dot with butter. Cover the casserole closely and cook in the centre of a preheated oven for 40 minutes.

Halve, peel and slice the avocado and arrange neatly overlapping slices to one side of the turkey fillets. Arrange wedges of tomato on the other side. Return the uncovered casserole to the oven and continue cooking for 10 minutes.

Sprinkle with finely grated cheese and return to the oven for a further 10 minutes until the cheese has melted.

■ COOK'S TIP

For an eye-catching garnish, sprinkle the turkey fillet next to the avocado with paprika, and the fillet next to the tomato wedges with freshly chopped parsley.

218 PLAICE WHEELS

Preparation time:	YOU WILL NEED:
30 minutes	*15 g/½ oz soft margarine*
	100 g/4 oz button mushrooms,
Cooking time:	*trimmed and chopped*
30 minutes, plus	*1 small onion, finely chopped*
cooling	*1 small red pepper, cored, seeded*
	and finely chopped
Oven temperature:	*1 tablespoon chopped fresh parsley*
200C/400F/gas 6	*salt and pepper*
	pinch of grated nutmeg
Serves 4	*1 teaspoon lemon juice*
	4 plaice fillets, about 175 g/6 oz each
Calories:	*150 ml/¼ pint fish stock*
241 per portion	*1 green pepper, skinned*
	4 tablespoons double cream

Melt the margarine in a flameproof casserole and sauté the mushrooms, onion and red pepper for 3-4 minutes. Remove from the heat, stir in the parsley and add salt, pepper and nutmeg. Stir in the lemon juice and set the filling aside. When cool, divide the filling between the plaice fillets and roll up. Secure with cocktail sticks.

Arrange the rolls in the casserole, pour on the fish stock and cover the dish. Cook in a preheated oven for 12-15 minutes, until the fish is just cooked.

Halve, core and seed the green pepper and slice it thinly.

Stir the cream into the casserole and heat gently on top of the cooker. Pour sauce on to each plate. Add a plaice roll and arrange pepper strips on top. Sprinkle with paprika, if liked.

■ COOK'S TIP

Garnish this dish with whole prawns and spring onion curls.

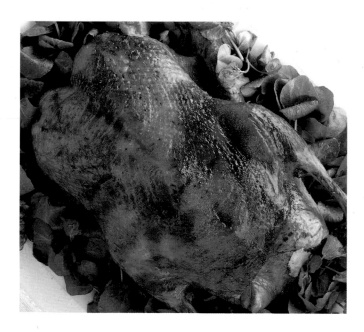

219 DUCK WITH WALNUT SAUCE

Preparation time:	YOU WILL NEED:
10 minutes	*1 x 2.25-2.75 kg/5-6 lb duckling*
	salt and pepper
Cooking time:	*1 onion, finely chopped*
about 1½-1¾ hours	*50 g/2 oz walnut pieces, chopped*
	300 ml/½ pint duckling stock,
Oven temperature:	*2 tablespoons honey*
200C/400F/gas 6	*2 teaspoons cornflour*
	2 tablespoons cream sherry
Serves 4	*1 teaspoon soy sauce*
	1 tablespoon lemon juice
Calories:	*1 tablespoon duck dripping*
934 per portion	*25 g/1 oz walnut halves*

Prick the duckling all over, season and put in a casserole. Cook in a preheated oven for 30 minutes. Drain the dripping from the casserole and reserve. Fry the onions in 1 tablespoon dripping until tender. Add the walnuts and cook for 2 minutes. Stir in the stock, then pour around the duckling. Cover the casserole and return to the oven for 45 minutes. Coat the skin of the duck with honey and cook, uncovered, for 15-20 minutes, until the duck is tender and the skin is brown.

Meanwhile, fry the walnut halves in 1 tablespoon of duck dripping until lightly browned, then drain well.

Transfer the duck to a serving dish. Skim any fat from the sauce in the casserole. Blend the cornflour and sherry, and stir in the soy sauce and lemon juice. Add a little of the hot liquid from the pan, blend, then stir the mixture into the pan. Bring to the boil and simmer for 1 minute, stirring. Garnish the duck with the fried walnuts and serve the sauce separately.

■ COOK'S TIP

To make the duckling stock, place the giblets in a pan with 600 ml/1 pint of water and simmer for 1 hour. Strain well and skim off any fat before using.

220 POT ROAST BONED TURKEY

Preparation time:	YOU WILL NEED:
30-45 minutes	*3.25 kg/7½ lb oven-ready*
	turkey, half-boned
Cooking time:	*stuffing (see Cook's Tip)*
about 1½ hours	*25 g/1 oz butter*
	150 ml/¼ pint red wine
Oven temperature:	*225 g/8 oz button mushrooms,*
180C/350F/gas 4	*25 g/1 oz butter*
	25 g/1 oz flour
Serves 6-8	*potato crisps and watercress to*
	garnish
Calories:	
719-539 per portion	

Spread the inside of the turkey with the stuffing and pull the flesh over to cover it. Secure with small skewers. Turn the turkey over and shape evenly; position the legs and wings and truss loosely.

Melt the butter in a large frying pan and brown the turkey all over. Transfer to a casserole. Add the wine to the pan and bring to the boil. Add salt and pepper and pour over the turkey. Cover and cook in a preheated oven for 1 hour.

Baste the joint, cover again and return to the oven for a further 30 minutes or until the juices run clear when the turkey is pierced with a skewer. Remove the joint and keep warm. Bring the pan juices back to the boil and add the mushrooms. Cream the butter and flour together, then whisk into the sauce a little at a time and bring back to the boil for 2 minutes.

Stand the turkey on a serving dish and garnish with potato crisps and watercress. Serve the sauce separately.

■ COOK'S TIP

For the stuffing: fry 1 finely chopped onion and 1 crushed garlic clove in 25 g/1 oz butter. Turn into a bowl and add 3 chopped celery sticks, 100 g/4 oz *fresh breadcrumbs, 100 g/4 oz liver pâté, 1 teaspoon ground coriander, 1 teaspoon dried mixed herbs and salt and pepper to taste.*

221 NEW ENGLAND BOILED DINNER

Preparation time:
15 minutes

Cooking time:
3¼ hours

Serves 6

Calories:3230
538 per portion

YOU WILL NEED:
1.5 kg/3½ lb salt beef in one piece
about 1.5 litres /2½ pints water
6 medium potatoes, peeled and halved
1 small swede, peeled and diced
6 medium carrots, thinly sliced
225 g/8 oz frozen sweetcorn kernels
12 button onions, peeled
freshly ground black pepper
pinch of sugar
2 tablespoons chopped fresh parsley

Trim the excess fat from the beef. Place the meat in a large flameproof casserole, pour on enough water to cover it, and bring to the boil. Skim off any foam that rises to the surface. Cover and simmer for 2½ hours, adding more boiling water, if necessary. It is important that the meat is well covered.

Add the vegetables, distributing them evenly around the meat, and season well with pepper and add a pinch of sugar.

Bring the stock back to the boil, cover the dish and simmer for a further 30 minutes, until all the vegetables are just tender. Taste the stock and adjust the seasoning, if necessary.

Slice the meat thickly, transfer it to a large, warmed serving plate, arrange the vegetables around it and sprinkle them with parsley. Cover with foil and keep warm.

Skim off the fat from the stock, bring it to the boil and serve a little of it separately as a sauce. (The remainder will make a tasty basis for a meat or vegetable soup.)

■ COOK'S TIP

If the beef seems very salt, and you dislike it, soak the joint in water for an hour before cooking. Drain, then cover with fresh water to boil.

222 POT ROAST PARTRIDGES WITH GRAPES

Preparation time:
15 minutes

Cooking time:
1¼-1½ hours

Oven temperature:
180C/350F/gas 4

Serves 4

Calories:
756 per portion

YOU WILL NEED:
4 partridges, prepared
salt and pepper
25 g/1 oz butter or margarine
100 g/4 oz streaky bacon rashers,
derinded and chopped
2 tablespoons brandy
2 tablespoons medium sherry
juice of 1 orange
300 ml/½ pint beef stock
100-175 g/4-6 oz green grapes,
halved and seeded
1 tablespoon cornflour
halved orange slices and green
grapes, to garnish

Sprinkle the birds with salt and pepper, melt the butter in a pan, then brown the partridges all over. Transfer to a casserole. Fry the bacon in the same fat until golden brown, stir in the brandy, sherry, orange juice and stock and bring to the boil. Add salt and pepper and pour over the partridges. Cover and cook in a preheated oven for 1 hour, basting once.

Add the grapes to the casserole and return to the oven for 15-30 minutes or until quite tender.

Drain off the juices into a pan and skim off most of the fat. Blend the cornflour with a little cold water and stir into the sauce. Bring back to the boil and pour back over the partridges. Garnish with orange slices and green grapes.

■ COOK'S TIP

When partridges are not available, pigeons can be used; or use poussin if you would rather not use game at all. Pigeons may take about 30 minutes longer

cooking and poussins 30 minutes less.

223 COQ AU VIN

Preparation time:
40 minutes

Cooking time:
1½ hours

Oven temperature:
180C/350F/gas 4

Serves 4

Calories:
758 per portion

YOU WILL NEED:
45 g/1¾ oz butter
100 g/4 oz thick unsmoked
   streaky bacon, rind removed,
   blanched and diced
12 pickling onions, peeled
1 x ½ kg/3 lb roasting chicken,
   jointed
2 tablespoons brandy
1 bottle Burgundy
salt and pepper
2 garlic cloves, crushed
1 bouquet garni
½ teaspoon ground nutmeg
225 g/8 oz small button mushrooms
20 g/¾ oz plain flour
heart-shaped croûtons

Melt 25 g/1 oz butter in a flameproof casserole, add the bacon and onions and fry until the onions begin to colour. Set aside.

Add the chicken joints to the casserole and brown on all sides. Warm the brandy, pour it over the chicken and set alight. When the flames die down, replace the bacon and onions in the casserole. Heat the wine in a saucepan and pour over the chicken. Season to taste. Add the garlic, bouquet garni and nutmeg. Cover and cook in a preheated oven for 1 hour.

Stir in the mushrooms, re-cover and cook for a further 15 minutes. Remove the bouquet garni. Mix the flour with the remaining butter and whisk into the sauce in small pieces. Bring just to the boil, stirring. Garnish with croûtons.

■ COOK'S TIP

*For heart-shaped croûtons,
as here, use biscuit cutters
to stamp out shapes from
stale bread. Fry on both
sides in butter or oil until
brown and crisp.*

224 HALIBUT CLARINDA

Preparation time:
10 minutes

Cooking time:
about 40 minutes

Oven temperature:
180C/350F/gas 4

Serves 4

Calories:
298 per portion

YOU WILL NEED:
4 halibut steaks
salt and pepper
25 g/1 oz butter
1 tablespoon finely chopped onion
25 g/1 oz flour
300 ml/½ pint milk
1 tablespoon lemon juice
1 teaspoon Angostura bitters
100 g/4 oz crabmeat
   (fresh, frozen or canned), flaked
whole prawns and cucumber
   sticks, to garnish

Place the fish steaks in a lightly greased ovenproof dish and sprinkle well with salt and pepper.

Melt the butter in a pan and fry the onion gently until soft. Stir in the flour and cook for 1 minute. Gradually add the milk and bring to the boil for 1 minute.

Stir the lemon juice, Angostura bitters, crabmeat, and plenty of salt and pepper into the sauce and pour over the fish.

Cover the casserole and cook in a preheated oven for about 40 minutes or until the fish is tender.

Transfer to a serving dish and garnish with whole prawns and cucumber sticks.

■ COOK'S TIP

*If using fresh crabmeat, use
only the white flesh for the
sauce as the brown
crabmeat will discolour it.*

225 SLOW-COOKED VENISON

Preparation time:
20 minutes, plus
marinating

Cooking time:
2-2¼ hours

Oven temperature:
180C/350F/gas 4

Serves 4

Calories:
549 per portion

YOU WILL NEED:
*1 kg/2 lb boned leg or shoulder of
    venison, cut into 4 serving pieces
    marinade (see Cook's Tip)
40 g/1½ oz butter
2 medium onions, sliced
2 tablespoons plain flour
300 ml/½ pint beef stock
2 tablespoons redcurrant jelly
1 bouquet garni
2 tablespoons port
1 tablespoon chopped fresh parsley
2-3 tablespoons orange juice*

Put the venison pieces in a large bowl, pour over the marinade, cover and set aside for about 12 hours or overnight.

Lift out the venison and pat it dry. Strain and reserve the marinade, discarding the flavouring ingredients in the sieve. Melt the butter in a flameproof casserole and sauté the venison pieces in batches. Set the venison pieces aside.

Fry the onions in the fat in the casserole for about 5 minutes, stirring to brown evenly. Sprinkle on the flour and stir well. Gradually pour on the reserved marinade and the stock, stirring all the time. Stir in the redcurrant jelly, add the bouquet garni and return the venison to the casserole. Cover and cook in a preheated oven for 1½-1¾ hours, until the meat feels tender when pierced with a fine skewer.

Discard the bouquet garni, stir in the port, and adjust the seasoning, if necessary. Sprinkle on the parsley to garnish.

■ COOK'S TIP

*For the marinade, mix
together 300 ml/½ pint dry
red wine, 3 tablespoons oil,
1 tablespoon chopped
parsley, 3 crushed black
peppercorns, 3 crushed*

*allspice berries, 1 small
sliced onion, 1 sliced carrot,
1 sliced celery stick, 1 thin
pared strip orange rind and
salt.*

226 BLANQUETTE DE VEAL

Preparation time:
35 minutes

Cooking time:
2¼ hours

Serves 4-6

Calories:
643-429 per portion

YOU WILL NEED:
*1 kg/2 lb boned shoulder of veal,
    trimmed and cut into cubes
1 onion, stuck with 4 cloves
1 carrot, sliced
2 bay leaves
150 ml/¼ pint dry white wine
salt and white pepper
225 g/8 oz button onions, peeled
150 ml/¼ pint double cream
2 egg yolks
1 tablespoon lemon juice
triangles of toast, to garnish*

Put the veal in a pan, cover with water, bring to the boil and skim off any foam. Add the onion, carrot and bay leaves to the casserole. Pour on the wine, season and bring to the boil. Cover and simmer over low heat for 1½ hours, or until the meat is tender. Strain the liquid into a pan, add the small onions, cover and simmer for 15 minutes, or until they are tender. Meanwhile, discard the whole onion and vegetables and keep the veal warm in the casserole.

Lift out the onions from the liquid in the pan and add to the veal. Measure the liquid and reserve 600 ml/1 pint for the sauce. Make the sauce (see Cook's Tip).

Beat together the cream, egg yolks and lemon juice. Add a little of the hot sauce, whisk well and pour the cream mixture into the pan. Add the rest of the hot sauce to the casserole and stir to blend thoroughly. Check the seasoning.

Garnish the dish with the toast and lemon twists, if liked.

■ COOK'S TIP

*To make the sauce, melt 40
g/1½ oz butter in a small
pan, stir in 3 tablespoons
flour and cook to make a
roux, then pour on the 600
ml/1 pint of hot stock,*

*stirring constantly, and
cook until the sauce
thickens.*

227 OSSO BUCCO

Preparation time: 20 minutes	YOU WILL NEED: 6 *pieces knuckle or shin of veal* 40 g/1½ oz plain flour
Cooking time: 2-2¼ hours	*salt and pepper* 2 *teaspoons dried oregano* 4 *tablespoons oil*
Serves 6	2 *garlic cloves, finely chopped* 1 *large onion, chopped*
Calories: 283 per portion	150 *ml/¼ pint dry white Italian wine* 150 *ml/¼ pint chicken stock* 1 x 200 *g/7 oz can tomatoes* 3 *tablespoons tomato purée* 1 *teaspoon sugar* 6 *anchovy fillets, drained, rinsed and finely chopped* 1 *tablespoon chopped parsley* *gremolata (see Cook's Tip)*

Cut away any excess fat or gristle from the meat. Put the flour, salt, pepper and oregano into a bag, shake well and toss in the meat, 1 or 2 pieces at a time, to coat it thoroughly.

Heat the oil in a flameproof casserole and sauté the meat for 3-4 minutes on each side, until it is evenly brown. Add the garlic and the onion and pour on the wine, stock and tomatoes. Stir in the tomato pureé and sugar and bring the sauce to the boil. Cover the casserole and simmer over low heat, stirring once or twice, for 1½-1¾ hours, or until the meat is tender and has shrunk away from the bones.

Stir in the anchovies and the parsley. Simmer for a further 10 minutes then sprinkle over the gremolata and serve very hot.

■ COOK'S TIP

For the gremolata, mix together 2 tablespoons chopped fresh parsley, 1 finely chopped garlic clove and 2 teaspoons grated lemon rind.

228 SCALLOPS FELIX

Preparation time: 10 minutes	YOU WILL NEED: 10-12 *scallops* 1 *bouquet garni*
Cooking time: about 40 minutes	150 *ml/¼ pint white wine* 150 *ml/¼ pint chicken stock* *salt and pepper*
Oven temperature: 180C/350F/gas 4; 220C/425/gas 7	1 *tablespoon lemon juice* 40 *g/1½ oz butter or margarine* 1 *large onion, finely chopped* 2-3 *sticks celery, thinly sliced*
Serves 4	25 *g/1 oz flour* 175 *g/6 oz button mushrooms*
Calories: 302 per portion	3 *tablespoons double or soured cream* *few drops of Tabasco sauce* 50 *g/2 oz fresh white breadcrumbs* 25 *g/1 oz Cheddar cheese, grated*

Prepare the scallops (see Cook's Tip). Put in a casserole with the bouquet garni. Bring the wine, stock, salt, pepper and juice to the boil, pour over the scallops and cover. Cook in a preheated oven for 20 minutes or until nearly tender.

Melt the fat in a pan and fry the onion and celery gently, until soft. Stir the flour into the onions and cook for 1 minute.

Drain the cooking liquid from the scallops and reserve. Discard the bouquet garni. Gradually add the scallop liquid to the onions and bring to the boil for 2 minutes. Add salt and pepper, the sliced mushrooms, cream and Tabasco and pour back over the scallops. Combine the breadcrumbs and cheese and sprinkle over. Increase the oven temperature and cook for about 20 minutes or until the top is crisp and brown.

■ COOK'S TIP

To prepare the scallops, cut away any black pieces and wash the scallops. Separate the roes from the body of the scallops and cut the white part horizontally into *2 or 3 pieces, depending on the size of the scallops. Slices of cucumber and lemon make an appropriate garnish for this dish.*

229 BRAISED SALMON STEAKS WITH ASPARAGUS

Preparation time:	YOU WILL NEED:
10 minutes	4 salmon steaks, about 2.5 cm/1 inch thick
Cooking time:	salt and pepper
40 minutes	1 x 350 g/12 oz can asparagus
	2 teaspoons cornflour
Oven temperature:	6 tablespoons double cream
190C/375F/gas 5	2 teaspoons lemon juice
	lemon wedges, to garnish
Serves 4	

Calories:
338 per portion

Place the fish in a shallow, buttered, ovenproof dish just large enough to take the steaks in a single layer. Sprinkle with salt and pepper.

Drain the asparagus, reserving 6 tablespoons of the liquid Reserve 12 asparagus spears for garnish and roughly chop the remainder. Scatter over the fish.

Blend the cornflour with the cream and then with the asparagus liquid, lemon juice and plenty of salt and pepper. Pour over the fish.

Cover and cook in a preheated oven for about 40 minutes or until the fish is cooked through. The cooking time depends on the thickness of the fish.

Garnish with the reserved asparagus and lemon wedges.

■ COOK'S TIP

Test the fish with a skewer after 30 minutes to see if it is done. Fish should never be overcooked as it then becomes dry and tasteless.

230 BEEF STROGANOFF

Preparation time:	YOU WILL NEED:
15 minutes	750 g/1½ lb fillet of beef
	50 g/1 oz unsalted butter
Cooking time:	2 medium onions, thinly sliced
25 minutes	225 g/8 oz small button mushrooms, (trimmed)
Serves 4	salt and pepper
	250 ml/8 fl oz soured cream
Calories:	1 tablespoon tomato purée
414 per portion	2 teaspoons French mustard
	1 tablespoon dry sherry
	¼ teaspoon paprika and sprigs of dill, to garnish

Trim the beef. Cut it into strips 5 cm/2 inches x 5 mm/¼ inch.

Heat half the butter in a flameproof casserole. Fry the onions gently for 3-4 minutes until they are translucent. Add the mushrooms, stir well, lower the heat and cover the dish. Cook for 5 minutes, shaking the dish frequently. Using a slotted spoon, lift out the vegetables, cover and keep warm.

Melt the remaining butter in the casserole and sauté the strips of beef over moderate heat, turning them so that they brown evenly on all sides. Return the vegetables to the casserole, season with salt and pepper, cover and cook over low heat for 2-3 minutes, to allow the flavours to blend.

In a small bowl, mix together the soured cream, tomato purée, mustard and sherry. Stir the cream mixture, a little at a time, into the casserole and bring slowly to simmering point. Do not allow to boil. Garnish with paprika and dill.

■ COOK'S TIP

Breaking away from tradition, you might like to try an alternative and less expensive cut of meat cooked in exactly the same way. You can substitute fillet of pork, cut into thin strips across the grain. The finished dish is equally delicious.

231 FESTIVE PHEASANT

Preparation time: 15 minutes	YOU WILL NEED: *4 pheasant breasts or joints* *salt and pepper*
Cooking time: 50-60 minutes	*25 g/1 oz butter* *1 tablespoon oil* *225 g/8 oz button onions, peeled*
Oven temperature: 180C/350F/gas 4	*225-350 g/8-12 oz chestnuts,* * lightly roasted or boiled and peeled* *2 tablespoons flour*
Serves 4	*200 ml/7 fl oz dry white wine* *150 ml/¼ pint chicken stock*
Calories: 502 per portion	*1 tablespoon redcurrant jelly* *rind of 1 orange, cut in strips* *juice of 2 oranges* *2 tablespoons brandy (optional)* *1 bay leaf* *orange slices and watercress*

Season the pheasant. Heat the butter and oil in a pan and fry the pieces until browned all over. Transfer to a casserole.

Fry the onions in the same fat until lightly coloured and arrange around the pheasant with the chestnuts. Stir the flour into the fat in the pan and cook 1 minute. Gradually add the wine and stock and bring to the boil. Stir in the redcurrant jelly, orange rind and juice, brandy and bay leaf. Season and pour over the pheasant. Cover and cook in a preheated oven for about 50-60 minutes or until tender. Discard the bay leaf and serve the pheasant on a platter surrounded by onions and chestnuts with sauce spooned over (serve the rest separately). Garnish with orange slices and watercress.

■ COOK'S TIP

To cook chestnuts, make a small cut in each shell, then boil for 25-30 minutes. Drain, then peel using a sharp knife.

232 NAVARIN

Preparation time: 20 minutes	YOU WILL NEED: *25 g/1 oz butter* *2 tablespoons oil*
Cooking time: 2¼ hours	*750 g/1½ lb lean shoulder of* * lamb, trimmed and cubed* *1 tablespoon sugar*
Oven temperature: 150C/300F/gas 2	*4 tablespoons plain flour* *salt and pepper* *1 tablespoon tomato purée*
Serves 4	*450 ml/¾ pint chicken stock, hot* *150 ml/¼ pint cider*
Calories: 506 per portion	*2 garlic cloves, crushed* *12 small new potatoes, scraped* *12 button onions* *12 small new carrots, scraped* *225 g/8 oz shelled broad beans*

Heat the butter and oil in a flameproof casserole. Sauté the meat in batches, turning to brown evenly on all sides. Pour off the fat and return the meat to the casserole. Sprinkle on the sugar and stir until it melts and caramelizes. Sprinkle on the flour, season and stir well to coat the meat. Lower the heat and cook for 3-4 minutes, stirring once or twice, until the meat is lightly browned. Stir in the tomato purée, then gradually pour on the hot stock and the cider, stirring all the time. Add the garlic. Cover the casserole and cook in a preheated oven for 1¼ hours.

Skim the fat from the surface. Add the potatoes, onions and carrots, cover and cook for 30 minutes. Add the broad beans, cover and cook for 15 minutes. Serve hot.

■ COOK'S TIP

To skim fat from the surface of a hot liquid, tilt the dish or pan slightly and let the liquid fat run into a large, shallow serving spoon. It may be necessary *to repeat this process several times if you used meat with a heavy fat content.*

233 COUSCOUS

Preparation time:	YOU WILL NEED:
50 minutes, plus	*450 g/1 lb medium couscous grains*
soaking overnight	*salt*
	3 tablespoons oil
Cooking time:	*1 kg/2 lb boned shoulder of lamb,*
2¾ hours	*trimmed and cubed*
	12 button onions
Serves 6	*1 teaspoon harissa sauce*
	2 teaspoons turmeric
Calories:	*1 x 400 g/14 oz can chick peas*
649 per portion	*1 x 425 g/15 oz can tomatoes*
	2 medium carrots, sliced
	2 celery sticks, sliced
	450 ml/¾ pint water
	2 green peppers, cut in large pieces
	3 small potatoes, peeled and halved

Pre-cook the couscous (see Cook's Tip).

In the base of the steaming set heat the oil and fry the meat and onions for 5-6 minutes. Lower the heat and continue cooking for 20 minutes. Stir in the harissa sauce and turmeric, add the drained chick peas, tomatoes, carrots, celery and water. Stir the ingredients together, bring to the boil and cover the pan. Simmer for 1 hour, then add the peppers and potatoes and bring back to the boil.

Tip the couscous grains into the steamer top and fit it over the pan. Continue cooking, uncovered, for 30 minutes, forking over the grains. Keep the liquid in the base boiling gently.

Spoon the couscous round the edge of a serving dish and pile the meat into the centre. Garnish with coriander.

■ COOK'S TIP

To pre-cook the couscous, wash in a sieve and drain well. Put in the top of a steamer lined with muslin, stir in a little salt and steam uncovered for 30 minutes, *breaking up any lumps with a fork. Lift off the steamer and pour cold water through the grains. Turn into a dish and break up any lumps.*

234 AVOCADO SEAFOOD

Preparation time:	YOU WILL NEED:
15 minutes	*120 g/4½ oz butter*
	1 large avocado pear, halved,
Cooking time:	*stoned, peeled and cubed*
50-55 minutes	*2 teaspoons lemon juice*
	350 g/12 oz cooked white crabmeat
Oven temperature:	*350 g/12 oz cooked peeled prawns*
180C/350F/gas 4	*350 g/12 oz cooked scallops*
	75 g/6 oz onion, finely chopped
Serves 8	*100 g/4 oz plain flour*
	400 ml/14 fl oz single cream
Calories:	*400 ml/14 fl oz milk*
614 per portion	*1 teaspoon Dijon mustard*
	175 g/6 oz Gruyère cheese, grated
	1 tablespoon fresh thyme leaves
	salt and white pepper
	garnish (see Cook's Tip)

Grease a casserole with butter. Toss the avocado with the lemon juice. Put the avocado, crabmeat, prawns and scallops in the casserole.

Melt the remaining butter in a saucepan. Cook the onion until soft and golden. Blend in the flour. Stirring constantly, cook for 2-3 minutes. Gradually whisk in the cream, milk and mustard. Increase the heat to medium and cook, stirring, until smooth and thick. Stir the cheese into the sauce. Remove the saucepan from the heat, then add the thyme, salt and pepper. Gently blend the sauce into the seafood mixture. Bake in a preheated oven for 30-40 minutes, until heated through. Arrange the avocado fan on top. Sprinkle over parsley, if liked.

■ COOK'S TIP

Garnish this dish with an avocado fan: stone and peel half an avocado and cut it into a fan shape, being careful not to slice it through as the base.

235 BOUILLABAISSE

Preparation time:	YOU WILL NEED:
1 hour	*6 tablespoons olive oil*
	large pinch powdered saffron
Cooking time:	*2 large onions, sliced*
30 minutes	*2 medium leeks, trimmed and sliced*
	4 large tomatoes, quartered
Serves 6	*5 garlic cloves, chopped*
	1 tablespoon chopped fresh fennel
Calories:	*salt and pepper*
633 per portion	*1.5 kg/3½ lb mixed fish, cleaned*
	3 large potatoes, sliced
	300 ml/½ pint dry white wine
	900 ml/1½ pints fish stock
	1 kg/2 lb mussels, cleaned
	pepper sauce (see Cook's Tip)

Put the olive oil into a bowl, stir in the saffron. Put the onions, leeks, tomatoes and garlic into a flameproof casserole. Stir in the saffron-flavoured oil and the fennel. Season with salt and pepper. Place on top the thickest fish, (e.g. monkfish) and cover with the potatoes. Pour on the wine and stock. Bring to the boil and fast-boil 5 minutes. Add another layer of fish (e.g. John Dory or red snapper) that requires less cooking. Fast-boil 5 minutes. Add the mussels, cover the casserole and fast-boil 5 minutes. Discard any mussels that have not opened. Remove the fish and the potatoes, then strain the fish broth. Cut the fish into serving pieces.

Make the pepper sauce (see Cook's Tip). Divide the fish, mussels and potato among 6 deep soup bowls, ladle on broth to cover and sprinkle with parsley. Hand the sauce separately.

■ COOK'S TIP

Pepper sauce: simmer 1 seeded and chopped pepper and 1 seeded chilli in water 10 minutes. Drain, discarding the water. Blend the pepper and chilli with 1 *200 g/7oz can pimientos (drained) and 2 garlic cloves to a paste. Gradually pour 2 tablespoons olive oil into the blender. Mix in 2-3 tablespoons breadcrumbs.*

236 CASSOULET

Preparation time:	*450 g/1 lb dried white haricot*
1 hour, plus soaking	*beans, soaked overnight*
	450 g/1 lb salt pork
Cooking time:	*1 large onion, studded with 6 cloves*
4½ hours	*2 large onions, sliced*
	4 garlic cloves, peeled
Oven temperature:	*2 bay leaves*
190C/375F/gas 5,	*4 tablespoons oil*
then 170C/325/gas 3	*selection of meats (Cook's Tip)*
	6 tablespoons tomato purée
Serves 8-10	*600 ml/1 pint beef stock, hot*
	150 ml/¼ pint dry white wine
Calories:	*salt and pepper*
870-696 per portion	*150 g/5 oz dry white breadcrumbs*

Drain the beans and put with the salt pork into a pan, add the onions, garlic and bay leaves. Cover with water, bring to the boil. Skim off any foam. Cover and simmer 1 hour, until the beans are tender. Remove the pork and drain the beans, reserving the liquid. (Discard the bay leaves and large onion.) Skin the salt pork and cut the meat into cubes.

Meanwhile, heat the oil in a roasting pan, add the meat (except sausage) and roast for 30 minutes to brown on all sides. When cool, cut into large serving-size pieces.

In a deep casserole, layer the beans and onion mixture, then the two types of pork, then more beans, the lamb, beans and poultry, beans and sausage, finishing with a layer of beans.

Mix together the tomato purée, stock and wine, season and pour over the casserole. Sprinkle the breadcrumbs on top. Cover and cook in a preheated oven for 3¼- 3½ hours.

■ COOK'S TIP

Suggested meats for this traditional dish are 450 g/1 lb boned shoulder of pork, 450 g/1 lb boned shoulder of lamb, 750 g/1 ½ lb boned poultry, such as goose, *chicken or duck (in large pieces) and 450 g/1 lb French garlic sausage (peeled and sliced).*

237 JUGGED HARE

Preparation time:	YOU WILL NEED:
40 minutes	1 x 1.75 kg/4 lb hare, blood
	reserved, cut into 6 pieces
Cooking time:	50 g/2 oz butter
3½ hours	4 slices streaky bacon, chopped
	300 ml/½ pint robust red wine
Oven temperature:	300 ml/½ pint beef stock
150C/300F/gas 2	1 teaspoon juniper berries
	½ teaspoon black peppercorns
Serves 6	2 bay leaves, crumbled
	350 g/12 oz button onions
Calories:	225 g/8 oz mushrooms, sliced
625 per portion	4 tablespoons ruby port
	2 tablespoons redcurrant jelly

Sprinkle the hare joints with seasoned flour.

Heat 25 g/1 oz of the butter in a flameproof casserole. Fry the bacon until it is crisp. Lift out and set aside. Brown the hare pieces in the casserole. Pour on the wine and stock. Tie the juniper berries, peppercorns and bay leaves in cheesecloth. Add to the casserole. Return the bacon and hare to the casserole. Cover and cook in a preheated oven for 2 hours, then add the onions and mushrooms and continue cooking for 45 minutes. Test that the hare is tender by piercing the thickest part of a leg joint with a fine skewer.

Lift out the hare pieces and vegetables. Discard the spices, strain the liquid into a pan and return the hare and vegetables to the casserole. Add the port and redcurrant jelly to the pan, pour on the reserved blood (to thicken the sauce), bring to simmering point and stir for 3-4 minutes. Pour over the hare.

■ COOK'S TIP

Use a biscuit cutter to cut out heart-shaped pieces from slices of white bread. Toast on both sides and serve with the casserole while still warm.

238 HARVESTER'S RABBIT

Preparation time:	1 kg/2 lb rabbit joints
30 minutes, plus	40 g/1½ oz seasoned flour
soaking	1 teaspoon dried oregano
	100 g/4 oz streaky bacon, diced
Cooking time:	40 g/1½ oz butter
1¼ hours	1 small onion, chopped
	1 garlic clove, crushed
Serves 4	2 tablespoons brandy
	150 ml/1/4 pint dry white wine
Calories:	100 g/4 oz seedless white grapes
532 per portion	450 ml/¾ pint chicken stock
	1 bouquet garni
	50 g/2 oz chicken livers
	50 g/2 oz blanched almonds

Toss the rabbit pieces in the flour. Fry the bacon in a flameproof casserole until the fat begins to run. Remove and set aside. Melt the butter in the casserole and fry the onion and garlic for 3-4 minutes. Remove and set aside. Brown the rabbit pieces for 6-8 minutes. Pour on the brandy, set light to it and shake the dish to distribute the flames evenly. Return the bacon and vegetables to the casserole. Put the wine and grapes into a pan, bring to the boil and simmer for 2-3 minutes. Remove the grapes and set aside. Pour the wine into the casserole, add the stock and bouquet garni. Cover and simmer for 1 hour.

Mince the liver and almond to make a thick sticky paste. Add a little of the stock to the liver mixture, stir well, and stir it into the casserole. Bring to the boil, cover the casserole and continue simmering for 15 minutes, until the rabbit is tender and the sauce thick. Scatter the grapes over the dish to garnish.

■ COOK'S TIP

When rich 'meaty' casseroles are less appropriate, it is a good idea to soak the rabbit joints in acidulated water before cooking, to draw out the strong flavour of the meat. This simple process also helps to tenderize it.

239 CIVET DE CANARD

Preparation time: 20 minutes	YOU WILL NEED: 1 x 2 kg/4½ lb duck, quartered 50 g/2 oz seasoned flour
Cooking time: 1¾ hours	25 g/1 oz butter 2 medium onions, finely chopped 750 ml/1¼ pints red wine
Oven temperature: 180C/350F/gas 4	1 bay leaf 1 teaspoon fresh thyme leaves 12 small onions, peeled
Serves 2	1 tablespoon cornflour 50 ml/2 fl oz cold duck stock
Calories: 751 per portion	1 teaspoon demerara sugar 1 tablespoon chopped parsley

Prick the duck pieces and toss in the seasoned flour. Melt the butter in a flameproof casserole. Add the duck and cook for 10 minutes on each side to brown. Remove the duck and set aside.

Pour off all but 3 tablespoons of the fat in the casserole. Add the chopped onions and cook 5 minutes. Return the duck to the casserole. Blend in the wine, bay leaf and thyme and season with salt and pepper. Cover and cook in a preheated oven for 1 hour, turning the duck pieces occasionally. Stir in the small onions and continue cooking for 30 minutes.

Remove the casserole from the oven. Skim the fat from the surface. Transfer the duck and onions to a platter and keep warm. Put the casserole on a medium heat on the stove. Whisk the cornflour and stock together until smooth and pour into the casserole. Add the sugar. Cook, stirring, until the sauce has thickened. Arrange the small onions around the duck. Coat with the sauce, then sprinkle with the parsley.

■ COOK'S TIP

To reduce the fat content of this dish you could skin the duck pieces before cooking -in poultry all the fat is contained in the skin.

240 HADDOCK FLAMENCO

Preparation time: 15 minutes	YOU WILL NEED: 750 g/1¼ lb haddock fillet, skinned salt and pepper
Cooking time: 30 minutes	225 g/8 oz courgettes, washed and sliced 1 medium-sized onion, sliced
Oven temperature: 200C/400F/gas 6	25 g/1 oz butter 2 medium-sized tomatoes, skinned and chopped
Serves 4	¼ teaspoon Tabasco sauce
Calories: 177 per portion	

Cut the haddock into 4 equal portions, and season with salt and pepper. Fry the courgettes and onion in butter until just tender, then stir in the tomatoes and Tabasco sauce. Place the pieces of haddock in a casserole, then top the fish with vegetables. Cover and cook in the oven until the haddock and vegetables are tender.

■ COOK'S TIP

Instead of fresh tomatoes, you could use a can of chopped tomatoes for convenience.

INDEX

Aduki bean and bulgar casserole 168
Alabama chilli 67
Artichoke chicken 105
Artichokes au gratin 179
Asparagus, braised salmon steaks with 229
Aubergines: Aubergines stuffed with pine nuts 189
Aubergines taverna 180
Avocado seafood 234

Baccala 25
Bacon: Bacon stewpot 73
Casseroled bacon joint 69
Beans: Boston baked 156
Cassoulet 236
Italian bean casserole 171
Speedy mixed bean goulash 172
Beef: Beef and butter bean marmite 74
Beef carbonade 71
Beef stroganoff 230
Boeuf a la bourguignonne 77
Boeuf a l'orange 52
Goulash 50
Lasagne 145
New England boiled dinner 221
Old English casserole 66
Sweet and sour beef 79
Black-eye bean stroganoff 144
Boston baked beans 156
Bouillabaisse 235
Broccoli: Broccoli in wholegrain mustard sauce 203
Broccoli Lorraine 192
Brussels sprouts and mushroom casserole 200
Bulgar: Aduki bean and bulgar casserole 168
Butter beans Breton 195

Cabbage: Cabbage and celery casserole 194
Stuffed leaves 178
Cassoulet 236
Cheese: Macaroni cheese with sour cream 150
Chick peas: Chick pea curry 190
Chick pea ratatouille 157
Greek baker's pot 164
Chicken: Artichoke chicken 105
Chicken and broccoli roll-ups 82
Chicken breasts in quince sauce 112
Chicken in egg and lemon sauce 114
Chicken Marengo 102
Chicken Marsala 211
Chicken Rossini 81
Chicken Smyrna 108
Chicken Veronique 107
Chicken with olives 109
Chinese five spiced chicken legs 98
Circassian chicken 117
Coconut chicken 91
Coq au vin 223
Coq au vin rose 215
Drumsticks in barbecue sauce 93
Gingered citrus chicken 97
Italian hunters' chicken 92
Mandarin risotto 154
Mexican chicken in green almond sauce 118
Mughlai chicken 101
Nigerian chicken and peanut casserole 103
Poulet chez-moi 88
Poulet en cocotte 89
Poulet Versailles 115
Smokey chicken parcels 111

Stewed chicken 84
Stoved chicken 90
Stuffed chicken rolls 120
Chicory casserole with toasted walnuts 162
Chinese cabbage with tomato and ginger 202
Chinese crab and rice casserole 24
Chinese five spiced chicken legs 98
Chinese vegetable casserole 183
Circassian chicken 117
Civet de canard 239
Cod: Baccala 25
Cod and Cheddar casserole 5
Corfiot fish steaks 207
Fish pie 15
Greek cod with courgettes 30
Honey and almond fish steaks 3
Malaysian fish curry 4
Mediterranean stove pot 29
Colcannon, baked 197
Coq au vin 223
Coq au vin rose 215
Corfiot fish steaks 207
Cotriade 9
Cotswold pheasant 138
Courgettes: Courgette and brown rice layered casserole 163
Courgette risotto 151
Couscous 233
Crab: Chinese crab and rice casserole 24
Crab and spaghetti bake 147
Crab-stuffed sole rolls 2
Cracked wheat and spinach pilaff 149
Curries: Chick pea 190
Malaysian fish 4
Smoked fish 31
Vegetable 177

Duck: Civet de canard 239
Duck fesanjan 83
Duck with orange sauce 212
Duck with walnut sauce 219
Jubilee duckling 116
Kentish duckling 85
Plum duck 96
Tuscany duckling 87
Wild duck in Cumberland sauce 127

Elizabethan rabbit 121

Fennel with mushrooms 187
Fettucine casserole 170
Fish 1-48
Bouillabaisse 235
Cotriade 9
Fish boulangere 12
Fish with horseradish cream 40
Mario's casserole 23
Matelote Normande 35
Mediterranean fish steaks 44
Mixed fish casserole 47
Seafood pie 48

Game 121-40
Gascony rabbit 125
Goulash 50
Speedy mixed bean 172
Vegetable 167
With dumplings 158
Greek baker's pot 164
Greek cod with courgettes 30
Greek prawn casserole 18
Green bean casserole, Spanish 174
Grouse: Grouse with red cabbage 135
Orchard grouse 136
Guinea fowl, braised 123

Haddock: Creamy finnan haddie casserole 19
Haddock cobbler 37
Haddock flamenco 240
Haddock with cider and vegetables 38
Haddock with grapefruit and mushrooms 8
Scot's haddie 22
Seafood casserole 32
Smoked fish curry 31
Smoked haddock and bacon pot pie 11
Smoked haddock special 46
Halibut: Halibut a la Grecque 42
Halibut Clarinda 224
Hare: Casserole of hare 134
Jugged hare 237
Konigsberg hare 126
Herries pork 68
Herrings: Marinated and baked in tea 28
Potted in Guinness 21

Italian bean casserole 171
Italian hunters' chicken 92
Italian market day 141

Jambalaya 205

Kentish duckling 85
Kidneys: Kidneys Victoria 59
Lamb's kidneys in red wine 72
Kitchen garden pottage 176
Kitchiri 152
Konigsberg hare 126

Lamb: Couscous 233
Crisped loin of lamb 58
Lamb and dill hot pot 80
Lancashire hot pot 54
Moroccan lamb 78
Navarin 232
Noisettes with hazelnut sauce 51
Orange lamb and rice 65
Pot roast leg of lamb 57
Tagine 53
Lancashire hot pot 54
Lasagne 145
Leeks: Hot leeks vinaigrette 185
Leek and Jerusalem artichoke casserole 175
Lentils: Lentil cobbler 148
Sag dhal 155
Liver: Orange and liver casserole 63
Piquant liver 62

Macaroni cheese with sour cream 150
Mackerel: Baked mackerel with rhubarb sauce 17
Mackerel with sesame and orange 25
Malaysian fish curry 4
Mandarin risotto 154
Mario's casserole 23
Matelote Normande 35
Meat 49-80
Mediterranean fish steaks 44
Mediterranean stove pot 29
Mexican chicken in green almond sauce 118
Monkfish gratin 213
Moroccan lamb 78
Mughlai chicken 101
Mullet: Baked red mullet in port wine 33
Mullet Mornay 43
Mushrooms: Mushroom and green bean pilaff 165
Mushroom and raisin pilaff 161
Mushroom casserole 143
Mussels: Mussels in cider 34
Portuguese mussel feast 1

Navarin 232
Neapolitan pasta casserole 159
New England boiled dinner 221
New England oysters 214
Nigerian chicken and peanut casserole 103
Noodles paprika 142

Okra and pasta casserole Nicoise 153
Old English casserole 66
Osso bucco 227
Oxtail: Oxtail with black olives 61
Oxtail with red kidney beans 75
Oysters, New England 214

Partridge: Partridge pudding 131
Partridge with red cabbage 139
Pot roast partridges with grapes 222
Pasta: Italian market day 141
Neapolitan pasta casserole 159
Okra and pasta casserole Nicoise 153
Pepperonata 198
Pheasant: Cotswold 138
Festive pheasant 231
Pheasant casserole 124
Pheasant in red wine 133
Pheasants with brandy 128
Pigeon: Pigeon with raisin sauce 137
Vineyard pigeon 130
Pilaff: Cracked wheat and spinach 149
Mushroom and green bean 165
Mushroom and raisin 161
Plaice: Plaice paupiettes with smoked salmon 14
Plaice wheels 218
Plum duck 96
Polynesian poussin 104
Pork: Herries pork 68
Jambalaya 205
Paprika pork chops 76
Pork 'n' pears 70
Spare ribs 64
Sweet and sour pork Hong Kong style 55
Portuguese mussel feast 1
Potatoes: Baked colcannon 197
Gruyere potatoes 188
Pommes Dauphinoises 196
Potato and tomato casserole 181
Poulet chez-moi 88
Poulet en cocotte 89
Poulet Versailles 115
Poultry 81-120
Poussin, Polynesian 104
Prawns: Greek prawn casserole 18
Prawn and okra in coconut sauce 27
Prawn, garlic and herb casserole 39
Prawn gumbo with rice 13
Wild rice fish casserole 7
Prunes, rabbit with 132

Quail casserole 122

Rabbit: Elizabethan 121
Gascony rabbit 125
Harvester's rabbit 238
Rabbit with prunes 132
St Mellons rabbit 129
Ratatouille: Baked 173
Chick pea 157
Red cabbage: Braised 186
Spiced red cabbage and beetroot casserole 193
Rice: Southerner's rice 146
Spanish rice casserole 166
see also Pilaff

Risotto: Courgette 151
Mandarin 154

Sag dhal 155
St Mellons rabbit 129
Salmon: Braised salmon steaks with asparagus 229
Poached salmon 41
Salmon corn casserole 20
Salmon in red wine 6
Sauerkraut with orange and raisins 204
Scallops: Casserole of 208
Creamed scallops fantasia 16
Scallops Felix 228
Scot's haddie 22
Sea trout, baked 45
Seafood: Avocado seafood 234
Seafood casserole 32
Seafood pie 48
Sole: Crab-stuffed sole rolls 2
Sole paupiettes 206
Southerner's rice 146
Spaghetti: Crab and spaghetti bake 147
Spanish green bean casserole 174
Spanish rice casserole 166
Spare ribs 64
Spinach: Mullet Mornay 43
Sag dhal 155
Squid Provencal 209

Tagine 53
Tomato, spinach and ricotta casserole 184
Trout: Rainbow trout with brown butter 10
Tuna carousel 36
Turkey: Pot roast boned turkey 220
Turkey and chestnuts 100
Turkey breasts with avocado 217
Turkey Cinzano 95
Turkey escalopes in creamed corn 113
Turkey fricassee 106
Turkey hash 119
Turkey Mexicana 110
Turkey mole 94
Turkey olives 86
Turkey rice casserole 99
Turkey terrine 210
Tuscany duckling 87

Veal: Blanquette de veal 226
Osso bucco 227
Paprika veal 60
Paupiettes de veau 56
Stuffed veal rolls 216
Veal ragout 49
Vegetables 173-204
Chinese vegetable casserole 183
Country vegetable casserole 182
Kitchen garden pottage 176
Kitchiri 152
Mixed green vegetables with coconut sauce 199
Vegetable curry 177
Vegetable dhansak 169
Vegetable goulash 167
Vegetable hot pot with orange dumplings 191
Winter vegetable hot pot 201
Vegetarian hot pot 160
Venison: Slow-cooked 225
Spiced 140

Wild rice fish casserole 7